Jim Redman MBE
– Six Times World Motorcycle Champion
The Autobiography

Also from Veloce Publishing:

Speedpro Series
Harley-Davidson Evolution Engines, How to Build & Power Tune (Hammill)
Motorcycle-engined Racing Car, How to Build (Pashley)
Secrets of Speed – Today's techniques for 4-stroke engine blueprinting & tuning (Swager)

RAC handbooks
How your motorcycle works – Your guide to the components & systems of modern motorcycles (Henshaw)
Motorcycles – A first-time-buyer's guide (Henshaw)

Enthusiast's Restoration Manual Series
Beginner's Guide to Classic Motorcycle Restoration, The (Burns)
Classic Large Frame Vespa Scooters, How to Restore (Paxton)
Ducati Bevel Twins 1971 to 1986 (Falloon)
How to Restore Classic Off-road Motorcycles (Burns)
How to restore Honda CX500 & CX650 – YOUR step-by-step colour illustrated guide to complete restoration (Burns)
How to restore Honda Fours – YOUR step-by-step colour illustrated guide to complete restoration (Burns)
Yamaha FS1-E, How to Restore (Watts)

Essential Buyer's Guide Series
BMW Boxer Twins – All air-cooled R45, R50, R60, R65, R75, R80, R90, R100, RS, RT & LS (Not GS) models 1969 to 1994 (Henshaw)
BMW GS (Henshaw)
BSA 350 & 500 Unit Construction Singles (Henshaw)
BSA 500 & 650 Twins (Henshaw)
BSA Bantam (Henshaw)
Ducati Bevel Twins (Falloon)
Ducati Desmodue Twins (Falloon)
Ducati Desmoquattro Twins – 851, 888, 916, 996, 998, ST4 1988 to 2004 (Falloon)
Harley-Davidson Big Twins (Henshaw)
Hinckley Triumph triples & fours 750, 900, 955, 1000, 1050, 1200 – 1991-2009 (Henshaw)
Honda CBR FireBlade (Henshaw)
Honda CBR600 Hurricane (Henshaw)
Honda SOHC Fours 1969-1984 (Henshaw)
Kawasaki Z1 & Z900 (Orritt)
Moto Guzzi 2-valve big twins (Falloon)
Norton Commando (Henshaw)
Piaggio Scooters – all modern four-stroke automatic models 1991 to 2016 (Willis)
Royal Enfield Bullet (Henshaw)
Triumph 350 & 500 Twins (Henshaw)
Triumph Bonneville (Henshaw)
Triumph Thunderbird, Trophy & Tiger (Henshaw)
Velocette 350 & 500 Singles (Henshaw)
Vespa Scooters – Classic 2-stroke models 1960-2008 (Paxton)

Those Were The Days ... Series
British Drag Racing – The early years (Pettitt)
Café Racer Phenomenon, The (Walker)
Drag Bike Racing in Britain – From the mid '60s to the mid '80s (Lee)

Biographies
A Life Awheel – The 'auto' biography of W de Forte (Skelton)
Chris Carter at Large – Stories from a lifetime in motorcycle racing (Carter & Skelton)
Edward Turner – The Man Behind the Motorcycles (Clew)
Jim Redman – 6 Times World Motorcycle Champion: The Autobiography (Redman)

'Sox' – Gary Hocking – the forgotten World Motorcycle Champion (Hughes)

General
BMW Boxer Twins 1970-1995 Bible, The (Falloon)
BMW Cafe Racers (Cloesen)
BMW Custom Motorcycles – Choppers, Cruisers, Bobbers, Trikes & Quads (Cloesen)
Bonjour – Is this Italy? (Turner)
British 250cc Racing Motorcycles (Pereira)
British Café Racers (Cloesen)
British Custom Motorcycles – The Brit Chop – choppers, cruisers, bobbers & trikes (Cloesen)
BSA Bantam Bible, The (Henshaw)
BSA Motorcycles – the final evolution (Jones)
Ducati 750 Bible, The (Falloon)
Ducati 750 SS 'round-case' 1974, The Book of the (Falloon)
Ducati 860, 900 and Mille Bible, The (Falloon)
Ducati Monster Bible (New Updated & Revised Edition), The (Falloon)
Ducati 916 (updated edition) (Falloon)
Fine Art of the Motorcycle Engine, The (Peirce)
From Crystal Palace to Red Square – A Hapless Biker's Road to Russia (Turner)
Funky Mopeds (Skelton)
Italian Cafe Racers (Cloesen)
Italian Custom Motorcycles (Cloesen)
Japanese Custom Motorcycles – The Nippon Chop – Chopper, Cruiser, Bobber, Trikes and Quads (Cloesen)
Kawasaki Triples Bible, The (Walker)
Kawasaki Z1 Story, The (Sheehan)
Laverda Twins & Triples Bible 1968-1986 (Falloon)
Moto Guzzi Sport & Le Mans Bible, The (Falloon)
Motorcycle GP Racing in the 1960s (Pereira)
Motorcycle Road & Racing Chassis Designs (Noakes)
MV Agusta Fours, The book of the classic (Falloon)
The Norton Commando Bible – All models 1968 to 1978 (Henshaw)
Off-Road Giants! (Volume 1) – Heroes of 1960s Motorcycle Sport (Westlake)
Off-Road Giants! (Volume 2) – Heroes of 1960s Motorcycle Sport (Westlake)
Off-Road Giants! (volume 3) – Heroes of 1960s Motorcycle Sport (Westlake)
Racing Line – British motorcycle racing in the golden age of the big single (Guntrip)
Scooters & Microcars, The A-Z of Popular (Dan)
Scooter Lifestyle (Grainger)
SCOOTER MANIA! – Recollections of the Isle of Man International Scooter Rally (Jackson)
Triumph Bonneville Bible (59-83) (Henshaw)
Triumph Bonneville!, Save the – The inside story of the Meriden Workers' Co-op (Rosamond)
Triumph Motorcycles & the Meriden Factory (Hancox)
Triumph Speed Twin & Thunderbird Bible (Woolridge)
Triumph Tiger Cub Bible (Estall)
Triumph Trophy Bible (Woolridge)
TT Talking – The TT's most exciting era – As seen by Manx Radio TT's lead commentator 2004-2012 (Lambert)
Velocette Motorcycles – MSS to Thruxton – New Third Edition (Burris)
Vincent Motorcycles: The Untold Story since 1946 (Guyony & Parker)

For post publication news, updates and amendments relating to this book please scan the QR code or visit
www.veloce.co.uk/books/V5044

Jim Redman MBE
– Six Times World Motorcycle Champion
The Autobiography

VELOCE PUBLISHING
THE PUBLISHER OF FINE AUTOMOTIVE BOOKS

First published in 1998. Reprinted in 1999, May 2006, March 2013 and October 2016 by Veloce Publishing Ltd, Veloce House, Parkway Farm Business Park, Middle Farm Way, Poundbury, Dorchester, Dorset DT1 3AR. Tel: 01305 260068 Fax: 01305 268864 / E-mail: info@veloce.co.uk.

ISBN 978-1-787110-44-1 / UPC 6-36847-01044-7

© Jim Redman and Veloce Publishing Ltd 1998, 1999, 2006, 2013 & October 2016.

All rights reserved. With the exception of quoting brief passages for the purpose of review, no part of this publication may be recorded, reproduced or transmitted by any means, including photocopying, without the written permission of Veloce Publishing Ltd.

Throughout this book logos, model names and designations, etc, may have been used for the purposes of identification, illustration and decoration. Such names are the property of the trademark holder as this is not an official publication.

Readers with ideas for automotive books, or books on other transport or related hobby subjects, are invited to write to Veloce Publishing at the above address.

British Library Cataloguing in Publication Data –
A catalogue record for this book is available from the British Library.

Typesetting (Palatino), design and page make-up all by Veloce on AppleMac.

Printed and Bound by CPI Group (UK) Ltd, Croydon, CR04YY.

Front cover photo: Jim Redman on his way to winning the 1964 Ulster Grand Prix (© BR 'Nick' Nicholls); rear: Jim and 'Ago' share a joke at Daytona in 1996.

Contents

    Introduction & Acknowledgements 6
1. Daytona Comeback 8
2. Hard Years 15
    Picture Gallery 1 33
3. The Promised Land 55
4. First Year in Europe 68
5. Life of a Nomad 74
    Picture Gallery 2 81
6. Some Dreams Come True 97
7. A Factory Rider 108
8. Tears of Blood 117
9. The Ultimate Dream Realised 124
    Picture Gallery 3 129
10. Expensive Victories 146
11. The Honda 6 168
12. Two Wheels, or Four? 174
    Picture Gallery 4 177
13. The Final Crash 209
14. Honda 218
15. Back to Normal Life 220
16. Salt in the Wound 241
17. A New Beginning 252
    Epilogue 270
    What Others Say 273
    Postscript 279
    Jim Redman's World Championship Results 283
    Sixty Years 287

Introduction

I've had a fantastic life. When in my 30s, if anyone asked my age I said I was 280 years old, as I felt that I had packed into my life as least four times as much as anyone else who expects to live to 70. I have lived my life to the full, doing more or less everything I wanted to do; this is one thing about which I am absolutely certain.

Like a book, my life goes from one event to another, from one chapter to the next. There is no personal attempt to find the sense in life, no effort to link events or facts - paradoxical for a motorcycle rider - yet this path is mine. When I see an opportunity, or if it simply crosses my path, I grab it with both hands.

Writing my autobiography was not my idea. I try never to look behind me except, perhaps, to tell a story. But this project was a challenge (although I am quite surprised that people want to read about me) and what I love about life is the challenge, the risk, the unknown. Hardship, effort, or hard work has never deterred me. The only thing which ever counted was the excitement and possibility of success; that's the fuel that makes my engine run, I've led my life as if I was in a series of races, trying to win each one in order to go on to the next.

Money, fame, fortune, the rewards are pleasant, but not my objective. I am a wandering gambler and at times cars, houses, jewels, antiques, clothes, horses, companies, and even airplanes, have been my stakes. In reality, material acquisitions weigh me down as I can be happy with a notepad, a pen, a telephone and my brain. I am certain I always play the game honestly and loyally.

The early days of my life were not easy, and I did not grow up with an idealized notion of life and human behavior. I had to face some very hard truths during my youth, and make some difficult decisions. I am a very good workhorse and think - somewhat naively - that everybody is like me.

I am a networker; that is to say, I know a lot of people and have always taken the opportunity of getting to know more and more. People of all ages, cultures and social spheres - different characters, different lifestyles. These people make up the network in which I operate. That means my family, too, as they are also my friends.

Proof that, fundamentally, not much has changed within me over the years is the way in which I approached this project. Two years ago it was a good idea, but a year ago only a possibility. Then, all of a sudden, I began typing on an old typewriter. As with most people with no literary experience it wasn't an easy task, and very often I had to do it again. However, in very little time, I found within my network and amongst my friends, a team of people who shared my excitement and devoted time and effort to the creation of this book. One day I decided to write a book. I wrote it. I told a story. I hope that my story inspires and interests a great number of people, and will encourage those who, like me, were not born with a silver spoon in their mouths to strive for a more exciting, satisfying and better life.

– Acknowledgements –

I would like to thank everybody involved in this project, and particularly the following people, who helped me put my life down on paper: Arnaldo Wittemberg, Pierre Pampini, Andy Kershaw, Toni Blumeris, Caroline Coates and, of course, my wife, Kwezi. Thanks too, to all the photographers who kindly allowed me to use the images which add so much to this book.

Then, of course, there are my sponsors, without whom the whole project would have never got off the ground. These are Honda, Giulio Barbieri and Special Modular Coverings, Cooper-Avon Tyres Ltd., Stan Lewis and RDBS Computers & Software, Luke and John Lawlor, Martin Jones, Tim Clinton, Steve and KIC.org.uk, Rob Iannucci and Team Obsolete, Castrol Oils, Vanson Leathers, artist Jim Blanchard, Shell Fuels, Ferry Brouwer from the Centennial GP at Assen and owner of Arai Helmets, Bruce Joelson from Elna Sewing Machines in South Africa, The Life Extension Clinic, Auto Riviera Limousine and Alpinestars.

I also offer my sincere thanks to Giacomo Agostini, Reg Bolton, Ralph Bryans, Maurice Büla, Nobby Clark, Stuart Graham, Rob Iannucci, Nanou Lyonnard, Frank Perris, Phil Read and Luigi Taveri for their kind comments. I would also like to thank my friend, Barry Hearn, for all he has done to help me.

Jim Redman
South Africa

— Publisher's Note —

We apologise for the poor quality of reproduction of some of the photographs in this book. Unfortunately, the originals of some pictures have been lost over the years and therefore relatively poor quality duplicates had to be used, however we felt the importance of the photographs justified their inclusion.

1
Daytona Comeback

— **DAYTONA SPEEDWAY March 1995** —
The flag man signalled the start of the last lap and, at the same moment, I was passed by my team mate, Dave Roper, which dropped me back into second place again. I had spent the last few laps working out a way to try and beat Dave: his reserve was an unknown quantity - as was mine, not having been tested for years. Then, a sudden swerve by riders we were lapping, a collision, and down in a heap went Dave and his bike with the other rider and his bike; leaving me to cruise the last half lap and victoriously take the chequered flag ... 26 years after winning the last race of my long career.

What a win this was for me: 63 years of age, my first race on an MV Agusta motorcycle, my first race on a banked circuit, my first race in America and my first race for 26 years, apart from a warm-up at a small meeting in Georgia a few days earlier just to get the feel of things once more. You can imagine the feeling of crossing the finishing line and riding down victory lane again, after all those years away from the thrill, excitement and adrenaline rush of motorcycle racing ...

It was wonderful to cruise in and see the excitement in the huge smiles on the faces of my wife, Kwezi, my sponsor, Rob Iannucci, and my mechanic of 33 years, Nobby Clark, along with the rest of the Team Obsolete crew, and to see the commentator, Richard Chamberlain, going red in the face and almost swallowing his mike with excitement as he yelled to the crowd. He was telling them over and over again: this man is 63 years of age and has not raced for 26 years ... The grins, the slaps on the back and handshakes from my fans, some of whom had made the long trip from Europe to America just to see me ride once more, everyone asking me how it felt to be back in the winner's circle, I told them it would be at least 6 months before anything could wipe the smile off my face.

This whole Daytona episode began towards the end of 1994 when,

Daytona Comeback

one day, I received a call, out of the blue, from Rob Iannucci, owner of Team Obsolete. He called to tell me that he now owned the 1964 250 Honda 6 that I had raced at Monza in the Italian GP of that year. He also told me that he had my old mechanic, Nobby Clark, who had worked on the bike back in the 60s, in New York working on it again. He asked me if I would be interested in coming to Willow Springs in Colorado, to ride the 250 on some exhibition laps. Since I was planning to go to the United States on business, I told Rob that I would be in New York and that we could meet there and have lunch and discuss the whole thing. "Lunch?" said Rob, "No way! Come and spend a couple of days at my place." So I ended up in Brooklyn Heights staying at Rob's house, where we agreed that I would try and come to Willow Springs in October 1994, but if, for any reason, I couldn't make it, it was agreed I would ride demonstrations at Daytona in March the following year, 1995. What a good time we both had during my stay in New York. We rode all over New York and surrounding areas, Rob on a Harley Davidson, and me on his road-going G50 Matchless. After a two hour uninterrupted ride, we stopped off for breakfast in one of the last of those old 1960s-style diners, with the juke boxes on the tables, and sat down to a hearty, good old-fashioned American breakfast. I realized during my stay with Rob that he was a junkie for the classic golden era bikes of the 60s, just like me.

Back in the 60s, when we were just riders trying to make a living and win some titles, we did not realize that we were making such motorcycle racing history - which would never again be repeated. Those days were unique as there were not the restrictions there are today; everyone was allowed to use as many cylinders as they wished on all the bikes and make as much noise as they liked. We were real pioneers. The races were much longer than they are today and, of course, a hell of a lot more dangerous, but there was such madness, such real warmth, and such a really unique atmosphere. I feel so lucky to have belonged to this very special era. Some people say that Honda invented a noise and then built the "6" to make the noise. Nowadays, the bikes are so bland, they look the same and don't make any noise; gone is that spine-tingling sound that brought enthusiasts from Europe to America just to hear one bike do a few laps. Now, it's totally different to what we knew.

After breakfast we dropped in to see an old friend of Rob's called 'Frenchy,' who was full of punch, with a great personality. He loved speed and wild challenges and showed us the plane he has been building in his workshop for years. He told us about his latest exploit, intended to give him one 'last thrill,' because he thought that, at 77 years of age, he was getting to the age where he should drive more slowly and 'carefully.' This last thrill would be a blast on his BMW, a rapid trip to Florida and back. Donning his leather suit, he asked his wife what she thought he should spend on fines for this trip? His wife replied that whatever she said he would go as fast as he wanted, so it wasn't necessary to have her approval.

With a large smile, he said that $300 dollars would be his budget for fines

Jim Redman

for this trip and that, once spent, he would slow down. He put the money in the outside pocket of his leathers and took off like a rocket for Florida. Of course, he was soon stopped for speeding, but what a surprise for the policeman when Frenchy took off his helmet to reveal a wrinkled, chiselled and weather-beaten 77 year old face, and greeted him with "Yes Sonny, what do you want?" Astounded, the policeman let him off with a warning not to go over the speed limit again, at least not in *his* jurisdiction. Frenchy obeyed until he was out of the area, and then went racing again, getting to Florida and back without paying a single fine by calling all the policemen "Sonny."

In the end, it turned out that I was unable to make the Willow Springs event, so we firmed up that I would demonstrate the Honda 6 at Daytona in March 1995.

Right away I started to get myself into shape. Years ago, when I was riding, I never had to exercise to get myself in shape as I always raced at between 40 and 45 meetings a year, riding 2 or 3 classes, so I was race fit and did not need any particular training. It was only after my crash, at Spa-Francorchamps in 1966, where I broke my wrist so badly and had to have a few months off because it would not heal properly, that I found out you have to be fit to race bikes. It came as quite a surprise to me as I had always said it wasn't necessary to be fit to race bikes, not realizing just how race fit I was from years of non-stop racing. I rode in the Rhodesian GP on a Honda 250 four-cylinder and found that, because I had not ridden for a few months, I ached all over - even after such a short race. I remembered this experience and started walking every day and took up roller blading, getting my body back into some kind of shape. I have always been lazy about exercise but now I had a rendezvous with Daytona.

A few days before leaving home for Daytona, I received a phone call from Rob Iannucci who asked me how I felt about racing a 1967 MV Agusta 350cc, ridden previously by Agostini back in the 60s. He added that in case I did feel like racing he had registered me to race in the 350cc Classic GP race, next to Dave Roper, the Obsolete Team's number one rider, who would also be racing on an MV Agusta. On hearing this I said to him "Hey Rob, wait a minute, are you bloody crazy or something? It's 26 years since I last raced!" To which he replied "OK. Well, just try the bike and you'll see how you feel ..." Inside, I heard myself saying "After all, why not? I've really got nothing to lose and it could be fun."

I contacted the AA of South Africa to apply for an international license (awarded depending on the points scored the previous year). Of course, I had to admit that I had not scored any points for 26 years, so the lady put me through to her boss who, when I explained the situation, replied "OK, Jim! I'll send you a license, but be bloody careful." What a tremendous attitude!

When I climbed onto the MV at the Roeblin Road Raceway, in Savannah, Georgia, to carry out my first trial laps in 26 years, I felt horribly uncomfortable and very, very rusty. Once back in the pits, the whole team gathered around

Daytona Comeback

me to find out how I felt. The only answer that came out was "Fucking awful; I'm all over the place, but at least I'm fair to the track, as I'm on a different line every lap!" Rob was clever enough to say to me "Don't forget that you have just done the hardest part, from now on you will feel better every time you go out." Of course, he was right; as training progressed I could only get better and start to feel more comfortable.

After a few more laps on the MV Agusta, I took to the track again, this time riding the Honda 6. All of a sudden, like magic, things fell into place as I immediately felt at home on the Honda. I started to feel comfortable again, as if I had always been welded to the machine, despite these 26 years away from all racing competition. Then, when I went back to the MV, I felt much better than I had during those first laps. In the following race, because I had never tried a clutch start before I made a false start and was given the black flag (which meant a 10 second stop/go penalty) on the second lap. Once I was allowed to rejoin the race I managed to catch up and pass all but the first six riders. In short, for a new beginning it was rather encouraging ...

Then came that fateful day - the race at Daytona. Once again I found myself on the MV Agusta 350, as the Honda 6 was not available for racing. There are no spare parts and, if the bike breaks, everything has to be specially made, which is very expensive, so we decided that it would be used for exhibition laps only. I was shocked to find myself in about 50th position on the starting line - out of a total of around 60! I complained and said I felt sure I had not practiced that slowly, but was told that, in classic racing, grid positions are allocated on points scored the previous years. Since I had not participated in any races for so long, they had placed me first in the group of riders without points.

I was having the same pains in the stomach I had when I was a young man, not butterflies this time, more like seagulls; which was exactly how I always felt before a particularly hard race. My heart was beating uncontrollably, my legs felt as though they were folding up under me, my hands and the rest of my body tensed and were damp with sweat, and my eyes could hardly focus on the track in front of me. Then the flag went down and all this stuff disappeared as it always did in that fraction of a second when the flag drops.

As we entered the first corner, all the riders lined up on the correct line and followed each other round - a very classic reaction. This left tons of room on the wrong line for me to go right round the outside of loads of them. Just passing them on my left, one by one, made me feel real good, so much so that, on that first lap, I was able to go from 50th to 12th place, which amazed Kwezi, my wife, as she had never seen me ride before. I was surprised too, as were a lot of other people.

The bike handled beautifully. I would have been happier on the Honda but only because I felt more at home on it than I did on the MV. Once a race is underway, you concentrate on how you are going to overtake the rider

Jim Redman

ahead of you. As you probably know, Daytona is a banked circuit, which was new to me, so I found it quite scary overtaking a lot of riders on those first two laps. You see, the fastest line is down at the bottom, and the faster riders follow in the slipstream and pass on the right, higher up the banking. The problem for me was that they were in big bunches and I was having to pass right up at the top, taking a deep breath and scraping through between the top rider and the outer wall. Not good stuff for an old fart of 63 who was not the rider he was some years earlier. However, by the third lap, I was up with the leaders, which is always the safest place to be as at least they know what they are doing. Then I got ahead and - once - was in the lead. I could have kept going for a hundred laps or more ...

There were a few other problems. When lapping the slower riders, the main one was being confronted with a multitude of different types of motorbike, and just as many different types - whether in talent or experience - of rider. Some, at over 50 years of age, were racing for the first time in their lives and were like mobile chicanes, cluttering up the road all over the place. However, this was classic racing and they were out to enjoy themselves, so good luck to them. The minimum age for classic racing is 36. Some of us had loads of experience to draw on; others were in a steep learning curve - and it showed.

Kwezi, who had come along to support and encourage me, was very surprised to see me, after the first lap, in twelfth position, then moving up into fourth place and finally in second place behind Dave Roper who was on the other MV Agusta. Before the race, Dave had said to me that he would try to beat the lap record on the last lap. For the time being, we still had five laps to go, and here we were, neck and neck. At this particular instant, I thought to myself, every lap I am improving a lot (believe me, there was plenty of room for improvement), and I knew this race was not over yet. I thought if Dave wants to win, which, of course, he did, he still has to beat me. I knew that on the last lap I had to try and keep close enough behind him so that I could try and slipstream him enough on the last straight to allow me to slingshot past him before the finishing flag. Ferociously engaged against each other, suddenly, a lapper seemed to surge out of nowhere and he brought Dave down. From where I was, behind Dave, I saw the accident coming and was able to shut off in time to avoid it. There are some consolations to getting older, particularly the experience you can call upon.

Now I was in the lead, out on my own, miles ahead of the second guy, without a worry in the world and only half a lap to go. I felt an incredible mixture of exhilaration and dizzying happiness overcome me. Just being in the lead made my adrenaline shoot up. I felt invincible. Andy Kershaw from the BBC had wired up the bike to make a recording of the race and the mike was in the centre of the handlebars so I leant forward and said into it "OK, BBC listeners we have got this race won." Then, as I accelerated up to maximum speed on the banking for the last time, I knew that, even if the

Daytona Comeback

motor exploded, I could pull in the clutch and coast over the finishing line, so nothing could stop me from winning! When I got to the finishing line, I was in a state of exhilaration - young again. How could I have expected that, 26 years after retiring, I would be winning again?

I made the usual lap of honour to allow me to unwind - in the back of my mind wanting this moment, unique in my life, never to end ... I stopped halfway round, next to Dave, and asked him if he wanted to hop on and catch a ride back to the pits, but he preferred to help the rider with whom he had collided. I left him there and continued my ride down 'Victory Lane.' I glimpsed the excitement and astonishment on my wife, Kwezi's, face, and the flabbergasted expression on Rob Iannucci's face, along with Nobby and all of the team. Everyone was grinning from ear to ear, including me inside my helmet, but if I wasn't wearing my helmet, they would all have seen my eyes filled with tears; tears of joy.

Over the microphone, the excited commentator, Richard Chamberlain, almost swallowed his microphone, while screaming incessantly "Ladies and Gentlemen ... this man has not raced for 26 years ... This is the first time that he has ever raced in the United States ... This is the first time that he has raced here in Daytona ... This is the first time he has raced on a banked circuit ... This is the first time he has raced on an MV Agusta ... And he's 63 years old!"

When I arrived back at the pits, everybody ran out to congratulate and interview me. They kept asking me how I felt and each time I replied that I would need at least six months to get the smile off my face. Riders, spectators, journalists, photographers, cameramen, were all so incredibly nice to me. Everybody was so fantastic, I couldn't believe that it was me over whom all this fuss was being made. Phenomenal pleasure, great pride and an almost irresistible need to cry, flooded my innermost soul. I thought to myself, there's still some life in the old fart yet. In fact, two years later I recounted this story to a group of fans at the Yorkshire air museum and one of them wrote: "All of us listening forgot our aches and pains, and high blood pressure and felt inspired." You can imagine how proud I felt reading that.

Rob and I had decided that I would demonstrate the Honda 6 alone on the circuit for all the fans, some of whom had travelled all the way from Europe to hear the 'music' from the exhaust pipes of this six-cylinder bike. The Daytona Speedway management liked this idea but, for some reason, Jeff Smith, an Englishman who runs the AHRMA meetings in the States, categorically refused. He wanted me to ride in a full parade of riders which would mean that the beautiful sound of the 6 would be lost amongst that from the other bikes. So many people had come to Daytona specially to see and hear the Honda 6, that we could not let them down on the whim of one man, so we agreed with Larry Bellucci, Vice President of Daytona Speedway, that I would ride my demonstration laps during the lunch break, when the circuit reverted back to the control of the Daytona Speedway. As I was starting up the motor, Jeff arrived and tried to stop me going out and went to Rob Iannucci

13

Jim Redman

to tell him the same. Then, while he was complaining to Rob, he heard me take off and immediately ran to the flag man to stop me, but was too late. For some reason this made him furious and he rushed over to me as I pulled in and stopped, and, in front of the world's motorcycle media, grabbed me by the arm and ordered me to remove this 'thing' from the circuit. He was like a madman and I felt very sorry for him, making such a pitiful spectacle of himself in front of the media people, who had just been enchanted by the beautiful sound of the "6."

Personally, I was so delighted with my victory on the MV that nothing and nobody could spoil my joy. I found out later that there had been problems between Jeff and Rob for years, and I was just caught up in the crossfire. Later, Jeff apologized for his behaviour, adding that he could help me a lot on my trips to the States, but I would have to break off my relationship with Rob Iannucci. For example, he could get me a ride in the BMW-sponsored Legends race. I told him that if they wanted me to ride in the Legends race, I would consider it, but this would have nothing to do with my relationship with Rob. Of course, I heard nothing more.

For the fifteen days of Daytona Speedweek, Daytona becomes motorbike city. A huge banner proclaiming "Daytona welcomes all motorcyclists" greets visitors as they arrive in town. Thousands of riders descend on downtown Daytona; some travelling across the country and the world just to be there. I was amazed to discover that, in main street Daytona, some motorbike shops only open during this two-week period and the two weeks of Biketober Fest, but still pay rent for the whole year.

For the time being, I was still coming to grips with this unexpected, undreamed of victory and was literally overwhelmed by fans wanting autographs on anything they had in their hands - pamphlets, programs, autograph books, and even expensive motorcycle books. I spent two hours signing autographs and, in the middle of the commotion of all these people fighting to be the first to get an interview or a photo, I could see only one person. My eyes were fixed on a little boy, a slightly puny, little blue-eyed child with a scrawny air about him. There he was in front of me. Quiet. Looking me straight in the eye, with a shy and fearful smile on the corners of his lips. Suddenly we were alone, he held out a clean piece of paper and a pen with a large smile. Why did this little boy touch me so deeply? Why did I want to pick him up and squeeze him in my arms? Why? Because this little boy looked just like me at that age ...

2
Hard Years

My earliest memory from childhood is of my first brush with authority. My older sister, Jackie, was three years old and was going to nursery school for the first time. I decided to follow along but, when we arrived at the school gate, I was gently returned home (which was just over the road). Nevertheless, the next day I went again, but I need not have bothered, as I was just sent home again. However, I was very stubborn and went after Jackie again and again until the school finally gave in and got the message that I wanted to go to school. I was two years old at the time and have no idea why I did this as I was never a good scholar and did not enjoy school, except for the sport.

This story always touches me each time I remember it as, without doubt, it exemplifies the 'why' of my existence and the fact that I have always had to fight for everything in my life, and often had problems with the powers that be. I was born on the 8th of November, 1931, in West Hampstead, England, into a family of modest means but with great dignity and lots of love. We were all cherished by a wonderful woman - my mother. To me she was a goddess and I would have done, and did do, anything for her. I loved her deeply. She was the one who convinced me that I could do anything I set my mind to. She was the one who taught me that everything should be done well, to the best of your ability. I remember her sombre look and long, dark blond hair; she was slim but also had that certain 'something' that made her stand out wherever she was. Despite her very short life and modest existence, she was always very gay, intelligent and cultivated, and was musically gifted. Above all, she possessed the most insatiable appetite for life. A shorthand typist by profession, she loved horseriding and, for a long time, assiduously practiced fencing, in fact, up until the day she met my father ...

My father, in his youth, was a rather handsome man, with red, curly hair. He was born in the country but made his way to London to try his luck. He had no particular skills yet had no desire to follow in his father's

Jim Redman

footsteps as a tradesman living in the country. He quickly found a job with the bookshop W. H. Smith, but experienced difficulty making friends until, one day, a colleague took pity on him and invited him along on an outing with his girlfriend and his girlfriend's sister. The girlfriend's sister turned out to be my mother and it was love at first sight. Their love affair began at this moment, despite the fact that my mother's parents did not fully approve of their liaison - but love was stronger than all else: in no time they were married and my older sister, Jackie, was born on May 7th, 1930.

At this time my parents had just started their own little shop, in which was sold all sorts of things like newspapers, cigarettes and sweets, with the approval of my maternal grandfather, "Grampie." These "Newsagents and Tobacconists" shops as they were called at the time, were very popular in England, as they still are today. So, thanks to their little shop, my parents led a quiet, peaceful existence, not a rich one, but they lacked nothing. This happiness turned out to be precarious as, although my father was capable of hard work, he had one terrible problem - he was a gambler and a born loser who ended up spending most of his time in the shop talking about horse and greyhound races with his fellow gamblers. He would bet on anything and everything. How many times my mother must have tried to persuade him to give up this destructive habit and, each time, feeling guilty, my father promised he would.

My mother, as a pastime, made ice creams or popsicles which she kept in the fridge, and these became so popular that people came from all over the area - some even by bus - just to buy hers. So, in its small way, the shop had a lot of possibilities, especially as my mother insisted my father must give up gambling completely before she would borrow the money from Grampie to open it. However - everything went up in smoke. It must have been that my father's urge to gamble was stronger than anything else as, one day, whilst working in the shop, a stranger came in to buy some tobacco. Just as he was about to pay, the man asked my father which horse he fancied for the main race of the day. This was the beginning of the end of the little business as my father began to bet again, until, in order to pay off his debts, my parents were obliged to sell the shop at a loss. From here on life was never again the same at home. After this painful event, the family had to move to Dornfell Street in Hampstead, close to Grampie and my grandmother, "Mumsie's," home - and it was at this time that I was born.

After my birth, my mother found a job in a bookstore, and somehow found time to teach Jackie to read and write until she was able to go to nursery school. My father, however, was unable to find a permanent job and accepted odd jobs here and there, which were mostly badly paid. It was for this reason that, despite substantial help from Grampie, we lived relatively poorly.

A lot of people were out of work, there were no jobs, it was the 1929 slump and, with the Great Depression that followed, we were not the only ones in this situation. At last, my father found a steady job delivering milk.

16

Hard Years

The problem was we had to move again so that my father could be closer to his work.

We next found ourselves living in Heber Road in Cricklewood. Here, every day, with his horsedrawn cart, Father went around delivering milk, with a long day on Saturday collecting payment from all the families who had milk delivered. A very ordinary job, but in times of crisis one couldn't turn work down and accepted anything. I was very young at the time, but I helped him with these deliveries and, in return, he gave me a few pence.

At home, things were not that good, in fact, far from it. Despite so little money coming in, my mother tried her best when it came to feeding us. Meat and fish were very expensive for her to buy, but at least we ate better than we had when my father could not find work. At that time we had lived on rice puddings, day after day she prepared them for the simple reason that they were cheap and, above all, nutritious and filling. One would think that today I would hate rice puddings - God knows I ate enough of them when I was young - but, no, I love them, although they *must* be made the way my mother made them. I was six years old when my twin brother and sister, Peter and Wendy, were born. Jackie was the one that chose their names from the book of the adventures of Peter Pan and Wendy. I can remember going down my street jumping for joy and saying "I've got a little brother and a little sister! I've got a little brother and a little sister!" They were not very big at birth: Wendy weighed three pounds, while Peter just made two and a half pounds and, afraid he would not survive, my parents had him baptized immediately. However, we hadn't counted on all the love and attention my mother showered upon him, which eventually saved him.

The whole family was crazy about the twins. Twins were a probability in our family as Mumsie had a twin sister, and Grampie's mother had given birth to several sets - his family had no less than 22 children and Grampie was the eighteenth. It was at this time that the relationship between my mother and father began to suffer; they were having more and more arguments and my father was bringing home very little money. He must have been miserable and felt responsible for the situation. Luckily for us children, we were able to spend a lot of time with Grampie and Mumsie. We loved going to their home where it was calm and peaceful. Their lives were comfortable.

My grandfather was employed as a street lamp lighter in London and was in charge of a whole area. Since the 19th century, the streets of London had been lit by gas lamps which cast a particularly uneasy and strange light on the Capital, and within which one could feel the phantom of Jack the Ripper floating. When Grampie went to Tower Bridge he always took his wife with him, and both of them, very romantically, lit the lights on both sides of the bridge. Sometimes access to the upper part of the monument was forbidden, because of the many suicides. Above all, my grandparents were musicians. Mumsie had a perfect ear. It was only necessary for her to hear a piece of music once to be able to replay it on her piano. As for Grampie, he played the

Jim Redman

flat tuba which, since he was only one-and-a-half metres tall, was practicaly the same size as he was. This didn't bother him at all as he loved entering competitions because he walked away with many prizes.

Each time Grampie left for work he was impeccably dressed in pure white false collar and white cuffs which he changed every day. One would have thought he was the director of a large business. He enjoyed people looking at him and at least could say that he did not go unnoticed. From my maternal grandparents I have warm and affectionate memories of happiness and gentleness. Then war broke out and, since at the time everyone was quite naive about how it would be in the blitz of London, and hoping to escape the bombings, we moved from Cricklewood in the London suburbs, 15 kilometers away to Enmore Road in Southall, which was near Greenford in Middlesex. At the same time, my father transferred to the Middlesex dairies and thought that we would be protected by being out there in the country. This seems such a joke today to think of moving 15 kilometers out of London and calling it "out in the country." This naivety led the family setting up house close to Northolt Airport, but it could not have been worse had we stayed in our London suburb. As a matter of fact, during the war, Northolt Airport became one of the Germans' favourite targets.

With our house being so close to Northolt, and Britain's Air Defence installations close by, we must have had more than our fair share of bombs and shells. It was at this time - the end of 1939 - that my father was called up into the Royal Army Ordnance Corps. My parents were fighting more and more, and my father on the quiet was still betting. Unfortunately for my mother, she found out and could not stop crying. I started to detest my father for all the unhappiness he was causing my mother and, because of this, his departure into the army was a great relief for all of us, and we quickly became accustomed to his absence. We soon became aware of everything concerning the war and, as children will, turned the blitz into a game. As for my mother, for the first time since her marriage she received a regular, although small, source of income - her army allowance, and there was no-one to gamble it away for her.

All of us children in the neighborhood had a little box in which was jealously kept all the pieces of shrapnel each had found. We all exchanged pieces of land mines, grenades, bullets, cartridges, bombs, and so on. The game consisted of collecting the most unusual trophies; we even came to recognize the sound of the German airplane motors when they flew over us and knew the difference between a German and British plane just by the sound. We even knew which were the pilotless planes, or "doodlebugs," as they were nicknamed. When we heard them getting close, we knew we were in the danger zone but that, once we were able to see them, we were safe. If the motor stopped there and then, the doodlebugs would still have enough momentum to fly over our heads and land on somewhere else further away. We never considered the potential danger, the only thing that excited us was

Hard Years

the possibility of finding new trophies. When an explosion occurred, we tried to guess if the impact was close enough for us to be able to go and pick up the pieces of shrapnel. It was a game like any other.

From 1940 onwards, the air raids had steadily worsened and we were bombarded, as Northolt became a prime target for the Germans. Our bathroom window exploded into tiny pieces during one of the repeated attacks by enemy planes; our attitude was that at least we did not have far to go to pick up the pieces of shrapnel - they were already in our own bathroom! The same evening the street next to ours was literally flattened. Furthermore, right next door to our house, our local school - with its very modern architecture - became the target for the air raids; we think the Germans mistook it for some kind of military building.

It was about this time that Jackie and I caught sight of our first corpse, it had just been extracted from one of the blown apart houses ... close to where we usually rode our bikes ...

My mother was a marvel in our eyes. She managed as best she could between the rationing, the air raids, looking out for our safety and, at the same time, exchanging clothing coupons for food coupons for us. She had started to take in lodgers to earn extra money and to help with the war effort, so it was not unusual for my brother and me to find ourselves sharing our bedroom with strangers. Very often the lodgers went to their own homes on the weekends and stayed with us during the week, because the war materials factory in which they worked was too far away from their homes to commute daily. Above all, my mother did not want us to be left alone and the most important thing for her was to make the house earn some money in order to pay for its upkeep.

My mother worked very hard to make our lives as pleasant as possible. She did everything in the house: I can still see her sitting on the floor with shoemender's tools putting new soles on our shoes, then cutting off the protruding leather and finally putting heavy weights on the edges so that they stuck down. Each of us did our best to help her: Jackie with household tasks, Wendy and Peter set the table and I took care of the heavy work. We even had a washing machine that had to be wound by hand, with a wooden bar for handles that was inserted in the machine, which we then turned. It was a long and hard job, which had to be done if we wanted to be as clean and decent as possible.

How many times during the night were we startled awake as the sirens went off and ran for cover in the Anderson shelter in the garden? How many cold and damp nights did I pass down there? These shelters, which were half buried in the ground, filled with water during the winter and we had to bail out the water in order for the ground to dry. Each time the sirens went off my mother used to grab Wendy and Peter under each arm and shout for Jackie and me to follow, and we would run to the shelter for protection. We had to sit or sleep on a mattress dotted with wet patches from the constant water

19

Jim Redman

leaks. Finally, fed-up with all these comings and goings I said to my mother "If Hitler wants me he's going to have to come and get me. I am not going to get out of my bed again for him ..." There was also the Morrisson shelter, a sort of very big, very heavy table made of steel, under which we used to sleep, the idea being that, if the house collapsed, we had at least a fighting chance of being found safe under this table among the debris. These shelters worked very well and saved a lot of lives, unless, of course, the house took a direct hit from a bomb.

In fact, if I had to describe my childhood, two words would be enough: incessant struggle. When I was eleven years old, we were all evacuated to the north of England. It was common at the time to move the children as far away from London as possible. Consequently, for the evacuation, we were all assembled in an old school which served as the point of assignment. It had an immense entrance hall and the floor was lined with mattresses. The girls were placed in one side of the hall and the boys on the other. Wendy and Peter stood up on their mattresses and made signs in the air to each other: they wanted to remain together. Finally, the people responsible for the evacuation process understood that they were twins and arranged for them to be kept together. Despite the sadness of being separated from our loving mother, they cuddled up against each other and quickly fell asleep. Five years old at the time, Peter and Wendy were sent to Berrington village, near Shrewsbury in Shropshire. They were taken care of by Mrs Lewis, a charming and loving lady, who had a house in the country where the twins spent many pleasant years.

Jackie cried for a whole week when she was told of our upcoming departure. The thought of leaving my mother alone with the bombardments was unbearable, so she was allowed to stay at home. I had less luck. Because of a mistake in the evacuation plan, I was sent to Shrewsbury in Shropshire (instead of Dewsbury in Yorkshire), not far from where the twins were, into the home of a school headmaster. He and his wife were impassive, mean-spirited and very cold people. As soon as I arrived, I could immediately feel their resentment at having to have me there; they only did it because everyone was expected to help and, in his position as headmaster, he could not very well be the odd one out. It would not be putting it too strongly to say that I detested this family. After my own warm home I could not stand being imprisoned in a family that seemed to despise me. Even though the neighbours and other residents seemed nice and were decent to us, I could hardly understand a word of what they said because their accent was so strong.

So, for most of the time, I felt completely alone, and missed my mother a lot. Since I was the only one to come from a secondary school, this caused a lot of problems in an area where there were only technical establishments. Finally, following another administrative mistake, I found myself left out without even having been integrated into a school. Of course, I made sure that the headmaster did not find out about this, and immediately looked for

Hard Years

a job which would allow me to earn enough money in order to return home as soon as possible. I found myself a job helping a bread delivery man - a job I had already learned with my father as it was more or less the same as the milk deliveries. The bread was delivered every morning, and we went to collect the money at the end of the week. I managed very well as far as tips were concerned and could start saving money for my return home.

The man I was helping had just been hired and did not know how to keep track of his accounts, so I took care of the accounts book for him, working out what the customers owed for the bread delivered, balancing his book for him and teaching him how to do it. He was very grateful, as it enabled him to keep his job, so for this he gave me double what I earned in London, 5 shillings a week instead of 2 shillings and 6 pence. The man had not had much schooling but, for me - who was already experienced and loved maths - it was a dream situation. Also, during this time, I invented all sorts of lies to tell the headmaster, pretending that I was going to school every day, whereas I was delivering the bread. I preferred, by miles, the school of life, rather than school!

This situation lasted several weeks until the day the headmaster discovered my little charade. Once I knew the game was up, I gathered up my few belongings, said goodbye to my new friend the bread man, and headed for the nearest bus stop. Just a few days before I had estimated that I had saved enough money and had written to my mother to tell her that I wanted to come home. I had also warned my new employer that I would be leaving shortly and given him a cram course in book-keeping. So, when the bus arrived at the railway station, I jumped on the first train to London and connected to Greenford on the underground. For my age I knew my way around London pretty well, so this trip held no fears for me; I felt I was a man who had held down a job, so a journey like this was nothing. It was with immense relief and happiness that I returned to the family home.

My mother had just received my letter, in which I had mentioned - amongst other things - the home to which I had been sent, and all the contempt I held for those with whom I had lived. As I arrived and knocked on the door, she was still reading my letter. How surprised she was to see me right there in front of her, my little cardboard suitcase in my hand. She immediately seized me in her arms and squeezed me tightly with all her strength, while covering me with kisses, almost in tears. Then she looked me straight in the eye and, in a very soft voice, told me I would never be forced to go away again. Strangely, the day before, she had had a premonition that I would be coming home and had even mentioned this to Jackie. Besides being a remarkable woman she was also a little psychic! The headmaster panicked about my sudden disappearance and called the police, who immediately arrived at my mother's house. She reassured the authorities of my safe return home, and that from then on she would take care of me. The twins stayed quite a while longer in the country as they were both very happy with "Mummie

Jim Redman

Lewis," as they called her; in fact Wendy kept in touch with Mummie Lewis until she died just a few years ago.

My mother was still renting out rooms and writing often to my father. It was months since she'd last heard from him and a lot of her letters were returned. The only thing she knew was that he had left England for another country and we thought he was in the Middle East.

In our neighborhood, as with a lot of England, all the houses were the same: identical, long terraced lines with the same small garden in front, the same doors, the same roofs. Only the colours of the windows and doors differed, giving the streets a very particular style, not always in the best of taste. As far as we were concerned, we had enough space to live comfortably, with two rooms and the kitchen on the ground floor, and three bedrooms, the bathroom and toilet on the first floor. We had a little vegetable patch in the back yard, where we grew a few vegetables, as well as an old henhouse. I hated weeding this little piece of earth, because it took a lot of time, but my mother insisted that everything should be neat and clean.

Our house was right next to the school, which was very convenient for us even though I had never been very good about studies (Jackie was a brilliant student) and liked only mathematics, physical training, football, cricket and gymnastics, with running another of my passions. I ran well for my young age. One of our school runners was a real champion, named Ellis and I got into the habit of training with him, running on the school football field. I had no chance of ever beating him as he was not only better than me but older and bigger, but just running with him allowed me to make great progress. I trained very hard, running, on average, ten to twelve laps of the field most days. In the school sports field there were two huge craters made by a bomb during an air raid. Jackie and I used to hide in these and play the card game Pontoon with other children until one of them was called and we were all discovered. As usual - and this seemed to happen often during this period - I was the one severely punished by the headmaster.

Another of our pastimes consisted of lying on our backs on the school grounds to watch the V1 and V2 missiles flying overhead, and cheering when they were hit by an anti-aircraft battery and exploded. When we did this the teachers generally thought we were at home, whereas my mother believed we were at school in the air raid shelters with the rest of the kids. The teachers were great and continued to teach, despite successive bombardments, if necessary right there in the shelters. When the noise became too unbearable they had us sing, very loudly, as if to provoke the Germans. It was not unusual for them to save their food coupons so that the children could eat when they were hungry. After the German planes left, my mother would emerge from her shelter at home and sometimes not be able to see our school, which was very close, through the dark, thick clouds of smoke. She said her heart would almost stop beating until the smoke cleared and she could see the school was safe!

Hard Years

When I was eleven years old there was a very important school exam, which was not to be failed if one wanted to be admitted to grammar school, it was known as the "Eleven Plus." If I failed this exam I would have to attend one of the technical schools, which was totally unacceptable to my mother, for whom grammar school represented the hope of a real profession and a better life. The year before, my sister, Jackie, had easily passed the exam but I knew it would be more difficult for me. Despite this, out of personal pride and in order not to disappoint my mother, I passed the exam, which, at the time, turned out to be easier than I was expecting. When I got home my mother wanted to know all the details, desperate to know if I thought I had passed. Pretending to be more sure of myself than I really was I told her "It was easy!" My mother looked at me for a long time and in a firm voice said "You had better pass." I tried to look confident in front of her, but admit I had some doubts. In the event I passed the exam and proudly started at grammar school.

During these school years I met and became acquainted with a very pretty little girl called Glendoline Elisabeth Evans, whom everyone called "Glen." She was a brilliant student and, year after year, we were in the same class, although she was at the top and I was near the bottom. I must admit that it's partly thanks to her I was able to pass my exams successfully and go on to the higher class. I copied her homework all the time, being careful to make some deliberate mistakes so that it would not look too perfect. It would have seemed suspicious to the teachers if it was too good, given the little enthusiasm I displayed in my lessons. In this way, I never had to really work hard at school. Outside of classes, Glen and I were always together and, even though I had a few other girlfriends with whom I went out, it was with Glen that I felt happiest. As the months went by Glen became my best friend and then the first love of my life. I did not know it at the time, but she would later become my wife.

I had a passion for football as well, and spent hours and hours kicking a ball around with the boys in the neighbourhood. Later, I played in some of the local amateur teams, but never dreamed of being a professional. The only desire I really had was to compete in motorbike races and become a professional rider. I already had a lot of very basic mechanical experience as all of us children in the neighbourhood had bicycles, which were quite old and always breaking down. In our eyes they were real treasures and I had started collecting spare parts so that I would be able to keep my bike running, and then gradually the bikes of most of the others. In the end, children came from all over the neighbourhood to ask my advice and buy my spare parts, which allowed me to make some extra pocket money. Little by little, I became quite an important person, the one who repaired the bicycles. Believe me, this was something ...

In 1944, my mother finally received news of my father, but it was not good, in fact, it was terrible. His mother was dying and he had tried in vain

Jim Redman

to get a few days' compassionate leave to be with her. He was categorically refused and my paternal grandmother died that year without seeing her beloved son for the last time. This tragic event was the turning point in my father's life. I remember later on that my mother told us that his letters changed and their tone became more and more bitter.

The war ended at last and, although England had been devastated by the continual bombings, its people were free. The twins returned home. We had not seen them for three years - three long years! They were now eight years old and nice and healthy. My mother was fascinated by their new accent and couldn't stop asking them about all they saw or did whilst in the country, so that she could understand their new ways and habits learned whilst away.

Little by little, the Redman family was coming together again, but this did not stop my mother from always being very strict about our household duties. Each one of us knew our tasks, which we did or were punished, and we were not allowed to listen to the radio in the evenings unless our homework was finished. At last, one day, we received the big news; our father was coming home. We were all so excited at the idea of seeing him again - at last, we were to be reunited and be a real family again! He had spent six years in Africa - six long, interminable years away from his family, in the most total loneliness - with the allied forces, and had not once in all that time succeeded in getting time off to come home.

We did not go to meet him because he preferred to come home by himself. Before he arrived my memory of him was of a gay, gentle and charming man, and I was holding on to this picture with all my strength for fear of finding myself in front of a stranger. When we saw him, he was terribly thin, his face was tired, his body bent, visibly used and bruised by all he had endured. He had even been hit by shell splinters and appeared greatly diminished because of this. It was a big shock for us, but even more for him. He seemed lost, unable to find his bearings. Days went by. He spoke little and closed in on himself more and more, despite all the love and support of my mother. His return to civilian life was going to be extremely difficult.

The army quickly found him a job delivering milk, but the take-home pay was low. Plus, since the return of her husband, my mother had stopped renting out rooms to factory employees who could now return to their normal jobs. I helped my father as best I could, going along with him on his deliveries whenever school time allowed. I loved being with him at these times. He let me drive the horse and cart and feed and clean the horse and I loved this. The arguments that had split my parents in the past now seemed forgotten, but after a few weeks of relative calm, the situation deteriorated again. Whereas before it was just words, now it was violent screams, during which my mother exploded into tears. As always, I defended my princess.

One time, when I became overwhelmed by my mother's screams and tears, I rushed into my parents' bedroom and violently pushed my father out of the room. He - who thought that his children would regard him as the

Hard Years

conquering hero, never imagined it would be our mother who commanded all our admiration. At the time, we resented him so much we couldn't stop mocking him and calling him "old man" or "sympathy," and all because one day he carelessly let slip, in a resigned way, that the only thing he wished from us was a little sympathy. A popular song of the time that everyone was humming was called *Sympathy* and we had taken to singing it behind his back. On another occasion, Wendy and Peter were preparing a sort of cocoa and sugar-based sweet in an old tobacco tin, into which they dipped their fingers. Our father surprised them and angrily screamed "What are you both doing?" The sound of his voice scared them so much that they ran upstairs and locked themselves in the bathroom. Father rushed up the stairs and knocked several times on the door, imploring them to open it. But Wendy and Peter, to whom my father was a complete stranger, didn't obey, so afraid were they by the anger of this man. After a while, however, they heard him crying and slightly opened the door. He was sitting down, completely lost, crying, and repeating softly "children, why are you so afraid of me?" Wendy and Peter looked at each other, didn't move, didn't say a word.

Despite their violent arguments, my father never once hit my mother. It was evident that they loved each other, but could no longer understand or tolerate each other, could no longer live together. For too many years they had been separated and now too many old and new wounds and misunderstandings separated them forever.

None of us children hated our father, just the fact that he made our mother unhappy. Jackie and I found out later that the first thing my father asked my mother, while holding her tenderly in his arms, was whether she had been faithful to him during his absence ... Finally, it was the army that decided my father's future by sending him to a rehabilitation centre on a farm, in the hope that he would be able to find his way back to civilian life. In his youth, my father had grown up in the country and worked on a farm. Before leaving, he asked my mother whether he could take with him some of his personal belongings, like his stamp collection and his precious piano as, without them, he would not leave. To my surprise, she agreed; she was so tired of the sudden arguments, the tension between them and the evil that constantly consumed my father and over which she had no control, that she would have accepted any condition which would remove him from our home. Some time later, he returned home and again life was calm. My father seemed to be improving, at least physically, but it was all an illusion: in fact, he never ever completely recovered. Each time his anxiety returned and the arguments with my mother became stormier, he returned to a different farm, up until the day when he gave up all hope of being cured and resigned himself, this time, to going away for good. The problem was he had seen so much and, as I found out much later, had been quite a brave motorcycle dispatch rider and ammunition truck driver, that he was "shell shocked," as they used to call it.

Jim Redman

In 1946 I had just turned 15 years old and was obliged to leave school, even before obtaining my Matric, because my parents could no longer afford to keep me there. My father had just been sent to a farm again, this time near Bath, for an indefinite period of time. Now, even though my mother received a small allowance from the army, she was not able to take care of the financial needs of the whole family. This was why I had to leave school and start looking for work. In any case, I knew deep down inside that I would not have passed the exam; it was becoming more and more difficult for me to accept the strict authority of school.

I found a job and started work immediately as an "Improver" in the car repair workshop of a big builder and civil engineering contractor in the area called Taylor Woodrow. With the future so uncertain in those days straight after the war, garage owners didn't sign apprenticeship contracts but instead used these Improver contracts for young men looking for work. As we advanced in our knowledge and competence, we were able to rise up the scale to finally become a fully-fledged mechanic. So, I swept the floor, cleaned the spare parts, and started to do simple repairs. Above all, I watched and listened and learnt quickly. My mother was quite proud of me. One day she returned from the public library with a book about Henry Ford. Standing close to me, and in a confident voice, she said "Here you go, you've started on the bottom step like Henry Ford and you, too, can become as big and as important as he has." She really made us believe in the impossible.

Even though I was bringing home some money, it was not enough, and we needed to increase the family income. At this particular time, there were many people from the north of England and Ireland who were looking for work, and so my mother decided to take in lodgers again. After the war, reconstruction went on everywhere: bridges, roads, buildings, offices, all had been damaged or destroyed by the bombardments, and so there was lots of work around, especially in the greater London area. We were able to lodge several people in our house, most of whom were nice, well-mannered men.

I remember one in particular. He was Irish, a married man, father of several children, who began taking me with him when he went fishing at the weekend. He was courteous and charming and, by the way he looked at my mother, it was easy to guess that he was infatuated but, of course, she pretended not to notice. Anyhow, she always remained polite and friendly towards him. I think, however, that she was not completely indifferent to him but remained totally quiet on the subject and if there *was* a secret between them, it was a very well kept one ...

Recently, as Jackie was reading a newspaper, she came across an article relating the story of an Irish vagabond who, for the last 50 years, had been wandering all across England. He had never returned to his home in Ireland and had recently been found dead at the age of 94. To her great amazement, the man in question had the same name, Paddy Duffy, as the young Irishman

Hard Years

who had lodged in our home 50 years before. The age was right, so the idea crossed our minds that this could be one and the same man who had, because of an impossible love for a woman - our mother- spent his entire life wandering, hankering after a love that could never be.

At the garage where I worked, two of the mechanics, Keith Starling and Bob Baker, owned their own motorbikes, so it was natural I should gravitate towards them as I had always been interested in bikes. As the days and weeks went by, we became friends, and often on weekends would go off for a ride together. I would ride pillion on one or other of the bikes, holding on tightly and becoming intoxicated by the speed and incredible sense of freedom. This wasn't enough for me though - I wanted to learn how to ride one myself, so eventually Bob taught me how. Right from the first time I gripped the handlebars of that motorbike, I knew I had to have my own.

It was just before my 16th birthday and I went from shop to shop, looking for the motorbike that would become mine. After a lot of indecision, I finally found one that I liked, it was by no means my first choice but my budget was very limited. It was a second-hand, ex-War Department, 350cc Matchless single cylinder, with girder forks and a rigid frame. My mother agreed that I could have it if I could work out a plan to pay for it: it was priced at £70. This was much more than I had, but a small deposit secured it and my mother signed the hire purchase agreement. At the time I was earning just 1 pound 15 shillings a week, most of which I gave to my mother since my father was not around, keeping only a little for pocket money. But I really wanted this bike and decided to find a job delivering newspapers early in the morning, before I went to work. This paid 10 shillings per week, but it would be all mine and all of it would go towards paying off the bike. While on my paper delivery route, I would read through the bike magazines. I could not afford to buy them and, of course, fell in love with the new bikes displayed, dreaming that one day I would be able to exchange my bike for one of these. I followed the motorcycle racing, too, and just knew it was something I had to do.

Years later, after paying off the Matchless and trading it in on a second-hand Triumph twin, I was able to buy the object of my dreams, a 500cc Vincent Comet. Using the Triumph as the deposit, I had enough for the down payment, the rest I would pay off little by little on credit. We called this the "drip feed" and, in fact, I spent more time cleaning and shining my motorbike than riding it as all my newspaper money went to pay the hire purchase. Frustrated that I had no money for petrol, one day at work I siphoned petrol out of the tanks of a few different cars to put into my bike. I was caught red-handed and told to resign immediately. The very same day, I found a new job at another garage about 100 metres away, called Ellbourne's Garage, whose owner, Colonel Ellbourne, was ex-army. It was a very imposing building, with its own service station, showroom and garage for repairs, and I worked here until I was twenty.

27

Jim Redman

Unfortunately, at the same time, the family was again struck by the hand of fate. One winter's morning, Jackie suffered violent pains in her back which prevented her from breathing. Our family doctor, Doctor Ginsberg, arrived almost immediately and his diagnosis was very alarming: Jackie was suffering from combined pleurisy and pneumonia. She was immediately rushed to hospital where it was discovered that she had also contracted tuberculosis. My mother was in a state of total collapse, but had to be strong for us all. I was - and still am - very close to my sisters, and it was unbearable knowing that Jackie was far away from me, in a hospital room surrounded by sick people. During the six months that followed, whenever it was possible we took turns visiting Jackie, so she could have the books she needed for studying, books that were taken away from her as soon as the family member had left the room.

She was strong-willed and, with this and some luck, she recovered from her sickness relatively quickly but, to her great disappointment, had still to remain a further six months at home for a complete rest. She, who adored studying and learning more than anything else, had to resign herself to the thought of leaving school forever and looking for a job once she was on her feet.

I was now earning more than the experienced mechanics, which made a big difference to me and my family, although I still continued to deliver the newspapers to pay for my new bike. Bob, Keith and I had bought three brand new Vincent HRD 500cc, single cylinder Comets and our license plates had consecutive numbers: LXH 767, LXH 768 and LXH 769. We really loved riding along the neighbouring roads in numerical order!

Jackie suddenly seemed very interested in our motorbike outings and, with Bob coming to the house regularly, romance blossomed between them. I was still madly in love with Glen, though I was seeing other girls at the same time when she was studying. Even while I was still at school, during the summer we would go every Thursday evening to see the Wembley Lions Speedway Team, whereas, in the winter, we would go and support the Lions ice hockey team at Wembley arena. Now, on weekends I would take Glen on the bike and go for rides with Bob and Jackie, Keith and Una, who was his girlfriend at the time and later became his wife. The six of us rode for hours on end, happy, free and far from all life's troubles.

For some time now, Colonel Ellbourne had watched me take apart and repair cars in the garage, I was always in a hurry and I hated being at work with nothing to do. After watching me quietly for some time, one day he said to me "This car just arrived this morning and you've already taken out the axle and the gearbox and repaired the gearbox ... I am going to have to pay you more, aren't I?" No sooner said than done and I became not only the youngest mechanic in his garage, but the highest paid, as I found myself with a substantial pay rise. I was proud, to say the least, and things settled down into a good routine. I worked hard, delivering the newspapers early in

Hard Years

the morning, working in the garage for the rest of the day and repairing the neighbours' cars in the evenings to keep up with the family expenses and pay for my motorcycle habit. I created my own little business for the evenings, and we jokingly called it "Curbside Motors" Whatever the weather, rain or snow, I worked relentlessly outside the house of whichever neighbour's car I was repairing. During winter, it was often so cold there at the curb that I had to keep going into the house to warm my frozen hands and tools so that I could carry on working.

I had been working a long time for the same newspaper shop and was able to choose my own paper route, which was perfect for me as I walked to the shop and then delivered papers all the way home, ending at my own street and house. One day, as I was delivering papers in my road, a policeman approached me looking for Enmore Road. I told him that he was in it but that it also went around the corner to the left. He thanked me and continued on his way. I do not know why, but suddenly I sensed that he was looking for my house. Forgetting about my paper deliveries, I went after him and caught up just as he was turning into our house. I asked him why he was going there, and if something had happened to my father. He asked me who I was. Before I had time to reply, my mother appeared at the door and I could feel that he was very uneasy in front of her, sorry to be there. After taking a few moments to gather himself, without even asking to come inside, he announced in a slightly trembling voice that my father had committed suicide and asked my mother to go down to the morgue to identify the body.

Even though she was badly shaken up by such news delivered in such an abrupt, unfeeling manner, my mother seemed simply weary and resigned, as if she had been waiting for a tragedy such as this. She took me into her arms and squeezed me tightly against her; I would have given my life for her not to have felt this shock and unhappiness. The news left us speechless; I did not want her to go to the morgue, afraid that she would suffer even more and that the experience might leave her marked forever. I tried to go instead of her but, since I was only 17 and a minor, it was not allowed by law. I was not even thinking about my sisters and brother, my focus was completely on my mother. The Policeman had been very vague about my father's death, and especially about the way in which it had occurred, but there was no doubt: it was suicide. In those days, suicide was considered a sin and we were sort of ashamed that it had happened in our family.

The next day, my mother and I took the train to Bristol, while Jackie stayed home with the twins. Once we had arrived at the morgue, I did my best to support my mother, ready to squeeze her in my arms at the slightest sign of faintness. The sheet covering the body was turned down to the chin and my father's face looked back at us. He seemed at rest, his features relaxed, as if, at last, he was free. In a very dignified manner, my mother said "Yes, it's him." Once the body had been identified, the corpse was quickly incinerated and the ashes buried next to the cemetery in a place reserved for

Jim Redman

poorer people, since we did not have the money to pay for a real funeral. We returned home and, throughout the entire journey, not a word was spoken between us; my mother seemed subdued and sad, but not overly so. Perhaps she had already prepared herself for such an eventuality and her sadness was mixed with a certain amount of relief? Perhaps she had always known how their relationship would end? As for me, I was more worried about her than my father. I did not love him anyway, each time he had come home he had hurt her, and she was my princess. Strangely enough, I suddenly remembered how, not long before, when my father had just argued again with my mother, he had turned to me and, with resignation had said "Now you are big enough to throw me out if I make too many problems." To which I had contemptuously replied "Yes, I won't hesitate!" Nothing in life any longer meant anything to him, the respect of his family, his work, his status as a man; he felt both useless and yet powerless to lift himself up. Too weak to fight his demons, too depressed to reconstruct a normal life, a stranger to himself and his family, what was left for him? The war had finished him, the separation between us and him grew deeper. He had decided to put an end to this perpetual suffering which ate away at him, little by little, and go silently far from the sight of others. God only knows the despair he must have felt and the courage it took to do what he did. I had always sided with my mother against my father but, as you get older, you come to understand that nothing is either all black nor all white, and that there are two sides to every story. I was not mature enough to understand that my father had suffered atrociously; I only saw that he made my mother cry. When he wanted a little understanding from us, he got only indifference and criticism.

Not too long ago, I learnt that my father had been a dispatch rider during the war, conducting himself very courageously and defying danger each time he passed enemy lines. Before this I had always believed that I was the only motorcycle rider in the family. My father was attached to the eighth army, which fought against Rommel. When the big offensive took place, he drove a lorry filled with ammunition right to the front line over and over again, despite seeing his friends blown to pieces doing the same job. I now realize what he had to endure; it must have been terrible.

At home, life resumed its normal pattern, with each of us returning to their jobs and tasks. The twins still went to school, Jackie continued her job as a receptionist for a dentist, and I divided my time between my paper round, work and Curbside Motors. My mother took care of the house, still with all her usual energy, while keeping a close eye on Wendy's and Peter's education. One particular day, after having glanced through several pages, her attention was caught by one particular article in the newspaper. As she read it, her face became pale and her features frozen. There in the title to the story was "... the decapitated body of Edward Albert Redman found on railway track ...," together with a photograph of my father. The article described in great depth the horrible way in which the poor man had killed

Hard Years

himself. These few words were enough to shake our entire existence forever. Imagining my father laying his head down on the railway track of his own will, and waiting for a train to come along and cut off his head, traumatized my mother greatly. At the same time, she could not imagine him so unhappy as to be unable to tell her, his wife, that the only alternative left to him was to end his life in the most horrible way possible. My mother had succeeded in more or less getting over the shock of his suicide but, upon reading the newspaper article, something seemed to explode within her brain.

At the morgue, we had only seen his face, smooth and unmarked, because the authorities had taken care to hide the rest of the body from us, at the same time remaining very evasive about the method of his suicide. Even in her worst nightmares, mother could never have imagined anything so monstrous. Now here it was in front of her, written down in black and white. For a long time she remained immobile, a haggard look on her face. From this moment my mother deteriorated daily, suffering migraine headaches which tortured her terribly. We did not know what to do to help her during these moments and it hurt us all a lot to see her in this state. She, who was always iron-willed, but with a playful personality, had become a shadow of her former self.

A few days later, in the evening, she was not feeling well so went up to her room and asked my sister to bring her a bowl as she said she was feeling sick. During the night I was awakened by a strange noise coming from her room: it was as if someone was scraping away at the door trying to get in. Being young, and tired from working hard, I did not get up to go and investigate but went back to sleep. In the morning I went into my mother's room and was horrified to find that the scraping noise had been caused by her 'mixing' in the bowl with her hand. The bottom of the bowl had a very rough finish and she had scraped most of the skin off her fingers. She was still mixing when I went in and the bowl had lots of her blood in it.

My mother was lying on the bed, with a tired, drawn face from a night without sleep, I ran to help her while Jackie called Doctor Ginsberg to come and help us. With an absent look, my mother told me that she was making a cake for us. It was obvious she was losing her mind. As soon as the Doctor arrived, he confirmed the gravity of her condition and called for an ambulance immediately. As she was taken out on a stretcher, my mother gave us a smile, gentle and anxious at the same time, as if to reassure us. In a barely audible voice, she still had the strength to tell my sister and me that, whatever should happen to her we, her children, should always stick together, through thick and thin and never separate. The doors closed and the ambulance took off sharply amid the sound of screaming sirens. As it disappeared from sight I could feel my heart squeezed by pain and tears welling up within me. I turned towards Jackie, who was also trying not to cry. During a minute which seemed to last an eternity, we looked at each other in silence, completely shattered.

Jim Redman

We were able to visit our mother later that day and, thankfully, she seemed a lot better and much more rested. Her face had regained its normal colour and the wild look had gone, her voice was clear and her most gentle smile was back in place. We had found our mother again, the mother that we loved so dearly. Who would have thought that her end was so near? On June 11th, 1949, while Jackie was doing some housework and I had just finished my paper round, a policeman appeared on our doorstep. With a cold face he told us the terrible news: our mother had just died of a cerebral haemorrhage, but I knew that it was the shock of finding out the details of my father's suicide that had killed her.

Completely devastated, Jackie and I left the twins at home and went immediately to the hospital morgue; we had to see her one last time. The pale creature in no way resembled our mother, but at least she was at peace. We gave her a last goodbye kiss, Jackie gathered together some of her belongings, including her wedding ring (which Wendy still wears). The nurse with us said that if our mother had survived the attack she would have been completely paralyzed on her left side and would have had to spend the rest of her life in a wheelchair. Knowing our mother's character, we knew she would have hated to feel so physically diminished, so thought that perhaps it was better this way ... Jackie and I took care of everything: signing papers, telephoning other family members and, above all, the future of the four of us. Our mother had always told us that, in the event of her death, she did not want her children to mourn her. Out of respect for her wishes, ours was the only house in the street whose curtains were not drawn closed.

In the space of just twenty seven days, we had lost both our father and mother; it was an enormous shock for us all. In this short span of time, I had gone from being a protected adolescent to an adult. At the same time, these events taught me early how to face up to life's hard knocks: I had to get a grip of myself, if only for Wendy, Jackie and Peter.

My work at the garage was hourly paid and the slightest amount of time lost meant money lost, which we could absolutely not afford to lose. For this reason, I could not even allow myself the luxury of crying over the death of my parents: I stayed at home just a little while to pay homage to my mother, and then returned to work at the garage. There were very few people at the funeral: only our aunts made the journey as their husbands could not afford the time off from work. Our mother was cremated and we kept her ashes in a little urn which for many years remained on the sideboard in the living room: in this way we felt that her protective aura was watching over us every day. Jackie and I first had to think about the twins who needed an enormous amount of love and tenderness, yet we all cried a lot. The important thing in our eyes, at that time, was to survive and above all to remain

Continued on page 49

Picture Gallery 1

MV 3 'triple' – Daytona 1995. It would take six months to wipe the smile off my face ...

Commentator Richard Chamberlain with Nobby, Jim and Kwezi, Daytona 1995.

Jim Redman

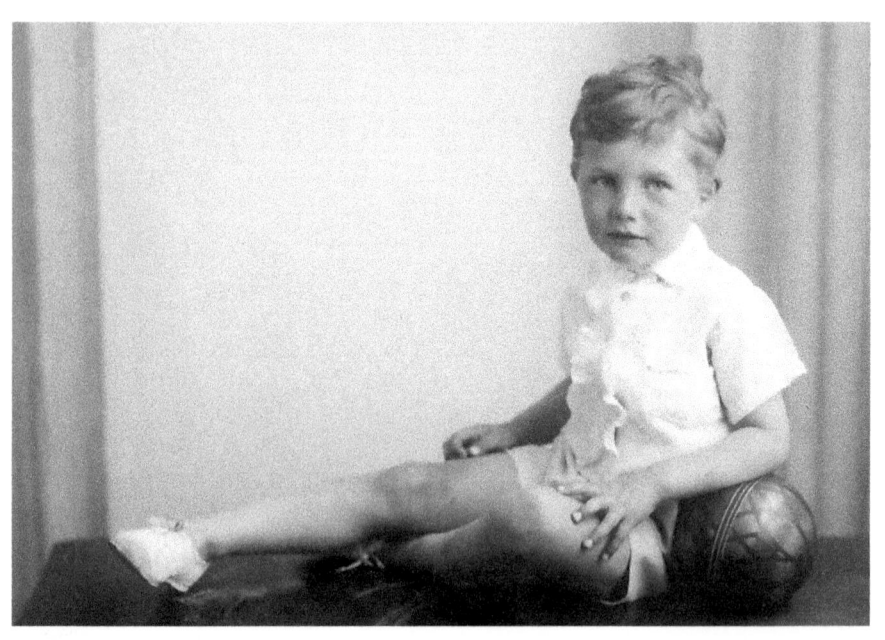

Quite an early picture of Jim, about 1935.

I always put my mum on a pedestal, seems like that's where she put herself, too!

Picture Gallery 1

1955 and the scene of my first business venture.

Typical South-African racing shot, 1957. Jim (50) leads Beppe Castellani (52).

Jim Redman

1958: bedroom, kitchen, workshop, transporter. The faithful ex-Pip Harris 3 way Austin van, with Paddy Driver and Jim.

Jim leads Harry Hinton and Paddy Driver on the cobblestones – probably Sachsenring.

36

Picture Gallery 1

The 'Bushmen,' the South African contingent 1958/59. L to R: Paddy Driver, Sox Hocking and Jim. Our combined results were not bad in the end.

An early shot. Jim leaping Ballaugh Bridge IoM, probably in 1959.

37

Jim Redman

A good friend, New Zealander John Hempleman – 'Hempo' – who still lives in Auckland.

The Australian, Ken Kavanagh, who lives in Bergamo, Italy, smiles quietly as he thinks about selling Jim his ex-works Ducati.

Picture Gallery 1

Assen, June 1959. Jim and 'Sox' have a problem and discuss it with one of racing's pure gentlemen, Mr. Burik – head of the Dutch federation and senior in the FIM. Whatever the problem was, I bet he fixed it.

July 1960. A good man. Bob Brown in pensive mood at Solitude in practice on his Norton. He was later killed on the Honda 250 four.

39

Jim Redman

1961. Now come on Sox, get me that ride. Frankie Stastny looks on highly amused ...

... and later discusses the situation further with Jim ...

Picture Gallery 1

... and, perhaps, says – "Jim you're too big for the MZ 125 & 250."

The dreaded cobblestones! Jim leads Tom at Brno, Czechoslovakia, in the dice that probably influenced Tom Phillis to recommend to Honda that Jim should take his place at Assen.

41

Jim Redman

Postcard of Sachsenring showing: 1) The vast crowds; 2) Dickie Dale on his BMW; 3) Jim leading Harry Hinton and Paddy Driver on the cobblestones; 4) Start of the sidecar race. The organisers were unhappy as their crowds had dropped to 'only' 250,000 that year.

A serious looking Dickie Dale. He was always checking his sparkplugs trying to 'read' the mixture.

42

Picture Gallery 1

1960, Montjuich Park, Barcelona. Jim hounds 'poor' Remo Venturi on his MV.

1961 visit to the Honda factory. It was so interesting that we could easily have spent all day there.

43

Jim Redman

The great man, Soichiro Honda – working as usual.

Jim and Tom in Tom's van. A friend (Rex Evans) bought this van when Tom was killed and has only recently sold it. He kept the number plate though, and it's now worth more than he paid for the van in 1962.

Picture Gallery 1

About 1960-61, Jimmy Junior tries to resurrect the carcass of a 1960 Honda 4.

Jim leading Tarquinio Provini at Cesenatico 1961.

45

Jim Redman

Hockenheim 1961: Takahashi just before he became the first Japanese rider to win a Grand Prix.

Kunimitsu Takahashi – 'Taksan'. We met again in Japan in 1996 and 1998, Taksan was still racing cars and hardly looked any older.

46

Picture Gallery 1

The boys in the backroom. Nobby Clark with some of the Japanese mechanics in 1965.

Jim up to his ears in winner's wreath, Solitude 1962.

47

Jim Redman

This get-up works on a touring bike, but nearly tears your head off as you sit up off the tank of a racer — The Turbo Visor.

Hard Years

together. Luckily, the love that united us seemed indestructible to us. It was us against the entire world.

For a while, my sister and I thought about asking our aunts and uncles for some help, but that would mean we would live apart from each other, so was out of the question. Jackie took on our mother's role, preparing breakfast, keeping the house in order, preparing dinner; while at the same time working at the dentist's office during the day. Peter and Wendy were eleven years old at the time and big enough to give a hand with the chores around the house. Jackie even found the time to acquire her motorbike license and, for the first time in her life, had her own transport: a BSA Bantam, which was her pride and joy. I was more than proud to have a sister who could ride a bike so well.

On the whole, we managed quite well. For dinner we ate a lot of potatoes and green vegetables, and on special occasions splashed out on meat and fish. Never once did we receive encouragement or help from the neighbours, who considered us the poorest family in the area. For our part, we responded as would our mother - too proud to ask them for anything.

We often received letters from our aunts and uncles asking us if everything was going well, and whether we needed anything? One day, between themselves, they decided that they would look after the twins as they felt that Jackie and I could not look after all their needs. When they told me this the blood rushed to my head and I became very angry. My reply was firm and final: in no way would we be separated from our sister and brother. We did not need anyone to take care of their education and upbringing as we could handle this and, anyway, we had been instructed to do so by our mother. I ordered them to leave us alone and to take care of their own affairs. In a way, I think they were glad that this was my attitude as another mouth to feed would cost money. Despite this victory, though, we were not at the end of our problems.

One day a man and a woman from the welfare knocked at our door: they had come to pick up Wendy and Peter and take them to an orphanage as the authorities had decided that, given our situation, there was no way the twins could stay with us. My reaction was most violent - I told them to get out and leave us alone, that we could take care of their needs without any problem as my sister was 18 years old and I just a year younger. We made enough money to keep them, ensure a good education and provide everything they needed. The discussion was long and exhausting but I refused to back down and accept any compromise. The reason for this was simple, just a few days before, inside the cover of one of my school books, I found a small piece of note paper upon which was written in my mother's hand these few words "If ever anything should happen to me, I want my children to stick together through thick and thin. This is my last wish." Almost the same words she had said to my sister and me just before her

Jim Redman

death. It was as if she had had a premonition that something was going to happen to her. Faced with our determination and anger, the welfare people gave in - we had succeeded!

In the days that followed, there were no luxuries, but at least we had enough to eat and for the bare necessities of life. What an appetite for life we had! Jackie and I were very careful, working day and night to ensure the twins' well-being and making sure we gave the authorities no excuse to interfere. Happily, the midday meal at the school canteen was free for all children, which meant one less meal to pay for. In the house everything was very well organized with each of us knowing what they had to do. In the past we would often quarrel because one of us had done the same task twice in a row, while the other hadn't done it once. After my mother's death we never squabbled over such nonsense.

The only pleasures I allowed myself were the Speedway races that I went to with Glen and the ice-hockey matches at Wembley plus, of course, my bike, which was my big luxury but still paid for by the newspaper deliveries. We also had a cat that was the joy of Wendy and Peter, and to whom we gave milk and the leftovers. From time to time, I took the twins for a ride on my motorbike which thrilled them. Of course, I envied my friends, Keith and Bob, who still lived with their parents and didn't have the same money problems that I did. I was always the poorest of the group and had to work myself almost to death to save up the little bit of money I needed to be able to go out with them. I earned good money, especially from Curbside Motors, but needed most of it to take care of the family. When my parents died, I had managed to save eight pounds in my savings account, which I never touched as it was my money in case of an emergency. It was strange; I felt safe knowing I had those eight pounds. Anything could have happened to us but I thought that I would be able to handle it as I was never broke, thanks to my savings. Now, when I think about it, I realize how foolish I was to imagine I could handle anything that came along with such a small amount of money; it really was nothing at all. All the same, I have fond memories of this very difficult period, because it taught me - amongst other things - never to give up fighting, to be independent and to take life's knocks like my mother had, with dignity and strength.

I can remember the first Christmas without our parents. As it approached, we managed to put aside some sweet things like jars of fruit and other delicacies, just like our mother had always done. Then, just two days before Christmas, while we were preparing everything, someone knocked on the door. It was a Colonel from the American Airforce who had arrived in a jeep from Northolt Airport, where his contingent had set up base during the war. In a very bluff, warm voice he told us he had asked the mayor of the town for information about the most needy families in the area, and our name was top of the list. He had hardly finished talking when several airmen placed two huge cartons filled with food at our feet;

Hard Years

some of the items we had only ever seen in magazines. There were all sorts of huge tins, containing ham, fruits, different meats, candies, as well as pots of jam, chocolates and nuts ... Wendy and Peter went crazy! They screamed with joy as they unpacked the cartons and ran around wildly in all directions. Jackie, her eyes filled with tears, and overwhelmed, watched them laughing, drunk with happiness, while I still could not take it in. I stood there, unable to speak, completely stunned with gratitude by so much generosity. In the middle of all these tins of food I discovered an old cigar box which rattled. As I opened it I turned to Jackie and told her that if it was money I would not be able to stop myself from crying. Money it was, and I burst into tears. The poor Colonel left in tears, a big handkerchief covering his face to hide his red eyes. What a fabulous Christmas it was for us, but what a pity that our mother could not be with us to share our joy and God knows how we laughed during dinner! Jackie - for her very first Christmas as a cook - decided to cook a goose and some pork. Unfortunately, she did not know it was necessary to repeatedly drain the fat from the meat. As she opened the oven to see how the meat was doing, the grease caught alight and she was almost burnt alive. When at last she came to sit with us and serve the food, she had no more hair on the front of her head, no eyebrows, and no eyelashes. The sight of her had Wendy, Peter and me in hysterics as, soon, was Jackie.

At the beginning of each week, Jackie and I took care of the accounts. Everything was decided very carefully and nothing left to chance. We first settled the question of the rent, then that of food, money for petrol and, lastly, new clothes for the twins who were growing fast. We always enjoyed being neat and clean in front of others and would never have presented ourselves in a neglected manner, or with old and patched clothing. From time to time, when the budget allowed, we would buy something for the house, and it was not unusual at Christmas to buy a useful object that would make life easier - a brush for the sink, an iron. But most of the time it was a struggle financially. Once it happened that we did not have enough money to buy a new pair of shoes for the twins, but I worked some overtime and we got them what they needed. Wendy and Peter had their own pocket money that Jackie and I gave them each week and, with it, went to the closest swimming pool and visited the museums in South Kensington. I continued delivering newspapers in the morning, working in the garage during the day and at my own business in the evenings, repairing cars in front of the house, sometimes with Peter helping me as best he could.

So, that's how we lived until I reached the age of eighteen, when all boys were obliged to enlist in the army for two years. However, it was possible to obtain a six month deferment in order to finish school or for exceptional circumstances. When I received my draft letter it was clear that I could never leave my family, so I went to the nearest Recruitment Centre and explained my situation in great detail to the committee. I was

Jim Redman

asked to leave the room while they came to a decision. The minutes went by very slowly until I was told to enter. As I had hoped, I was allowed a first deferment of six months in order to continue looking after the twins. However, I was to report to the committee every six months for a re-evaluation of my situation. Each time I did so my blood ran cold at the thought of being told I must join the army, although I knew that one day this must happen. Nevertheless, I managed to delay my departure for two years.

When I was twenty years old, the Army finally decided it was time for me to join its ranks. The twins had grown and were now fourteen years old; an age at which they would be able to manage with my older sister, the committee told me. The committee this time comprised about a dozen people - soldiers, but also representatives of the welfare system. I agreed to join the army, but first wanted to know how they were going to take care of my family whilst I was gone. It seemed there would be an allowance for the upbringing of the twins. I had checked how much the allowance would be, the maximum was 15 shillings a week each, which would not even pay the rent, never mind the food for three people. My army pay would be one pound fifteen shillings per week, plus fifteen shillings per child; a grand total of three pounds five shillings. With rent of two pounds per week, there was not much left. With all my different jobs, I was earning around thirteen pounds per week, and, even then, there was not much over for the small luxuries, so it was out of the question to manage on a quarter of that. I explained all this but the committee was not really listening: it was my problem. Faced with such indifference I was livid with rage and could not control my temper. I insulted them royally, calling them armchair warriors who didn't give a damn about other people's problems, and who were only good enough to sit there and put crosses in the little squares. Disgusted, and mad about the way the interview had gone, I walked out on the committee and immediately returned to the garage where Colonel Ellbourne was waiting for me.

On the way back I decided that, if this was England, I would rather get the hell out and go and live somewhere else! I recounted everything that had just happened, my disgust for what seemed to me to be blatant injustice and, above all, my decision to leave the country as soon as possible. The Colonel seemed shaken and tried to calm me. Previous to this he had asked me to manage the garage whenever he was not there so that he could be free to look after the service station, the car sales and a new garage he was buying. He told me that, once he acquired the new garage, he wanted me to run the old one completely. He now took me into his office and gave me the following advice "If you leave the country the day after you have been drafted, you'll be considered a deserter and the police will be looking for you. On the other hand, if you leave before being called up, they can do nothing. If you want to do that, you have to move quickly or

Hard Years

it'll be too late ..." I thanked him for everything he had done for me and gave him my resignation.

We had this conversation on a Thursday. The following Tuesday I was on a cargo ship leaving for Cape Town, South Africa, the only ship on which there was an available berth, the next one being in six weeks. My call-up was due in three weeks so I had to take this ship. The very next day, Friday, I sold my motorbike, the Vincent Comet, for 200 pounds and reserved and paid the 100 pounds for my berth on the Cape Town Castle. I packed my spanners and meagre belongings, and had a long discussion with Jackie. I knew that the decision I had just taken would change the course of our lives forever. Maybe I would not see my brother and sisters for a very long time. I was really scared; not for me, but for Jackie, Wendy and Peter, whom I felt in a way I was abandoning at a time when they needed me most.

Jackie reassured me, dispelling my fears by announcing that she was going to marry Bob Baker, and that together they would be able to look after the twins. To my great surprise, she even seemed excited at the idea of my going to Rhodesia as she hoped to be able, one day in the future, to join me with the twins. Together, we worked out that they would need money for two months, the time it would take for me to get to Rhodesia and get set up and find work, after which I would do my best to send them some money each week to help with the bills until the twins had finished their education. I still had 100 pounds left from the sale of my bike after paying for the boat ticket. I decided I would have to manage with 30 pounds for the train fare from Cape Town to Bulawayo and leave the other 70 pounds with Jackie to keep her going.

The Cape Town Castle was a cargo ship and would take a month to get to Cape Town, compared to the mail ships which took only two weeks. But there was not a single berth to be had on a mail ship for six weeks, by which time I would have been in the army.

I was so pleased that Bob and Jackie were going to marry. Now that I had no worries about the other three, I got very excited about the new life I was going to make in Rhodesia. Bob, Jackie and I were scheming and planning how, once I was settled, we would get all of them - Bob as well - out to Rhodesia. Bob moved into the house and I left for London to board the old cargo ship heading for Cape Town, travelling on to Bulawayo on a two or three day train journey. The only reason I picked Bulawayo was that my friend, Keith Starling, had already left the UK to go there and had written to say it was a wonderful country and we should all come. Keith and his wife, Una, were the only people in the world that I knew outside of England and in his letters Keith told me that there was plenty of work out there for mechanics, and it was a far better life than in the UK. Of course, I had wanted to go then but could not see any chance of being able to do so until the army stepped in and changed all that.

Jim Redman

Keith said that the wages were twice as much as in England, his boat fares for him and his wife had been paid for by the CMED (which was the government garage in Rhodesia that had recruited him.) He added that if I wanted the same conditions, all I would have to do was find a Rhodesian employer looking for someone with my qualifications, and there were plenty of them. Obviously, I did not have time for this as my situation was urgent. I couldn't wait any longer so had to buy my own ticket and take my chances.

3
The Promised Land

All twelve passengers on the ship watched the hustle and bustle as the ship left the docks. As we headed out of the Thames Estuary, I found a place at the stern and contemplated, possibly for the last time in my life, this country of mine that I loved so much. The sun was shining very brightly and I felt like the loneliest man in the world and wondered if I was doing the right thing. I felt very bitter towards the army for forcing this decision to leave on me, although part of me was excited about the future.

All of the passengers were English, and most of them lived and worked in Rhodesia or South Africa, and had been spending their holidays in the country where they were born. We quickly introduced ourselves and became a small, united group. That first evening we met around the bar for drinks before dinner. As each bought a round of drinks, I had to refuse as I had no money to reciprocate: so I told them, right from the beginning, that I did not drink alcohol, nor even soft drinks: just tea, coffee and water. The coffee and tea were free, as was, of course, the water. This was going to be a long voyage, to go a whole month without touching a penny of my money was going to be quite a feat, and yet, somehow, I managed.

They all offered to buy me drinks: if only they had known how much I yearned for the taste of a good beer during those hot days on the ship - even a soft drink would have been better than the endless glasses of water - but I just had to go on sipping my glass of water. When someone asked me if I wanted something else, it was a little sadly that I refused, saying that water was the only thing that quenched my thirst.

The price of the boat ticket included breakfast, lunch, morning and afternoon tea and dinner, so I did not have to spend any money on food. I did not tell anyone in the group about my problems with the military authorities: it was too soon after the war and might appear as if I was shirking military duty. Nor did I tell them too much about myself and my problems but tried

Jim Redman

hard to put up a good front, being pleasant and friendly and, above all, hiding my shame at being so poor.

During the first two days of the voyage I was seasick but, after that, the trip became much more enjoyable and the weather was superb. I have always loved the sun - something we did not see enough of in Greenford - so I spent a lot of my time in the fresh air, getting a tan. The days seemed endless but, luckily, there were a lot of books and magazines available to us in the ship's library and, as I am an avid reader, I read whole books on Rhodesia and South Africa. Then, when I started to miss my family, I sat down and wrote them many letters describing as best I could ports of call like Dakar and Walvis Bay. Also, I wrote to them about the marvels of nature I had seen, like the dolphins which, from time to time, followed the ship and kept us company, and the huge flocks of flamingos in Walvis Bay.

At last, one beautiful sunny day, the ship arrived at Cape Town. It was July 1952 and Table Mountain looked fantastic; in fact, everything was breathtaking. I was a little apprehensive, but more excited than afraid. I hoped that by going to Africa I could manage to carve out a better life than we would have had in England. (I have not been disapointed; I love Africa, it's in my blood now.) Despite my optimism, I felt really on my own. With a slight twinge I left my 12 companions, and descended to the dock with my baggage. I had managed to hang on to all of my 30 pounds without spending a penny on the whole trip. Now I had to get the next train to Rhodesia ...

Luckily, one of our group was heading for the railway station to take a train to Johannesburg, and invited me to share his taxi. Once there, we took leave of each other and went our separate ways. At the ticket booth I was told there were no available berths on any train going to Bulawayo for the next 10 days. Upset, I did not know what to do. Here I was, alone in a country that I didn't know, in the middle of a city that was completely foreign to me, with strangers all around me, virtually no money and thousands of miles from home. I gathered my courage in both hands and went to look for the nearest, cheapest hotel I could find. I strolled around the city and finally found one in the worst possible area, where the price of the room was ridiculously low; so cheap, in fact, that I had to wedge the handle of my door with a chair for fear that someone would come in and cut my throat and steal my fortune! I hid my money in one of my socks and put it under my head under the pillow; no point denying that I slept with only one eye closed.

The next day I returned to the railway station, hoping, with not much conviction, that my new plan to bribe the ticket seller would work and I would be able to get a ticket for the train that day. At the booth it was the same man as the day before. I put one of my precious one pound notes on the counter and asked him what my chances were of leaving on a train today. He quickly slipped the note into his pocket and, with a big smile, told me there would be no problem. I paid around twenty pounds for the train ticket, which included a shared sleeper, bought my meal tickets and found myself left with three

The Promised Land

shillings in my pocket! The journey lasted three days and three nights and was quite nice, even though it was a little boring. It was strange to hear all the people around me talking in Afrikaans, a language I'd never heard before I left England. I battled to find anyone who spoke English but, of course, did not have the money to sit in the bar and strike up conversation there.

Finally, the train arrived in Bulawayo and it was with immeasurable joy that I found Keith Starling and his wife, Una, waiting for me on the platform. I could never have imagined how nice it would be to see familiar faces after so many weeks of loneliness. Suddenly, I felt great; all my fears and anxieties were blown away, gone was my hate for the army committee, gone was my shame at forever being poor. From now on I was going to be a new man with a completely new and better existence! Someone who would at last know what it was to be truly happy ...

Keith had already reserved a room, in the residential hotel where he and his wife were living, for fifteen pounds per month with all three daily meals included and a packed lunch if you could not get back to the hotel. Best of all - and most importantly - I could pay the bill at the end of the month. After collecting my belongings, we stopped on the way to the hotel at a café to have a slice of cake and a cup of coffee; we wanted some time to catch up with all the news and each had plenty to tell. I wanted to pay this bill but, unfortunately for me, it came to four shillings and I only had three. Keith smiled and told me to keep my money, when I had earned some more I could buy them a drink. I had to get a job as soon as possible!

The next day, early in the morning, I dropped Keith off at work and borrowed his car to go round to all the garages in the area. Jobs were plentiful as the garages were really in need of car mechanics, and Keith had made some enquiries and told me the best ones to go to. Most of them were ready to give me a very good salary and I could start right away, so I took my time choosing as I wanted to get the right one first time as I hate swopping jobs. Finally, I chose Duly and Co. as this concern was the Ford agent in the city (as was Ellbourne at home) and I knew I could hold my own with anyone working on Fords. The pay was perhaps a little less than some of the others, but the company looked solid and I liked the foreman who interviewed me.

I had arrived in Bulawayo on a Monday evening at 11pm, had found a job on Tuesday and on Wednesday began working (with my own tools which I had brought with me from England). I received my first pay on the Friday and, as the weekend was a long one, with the Rhodes and Founders holidays on Monday and Tuesday, Keith and Una wanted to go to Victoria Falls and thought that I might enjoy going along. Do donkeys eat strawberries? Of course I would go; I had three days' pay in my pocket - I was rich again! We spent four idyllic days at one of the seven wonders of the world, and what a beautiful place it is. Keith and Una slept in a tent and I slept in the car.

I had already begun to love Rhodesia, a feeling which has grown and grown over the years. The people are somehow warmer than people in

Jim Redman

England, which is strange, as lots of Rhodesians are either immigrants from England or descendants of immigrants. I had the feeling and impression that here in Rhodesia and, in fact, Africa, anything and everything was possible! There was such energy, such a desire to create, it was all so dynamic that I seemed to draw strength from the environment and wanted to live as hard as possible! I felt ready for anything and looked forward to everything!

The following Wednesday I was back at work, my three days' pay of the previous week had paid for my unforgettable long weekend, but now I had to get back to serious things. My main aim at the time was to save up enough money to be able to bring my family to Rhodesia to be with me. And of course there was Glen, to whom I wrote many loving letters, describing the country and telling her of my wish to have her here with me. I knew that Jackie, for her part, was working hard to pay for the twin's keep, as she had told me not to send any money because she and Bob could manage the day to day living if I could save hard for the fares for the twins and Glen. It was now July 1952 and I had until August 1953, when Peter and Wendy would finish school, to do it. In Greenford, things seemed to be going well and I made sure that at the end of each month I had saved something towards the price of the fares.

I was impatient to get things moving more quickly, so Keith and I restarted Curbside Motors. In the evenings after work we repaired cars for our friends, but this time we could do it in great weather and with a garage of our own, not on the edge of the pavement. Life became much easier for me, even though I still had to work very hard but, having an optimistic and positive nature, I knew that I was moving steadily forward and living a great adventure.

Keith and Una rented a house and suggested that I share it with them. I paid them each week for rent and food, and saved money by not having to buy a car as Keith lent me his whenever I needed it. We had made friends with quite a few people, and Una, Keith and I used to go to all the motorcycle races all over Rhodesia, which were held at three centers: Salisbury, Umtali and Bulawayo. I was twenty years old and crazy about motorcycle racing - and, of course, girls. Each time I was unfaithful to Glen I felt a little guilty, but reasoned that we were not yet married and a man has to sow his wild oats. The temptation was so great I could not resist, but Glen was still the love of my life.

By now, Jackie had looked after the twins for nearly eighteen months and they had just turned fifteen years of age and where old enough to leave school. I had saved enough money for Wendy and Peter and Glen to join me in South Africa and, at last, they were on their way on board the Athlone Castle mail ship. I had made plans to meet them and Keith and Una came along with me. We covered the 1500 miles (about 2400 kilometers) from Bulawayo to Cape Town and were there to welcome them when the boat arrived. What a reunion! We wasted no time and jumped into the car and drove straight to

The Promised Land

the port of Simonstown, which was British-owned at the time, where I had arranged for Glen and me to be married.

After the wedding we returned to Rhodesia, where I had found a little house that I was buying. Both the twins and Glen found jobs fairly quickly, Glen with an insurance company, Wendy at the Criminal Investigation Department as a trainee in the Finger Prints Department (which was the beginning of an exceptional career as she became one of the top experts in this field). Lastly, Peter became an apprentice tool maker. Now there were four salaries coming in and things were really going very well for us.

A little while later, it was the turn of Jackie and Bob to leave England and join us. Wendy went down to Cape Town to meet them and had a great reunion. They arrived in Bulawayo and soon bought a house close to ours. All of us loved Rhodesia, except Bob, who detested it.

In the meantime, I had left my job at Duly and Co. and joined Keith at the CMED - Central Mechanical Equipment Department. We repaired the police vehicles and motorcycles, and other cars and lorries belonging to the government. Keith worked with me and soon we were able to get Bob in there, too. It was just like the old days back in England and we were all very happy.

As time went by, I became acquainted with John Love, who also worked there. He was a born and bred Rhodesian, a motorcycle racer, with whom I became good friends. What I did not know at the time was that John would later become six times South African car racing champion; when we met he was a bike racer who was already interested in a career in car racing. John had just bought an ex-Stirling Moss Cooper JAP, which was being sent over from England and was due to arrive in Port Elizabeth. I went with John to pick up the car and, on arrival, it didn't take us long to discover that the vehicle was in a pretty bad condition. We returned to Bulawayo, where I helped John get the car in shape.

At the same time, John was trying to sell his racing bike, a Triumph GP Twin. Luckily for me, he could not sell it and to thank me for all the time I had spent helping him on his car he asked me (knowing full well I would have killed for this opportunity) if I wanted to race on the Triumph? I had no experience of racing but knew I would soon pick it up - all I could think of was that, at last, I was going to compete in a real motorcycle race! The whole family was very excited at the idea of seeing me in action.

So, in 1954, I found myself on the starting line of my first bike race, on the Belvedere Circuit in Salisbury, to which the whole family had come to encourage me. Besides the bike, John had lent me his leathers, helmet, boots, gloves and goggles - the whole shooting match. Despite being very nervous and very excited at the start of the race, I managed to finished 7th. I was over the moon with excitement and offered John the 100 pounds he wanted for the bike. Of course, I did not have that amount of money, but said I would pay him 25 pounds a month for the next four months. John asked me if he

Jim Redman

could think about it for a bit, which was good for me as, in the meantime, John exchanged his Triumph for a Norton. According to John, this machine was far superior. Once John accepted my offer he threw in all his racing kit as well, so I was fully equipped and ready to race. Glen supported me totally as she knew that this had been my dream for so long.

The circuits in Rhodesia and South Africa were excellent training grounds, especially as the standard of riding was very good. The distances we had to travel to get to the meetings were vast, and a lot of the time were on bad roads, or roads that were almost non-existent. The main danger came from farm or wild animals, which could when we were least expecting it, decide to cross the road. I can't count how many accidents with cows, monkeys and even elephants I avoided by the skin of my teeth. At this stage of my life, racing was just a hobby, so we would work during the day and repair my bike in the evenings. Then we'd go racing at the weekends and often had to take a day off to travel to the meetings.

That same year a friend of John's, Cliff Nesbitt, wanted to sell his bike, a 7R AJS, an absolutely superb machine for which he was asking just 150 pounds. I made my usual offer to pay him 25 pounds a month. I had just finished paying John for the Norton and already wanted to sell it to buy this little jewel. The problem was that Cliff would not deliver the bike until I had paid for it completely. I wasn't bothered as there were no races during this period. After a few months I managed to sell the Norton for a good price and finished paying for the 7R AJS. The third time I rode this bike I gave it everything I had and achieved my first victory - the Umtali 100 handicap race - and first prize of 100 pounds! My family joined in my celebrations and I thought about my mother; how proud she would have been of me ...

For many days afterwards my feet didn't touch the ground, and the 100 pounds came in very handy, too. Then, the biggest sums of money were put up for the handicap races to give the whole field a chance of winning the big prize. This meant they were all - the 125s, 250s, 350s and 500s - mixed together and generally involved 50 to 60 competitors, who were all on the circuit at the same time. This was, to say the least, pretty dangerous, because of the big differences in speeds, especially as some of the circuits were on public roads around factories or houses. Also, the bikes ran on Methanol, with the compression ratio pushed right up on the motors. Luckily, my 7R AJS was very solid, even with a compression ratio of 14.1, and I had no problems. For this reason, I won a lot of prize money.

I started getting ideas about what I wanted to do in the future, and one thing was clear: I would never again be able to give up motorbike racing. I reinvested my winnings in a new bike, a 500cc Manx Norton, which I bought from a guy from Northern Rhodesia, known now as Zambia. Then, in 1955, John Love and I quit the government garage in order to open our own little motorbike shop in Bulawayo, "Love and Redman Motorcycles." Each of us invested the princely sum of 250 pounds, with which we rented small

The Promised Land

premises where we had a few secondhand bikes for sale in the window, plus spare parts, with our repair workshop just behind the shop. Both John and I took care of the selling and the repairs with the help of two labourers who did all the cleaning.

Before we had the shop, we had built up a small clientele, and had been proudly telling our customers that we were going to open a motocycle shop to rival Van Rooyen's Motorcycles, at the time the biggest motocycle shop in Bulawayo. I have to say, though, that this was not really the case as we did not have the money, and we bought all our spare parts from Van Rooyen's anyway, which gave us a discount. Our business was tiny and could only handle about six bikes at a time as the workshop was so small, and even then we had to push all the bikes waiting to be repaired outside in order to have room to work. We had to do all the work ourselves, often late at night, but despite everything we were reasonably satisfied.

"Love and Redman Motorcycles" was successful, even though both of us were involved in racing. We had to ensure that all the bikes being repaired were finished before we left, leaving Murrell, John's wife, to take care of the shop. No matter where the races were or how far away, we still went, even if we had to leave in the middle of the week, which was the case for the Cape Town event because it was 1500 miles away. Most of the time we left work on Friday evening or Saturday morning, and always at the last minute. We owned a nice Chevy van which took my bikes in the back, with John's car on a trailer behind, and, like this, we crossed and re-crossed Rhodesia and South Africa. We took turns driving and sleeping, often driving the whole night in order to arrive in time for practice. Then we left immediately after the race was over and the prizes distributed, driving again all night to be there to open the shop the next morning.

It was really hard sometimes but it was worth it; John was getting good results with his car races and I was doing well on the bikes. Glen and I were getting on well, though we had no thoughts of children: I had looked after the twins for many long years and felt that this was 'my time.' Despite my love for Glen, the temptations during the race meetings were many and I started to have affairs without Glen knowing. I was young and impressionable, and wanted to enjoy all the good things life could offer which I felt I had missed out on when growing up.

John's wife, Murrell, had never been keen on John racing, and began saying that we were neglecting the business with so much racing. My reply was "Then let's give up the business," which, of course, upset her even more. Things reached such a pitch that one day I said to John, who was looking miserable "Okay, let's have it - what's her complaint for today?" This cleared the air and John saw the funny side of it, but we decided that he would buy me out and I would be free to go off to Europe and race full time. For quite a while now I had been concentrating all my efforts on winning the 500cc South African Championships with the idea that, if I did, I could go

Jim Redman

to Europe as South African Champion and have a chance of competing and being accepted there.

So, with my mind set on Europe - and Murrell stirring up trouble between John and me - I offered my half share of the business to John. Knowing that I wanted to go, he made me a low offer which was immediately countered by me offering the same amount to buy him out! I had spoken to Bob and was convinced that, at this low figure, it would be a good investment for Bob as he could have kept his job at the CMED whilst everything was being set up, and I could have run the business for the rest of the year for him, until I was ready to leave for Europe. Bob actually turned down my proposition, then changed his mind a week later upon Jackie's insistence. But, by now, it was too late as John had come up with a much better offer, to my great satisfaction, as I wanted to be free to go as soon as possible.

In a funny way, destiny later turned Murrell's scheming against her, because as soon as John found out that I was beginning to become successful as a motocycle rider, he wanted the success too, and left immediately for England, to compete in car races ... For the time being, the most important thing for me was to win the 1957 500cc Championship in South Africa but, unfortunately, I was beaten by Beppe Castellani, the current South African Champion, untouchable at the time. I was so upset about my defeat I had not even thought about the points for the 350cc Championship. What a surprise when I found out I had won it and was now the new 350cc South African Champion. The dream was slowly taking shape.

In the meantime, whilst competing in different races in South Africa, I had made the acquaintance of Paddy Driver. Some character, this Paddy! The first time he invited me to sleep at his home was one night during the Grand Central meeting, which was held halfway between Pretoria and Johannesburg, near to Paddy's home. As we arrived at Paddy's house, he jumped out of the car and ran full speed into his house, reappearing a few seconds later brandishing 45 and 38 caliber pistols, shouting and screaming and firing them into the air. We were petrified and stayed nailed to our car seats. Apparently, this was his way of welcoming us but, since we did not know how many beers he had already downed, we prudently waited until the bullets ran out. When we entered the house, I noticed a bullet hole in the radio, another in the roof and several others in the wall and knew then we had done the right thing by in staying in the car! Despite a flamboyant personality, Paddy had a negative characteristic. He was very economical in his spending, even though he was certainly one of the richest in our group, and this was something which would cause friction between us later on.

Besides the friendship which linked us, we had in common this crazy desire to race in Europe and spent hours and hours dreaming and speculating about our chances of ever getting there, and planning our departure date. Paddy had learned from another South African rider, Eddie Grant, that it was possible to do a whole season in Europe on 1500 pounds, but this was the

The Promised Land

bare minimum and entailed making a lot of sacrifices and living rough, with, of course, that little bit of luck to hold out for a whole season over there. All I had to do was find this money and I would be on my way in March of 1958. What amazes me now is just how simplistically I made my plans - Eddy says 1500 pounds so just save that and go, you can make it!

Eddy Grant was killed whilst racing in Europe and the rumour we heard back in South Africa was that he died due to neglect. Apparently, he crashed at Villefranche de Rouergue and, when the marshals picked him up, was unconscious but breathing normally and seemed okay. In their wisdom, the marshals decided to keep Eddy there until the race finished, to avoid having to stop the race in order to get an ambulance to him. Rumour has it that, as it was a hot day, they did not think to cover him with a blanket and keep him warm for the shock but just let him lie there. Eddy died from pneumonia and not his injuries. As I've always said, one of the hardest parts of surviving a crash is to survive the first aid.

Once again, fate played into my hands. I needed to earn some money as I could not touch the money I was getting from John for the business, which was earmarked for Europe. I could not get a job as I also had to attend every meeting in 1957 to try and win the SA Championship. So I went to see Mick Gammon, who had a small motorcycle shop in Bulawayo, and made him a proposition which I thought could work for both of us. Mick was getting quite old and could not handle all the repairs that came into his workshop, so he turned most of them away. We came to an agreement that I would do all the bike repairs and pocket the money for the labour charges, and Mick would get the profit on the spare parts that I used in these repairs. I quickly knocked up a small, open-air lean-to at the back of his shop in which to work, and our association went well immediately.

Mick was a dyed-in-the-wool racing fanatic who had been to the Isle of Man in the thirties, so was right behind me in my efforts. I was able to compete in all the races without upsetting Mick at all, in fact, he helped me by booking in all the work while I was away. Most of my customers knew my plans and were very understanding about my constant departures on Fridays to get to a race, or my late arrivals on Mondays as I came home from far-away meetings down in South Africa. I was very conscientious; even if it meant continuing late into the night, I always made sure my work was finished before going off to a race meeting so that there would be no complaints from customers. Many took a great interest in the races and it wasn't unusual to see them back on Monday morning to find out how I had done over the weekend.

My wife, Glen, was behind me all the way and was never critical of my plans, or for selling my half of the shop to John. She had a good job, made a pretty good salary and we owned our own little house, with a mortgage. Glen was always very enthusiastic about the idea of me going over to Europe, knowing it had always been my dream to make motorcycle racing

Jim Redman

my career.

Jackie and Bob were now divorced as Bob, unlike Jackie who loved it, was never able to settle down in Rhodesia. Jackie would not go back to England and Bob would not stay, so quite amicably they decided to part. Jackie worked for the Rhodesian Railroad in the Department of Mechanical Engineering, and fully enjoyed a very agreeable life in her little house, round the corner from ours in Bulawayo, which Bob had let her keep. Wendy lived with her as they had always got on well together, and they never stopped improving and decorating that house. Jackie had bought herself a little Morris Minor Coupé, that leaked like a sieve when it rained. However, it took a lot more than this to discourage my older sister and you would often find her lying under the car, with Wendy at her side, carrying out repairs.

Wendy seemed to be blooming in her new adoptive country and, after finishing training, was steadily making her way up the ladder in the local Fingerprint Identification Office, doing very well and earning a good wage. There was a very good social club with a superb swimming pool where Wendy and Jackie spent a lot of their time. Wendy, always the tomboy, could often be found, with the boys from her office, playing waterpolo.

Peter was learning fast in his job as apprentice tool maker. He attended evening classes and worked hard, as it was his goal to eventually own his own machine tool company. Since he was a small boy, he had always been very talented with his hands. I loved Wendy because she was full of life and had an incredible personality. At the same time I had a great affection for my brother, to whom I felt very close; besides being brothers, we were best friends as well, which does not often happen. As soon as I could, I helped him buy his first motocycle, then his first car and later his first house.

1957 marked a turning point in my private life. I was competing in a race at the Roy Hesketh circuit in Pietermaritzburg, a town some 85 kilometers away from Durban, and met Marlene Setaro. Ken Robas, a mutual friend and one of the great riders of that time, introduced us. Marlene was 21 years old and was lap scoring at this race meeting. She was married to another rider, Stan Setaro, who was overseas in Europe racing at this time. It took us only a couple of minutes to realize we were attracted to each other and I asked her if she would accompany me to the prize-giving that evening. She replied that she did not have anything suitable to wear, so I drove her the 85km to her home to change, drove back to the party, then to her home again afterwards and finally back to my hotel, in all, covering about 360km that evening. From then on we saw each other as much as possible, always without Glen knowing, Marlene even came to Bulawayo to visit relatives there so that we could have some time together. I loved her deeply and decided that I wanted to share my life with Marlene, who felt the same way. One thing was certain, after meeting Marlene my life would never be the same again. There were big obstacles in our way as we were both married and divorce was not as commonplace as it is today.

The Promised Land

Marlene was indirectly responsible, some months later, for getting Mike Hailwood - at the time a young inexperienced racer who was out in South Africa to acquire racing experience - to realize his capabilities. Mike was racing on a 250 NSU, but never used the brand new 350 Manx Norton that he had brought with him. It seemed that he was nervous of riding the bigger bike, but when he saw Marlene riding my 500 Manx Norton to get the bike to the race circuit he immediately started riding his 350.

At last the time had come for me to pack up in Bulawayo, travel down to the last couple of race meetings in South Africa and then on to Cape Town to catch the ship to Southampton. Before I did this, though, I had to take care of one last thing. I went to see a friend, Gary Hocking, who had just started racing and worked on the railways, and asked him if he would like to take my place working at Mick Gammon's. Gary and I had met each other a little while before at a race meeting in Bulawayo and quickly become friends. Then, we were just two young riders who thought only about winning a local race, certainly not a world championship, since racing was still a hobby for us both. Gary immediately accepted my offer, only too happy to be able to be his own boss and earn more money with more freedom. Once Gary was installed, I left Bulawayo in February 1957, after competing in the last races there, and joined up with Paddy Driver in Cape Town so that we could embark for England, this time on a luxury passenger liner and not an old cargo ship.

It was the month of March and the voyage was magnificent, we were both so excited that, at last, we were on our way after the months of planning. I took deep breaths of this fine sea air, this very special air of freedom and excitement. I had to leave both Glen and Marlene behind as, obviously, I could not take either one of them with me, I only had enough money to barely survive by myself, living in the van I planned to buy with Paddy. It was probably for the best as it would give me time to sort out my thoughts and plan the future. I carried memories of them both in my heart, even if it was Marlene who was more often in my thoughts. The voyage lasted two weeks and we had a fantastic time; in fact, I said to Paddy as we arrived in England that, even if I got killed in my first race in Europe, I felt I had lived my life to the full during that voyage.

At Southampton we were met by Bob Foster. Bob had been World Champion in 1950 on a 350cc Velocette and we had become acquainted during his recent visit to South Africa, when he was in the company of a certain Mike Hailwood during the 1957/1958 South African season. Bob had invited us to stay with him if we made it over to race in England.

Bob took us first to his house in Bournemouth where we spent the first night, then we left all our bits and pieces and took the train to Chiswick, a London suburb near Heathrow Airport, in order for us to pay Hugh Ray a visit. Hugh owned a motorcycle shop and was very keen on racing. I knew of his reputation and had taken the initiative of writing to him the year before to ask if he would be interested in sponsoring me. Unfortunately, he had

Jim Redman

just signed up Geoff Tanner, an English rider who had won the Manx GP on Hugh's Norton. Even though he could not sponsor me, he promised to do all he could to help us. He was as good as his word and lent us a van so that we could travel to the north of England to meet Pip Harris, the side-car rider, who had a second-hand van to sell. We bought it from Pip for 200 pounds, paying 100 pounds each.

The van was already equipped with two bunks and mattresses, a gas stove, water tank and pump over the sink, and enough cupboards to pack away all our food and spares. More importantly, it was just large enough to hold four bikes. We left with both vans, heading for Birmingham and the Norton factory to take delivery of the four Manx Nortons we had already ordered, which cost 400 pounds each. We then drove back to Hugh Ray's workshop where we spent two days preparing the bikes, making the necessary adjustments and tuning them in order to be ready for the race at Brands Hatch that weekend. We slept in the van, which we parked inside the workshop, to save what little money we had left. My bikes were ready, our van filled with all sorts of supplies and spare parts in case of accidents. In short, I was ready at last for the big adventure and off we went to Brands Hatch.

Having spent 800 pounds on the two bikes, 100 pounds on the van, 100 pounds on the boat fare and about 250 pounds on Norton spares, by the time I arrived at Brands I had 50 pounds in my pocket, all the money I had in the world, and obviously not enough for a long career. All the best short circuit specialists were there - Derek Minter, nicknamed 'the King of Brands', Bob McIntyre and Alistair King, Alan Trow, Bob Anderson, Mike Hailwood - the list was endless and all of them very difficult to beat. I was like a child in wonderland, pop-eyed and completely overwhelmed with happiness at just being there. I had read so many things about this circuit; the phenomenal atmosphere and the champions that were regarded as gods by the crowds, and now I was here and was going to compete with them. I could hardly believe it! Having become a Rhodesian, I found I was quite well received by the motorcycle world and I am sure this was because of Ray Amm, the fantastic Rhodesian Norton factory rider, nicknamed 'The Angel of Death', who was very popular and famous due to his lurid riding style. It was Ray who put Rhodesia on the motorcycle racing map and, sadly, he had been killed a year or two earlier in a crash at Imola in Italy.

During this first meeting in Europe I managed 4th place in the 350 race, 3rd in the 500 race and 2nd place in the final invitation race, where only the top 20 of the 500 riders were invited to compete. My ambition, in coming to Europe, was to join the "Continental Circus," as it was called, because, just like a circus, it arrived in town for the race meeting, then packed up and moved on to the next one. The circus riders had to live rough in their vans but this is where the factories looked to recruit their riders.

Murray Walker, then fairly new on the scene and not yet the famous Formula 1 car race commentator he was to become, had interviewed me

The Promised Land

before the race. Murray covered the Tourist Trophy races with his father and the short circuits on his own. To my very great surprise, I found he was not at all interested in my Champion of South Africa title; what he found more important and interesting was that, on my privately-owned Norton, I had just beaten Geoff Duke's lap record, which he had set on his factory Gilera at the Roy Hesketh Circuit in Pietermaritzburg. Murray asked me what I was going to do that day and I told him I had to run-in my two brand new Nortons which I had collected only two days previously. I explained that South African circuits were very bumpy, whereas Brands was very smooth, and it was possible to lean the bikes over so much more on the smooth surface, so it was necessary to cut down or shorten the foot rests so they would not scrape on the road. I finished up cutting a little more after each race and then finally learnt enough to bend them up as well, so I no longer left trails of sparks during my races.

In the final 500 race, Murray remembered this conversation and passed it on to the fans as I was still leaving a trail of sparks in the last race. Murray Walker said afterwards he couldn't believe his eyes when I tried to ride right round the outside of Minter on the famous clearways bend, and was shouting into his mike that I had said I was only going to be running-in the bikes. At the finishing line the British journalists crowded around me, repeating over and over that I had tried to take Minter, considered the King of Brands, on the outside, as if I'd committed a crime. As far as I was concerned I had ridden in exactly the same way as I did in South Africa, that is, as fast as possible and without thinking too much about a particular strategy. At the very least, this incident caused a lot of fuss at Brands, where I was dubbed "An accident looking for a place to happen." The only important thing in my eyes was that I had finished in front of people like Bob McIntyre, Alistair King, Bob Anderson, Michael Hailwood and Terry Shepherd (no relation to Alan).

Then it was Hugh Ray's turn to congratulate me; he was excited and also could not get over the way I had ridden round the outside of Minter. He seemed very impressed by my performance and seemed to be regretting he had not sponsored me. Whatever, thanks to these three races, I pocketed the neat little sum of 75 pounds for my day's work, which increased my reserves by a cool 150 per cent.

4
First Year in Europe

After the race, Mike Hailwood's, father, Stan, said I should have asked the organizers to give me a silver plate showing my excellent results, instead of taking the money, to which I replied that the £75 was much more important as I couldn't eat the silver plate!

I learnt a lot in those first few weeks in England. In South Africa, because we raced only once a month, we raced as fast as possible from start to finish and didn't bother with any sort of race strategy, the important thing being the thrill of speed! After Brands Hatch, Paddy and I went to Oulton Park and Silverstone, and it was at Silverstone that I had an quite a bad crash. The circuit was very fast and, as usual, I got away to a very quick start but crashed and badly damaged my Norton. Luckily for me, I didn't have to go to hospital, but I was mad with myself for damaging my bike so much and having to use much of my meagre stock of spare parts to repair it. Of course, I didn't say anything to my family about this accident in order not to alarm them and, in any case, in my letters home I always preferred to tell them the good things rather than the bad.

Then we left the UK for Salzburg, in Austria, which was an old and very difficult circuit, even though its layout was very simple, because all the bends were on cobblestones, which look very quaint in little villages but are not so good to race on. This was followed by the St. Wendel meeting in Saar, Germany where, once again, I fell (on the cobblestones) during practice, but finished third in the 350 race. I was leading the 500 race by 15 seconds when I again overdid it and had a huge crash, sliding right under a bridge over the road. I was saved from going over the edge and into the canal by the strong iron railings, but the crash was disastrous for the bike and myself and I was taken to hospital with a serious leg injury.

The race organizer, August Balthazar, was a great guy who loved the bushmen, wild colonials like myself who always went for it. August drove

First Year in Europe

over 50 kilometers each way to Saarbrucken, a larger town, to buy me some English books to read whilst I was lying in hospital, and brought them to me with a bottle of cognac to ease my pain and had a couple of shots with me. He then had me transferred by ambulance to Heidelburg hospital for a second diagnosis on my leg injury as he knew I was eager to get out of hospital to race again the following Sunday. The Heidelburg hospital was right next to the Hockenheim circuit, where the racing was to be held, and some 150kms from St.Wendel. Having me transferred by ambulance was August's way of getting me to the circuit at no cost to myself as he knew money was very tight. Right afterwards, he left a message for Paddy - who had gone on to Hockenheim without me - to pick me up at the hospital.

So, with me barely able to walk, Paddy came to pick me up and I discharged myself and left, limping badly. I headed immediately for Hockenheim and started repairing my crashed bike in order to be ready for the races the next day. Even though I was suffering atrociously with my leg, I had to race as I needed the money to keep afloat financially; everyone told me I was mad to try and ride but no-one knew just how broke I was. All of the riders had other funds they could call on in a crisis whereas my entire worldly wealth was in my back pocket. Paddy refused to help me fix my bikes because he said I was crazy to ride and just buggered off and left me to it. Grim-jawed and determined, I limped around awkwardly as it hurt like hell to bend my leg. Of course, it's nearly impossible to work on a motorbike like this, but the more everyone refused to help the more determined I became and, finally, the bike was ready.

It was a terrific battle to push-start the bike in the race, and I was left on the start line in both races, but at least I competed, collected my start money and stayed afloat for another week or two. Riding like that was known as a "start money special," an event where you have no chance of doing anything in the race, but participate just to collect the start money. I was not the only one to do this; loads of riders have done it in their careers, especially those at the bottom where I definitely was that weekend.

However, I was not stupid and realised I would have to radically change my way of riding - and my whole approach - if I was going to survive. Much easier said than done ... For example, during practice for my first year in the Tourist Trophy races on the Isle of Man, as I dropped down the steep, impressive downhill road just after the start called Bray Hill, I was not concentrating enough on where I was going and on what I was doing. Instead of lining the bike up to just miss the curb at the apex of the kink at the bottom of Bray, I was watching my rev-counter to see what revs I was doing down there in top gear - don't ask me why, but I was. As I looked up, I found I was heading straight for the pavement, going at full tilt. Somehow, I managed to steer to the left, missing the pavement with my front wheel but hitting it with the underside of the engine, which knocked me into a broadside at well over 160kph. The huge impact knocked my backside right

Jim Redman

over the back of the seat and the bike headed back in towards the pavement with me clinging on. The saddle of the bike was in my chest and my legs were flying wildly in the air behind. I had no control over where I was going but, luckily for me, the spot at which my front wheel hit the pavement again was the slope of someone's driveway so, instead of crashing, I shot up onto the pavement with the back wheel sliding from side to side, leaving black marks on the pavement. There I was, lying prone on the bike with my feet still waving in the air behind, hanging on grimly to the handlebars and saying to myself "Let go of these handlebars, Redman, and you're dead." In this very uncomfortable position I had to grip the handlebars with all my strength, while my Norton zigzagged its way up the hill which followed. I was still on the pavement, missing garden walls and anything else there by inches, the wheels skidding from one side of the pavement to the other. Gradually, the bike straightened up and I heaved myself over the back of the saddle and suddenly was in control again. Without stopping, I carried on and finished the next 60km of the lap, which give me time to compose myself for when I got back to the pits at the start and finish.

I quietly said to Gary Hocking, Paddy Driver and Bob Anderson "Guess who's been up the pavement at the bottom of Bray Hill?" Needless to say, they didn't believe me at first, and Paddy even said that there was no way I could have gotten out of that one alive, I would have crashed. I told them about my engine hitting the curb and when we all looked at the underside of my bike the four bolts on the bottom were cut off, as with a knife. Then they began to believe me, but it still seemed so impossible that all four of us went down to the bottom of Bray on our racing bikes. When we stopped, the Course Marshal, who recognized me from my number, came over and said "You gave me the scare of my life, I had to rush to the loo when you did that." He didn't understand why I didn't stop, once I had regained control of the bike. I told him "If I had got off my bike at that point, perhaps I would never have been able to get back on again." For sure, this was the first time I had come so close to death.

My aversion to the TT dates from this time. I was young - especially in terms of experience - and I still had a lot of things to learn about motorcycle racing. Plus, I had not had enough time to familiarize myself with this circuit, although that doesn't excuse what happened as it was a stupid mistake on my part which should never have happened. Also, I was suffering the after-effects of my accident and was still limping the day I arrived on the Isle of Man. One cannot afford the luxury of making mistakes at the TT, as there is just nowhere to go except into something solid: a house, a telegraph pole, or maybe a wall .... Nevertheless, this fear of the TT taught me to be very cautious and, in all the years that I raced and practiced there, mostly in three classes (which means a lot of practice and racing miles), I never once fell off.

It was about this time that I first heard the saying "There are plenty of old riders and plenty of bold riders, but not too many old, bold riders." I later

First Year in Europe

discovered that the older hands on the circuit were not at all impressed by young upstarts like me coming along and having a go right from that start. They would just nod and say "Another accident just looking for a place to happen." This hit home with me and, from then on, I decided to try and win as slowly as possible. I became a much shrewder rider, pacing myself to hold my position in a race but not riding over the top unless it was really called for: to think with the head and not with the guts. Win, yes, but not at any price! This attitude stood me in good stead once I made it into the Honda Team as they liked my approach, whereas riders like Mike Hailwood or Bob McIntyre had a completely different attitude. They pushed their bikes to the limit, often even when they had no need to go that hard as they had a comfortable lead over the other riders. Bob, who was always one of the journalists' favourite riders, said he didn't see the point in working hard if the bike is not working hard, too.

However, back to that first year. Despite these little incidents along the way, I greatly appreciated this first year in Europe and we had a great time. Certainly, we did not have a lot of money, we were thin and very often hungry, even though food was cheaper in England than in Rhodesia. But we had such a passion for racing that we went to all of the circuits that would have us, just for the pleasure of racing and the pleasure of discovering other countries and, of course, provided they would pay us to go as the prize money was quite small and hard to win, so we existed on our starting money. Paddy was financially much better off than me (although I didn't know this at the time) but his happy-go-lucky attitude disguised a reluctance to pay his share of the expenses, which caused tension from time-to-time. With the starting money and occasional prize money, we repaired our bikes, serviced our van and took care of all the maintenance; I even managed to save almost 600 pounds. The difficulty was that it only took a fall, or one of the motors to explode, or the van to need repairs, and the money was gone. The fact that Glen, my sisters and brother each had jobs in Rhodesia meant that I did not have to send any money home, which took an enormous weight off my shoulders.

During this period I had become very friendly with a New Zealand rider called John Hempleman. His opinion was that riders who could not afford to buy their own bikes and had to look for a sponsor, had to ride where and when the sponsor wanted them to, which was not always in the best interests of their personal ambitions. I had been looking for sponsors, thinking that this would take the pressure off in the constant struggle for money, but "Hempo" (as he was nicknamed) convinced me that the thing to do was battle on with my own bikes, whilst trying to get a ride in a full factory team. I remembered Hempo's words when Reg Deardon offered me the chance to race for him and refused. I wanted to control my own destiny as I had always done in the past.

I managed to persuade Reg, during the TT races in the Isle of Man, to lend Gary Hocking the two Nortons and the van that he was offering me

Jim Redman

with his sponsorship. A few days earlier, Gary - having heard of my second place at Brands Hatch - had actually sold everything he owned in Rhodesia to buy his plane ticket to England. He arrived in the UK with only 200 pounds in his pocket, and a cheap, small cardboard suitcase in very bad shape, in which were thrown his few personal belongings, and it still rattled! He, like me, had always wanted to make a career of motorcycle racing so he took the chance that someone would give him bikes and just came. Reg did not regret his gesture, for Gary turned out to be particularly gifted. Getting Gary the ride with Reg cemented our already very strong friendship, and so Gary joined the "Continental Circus" and we competed all over Europe, racing practically every weekend.

There were an incredible number of races during this time, and it was not unusual to practise in the morning and then race in the afternoon. We were always very glad when there was a long weekend with a public holiday, because it meant we could ride in more than one race meeting, which always helped the finances. So, during the Easter long weekend, I rode at Brands Hatch on Friday, Snetterton on Sunday and at Oulton Park on Monday. Even though I never won a race during this season of 1958, I managed to earn enough money to buy my own little van, which would allow me to travel alone for the 1959 season.

At the end of the '58 season I sold Paddy my half of the big van and, with this money, bought a second-hand caravan for a good price. The time had come for us to go our separate ways. We had dreamed together and shared magnificent and intense moments, but now I knew that I wanted, above all, to share this nomadic existence with the woman in my life. I missed Marlene, terribly. To live any longer without her seemed impossible: starting next season, we would be together, for better or for worse.

I had also saved up enough money to deposit 1000 pounds in the bank, and so, on my return to Europe, my van and caravan would be waiting for me, my new motorbikes would already have been ordered and I would have money in the bank as well. Now I knew I had them beaten!

Before returning to South Africa I felt the need to go back to the places where I had spent my childhood. As I saw what had been my parents' house, I felt a big lump in my throat. It hadn't changed, this place that had witnessed so much happiness, so much sadness. Many memories came flooding to the surface and I couldn't stop thinking about my mother: it was as if she was in front of me, talking to me, smiling at me. Later, I walked past my old school and decided to pay a visit to my old friends and workmates at Taylor Woodrow and Colonel Ellbourne's. What struck me most was how little their lives had changed since I had left for Rhodesia and Africa. Watching their faces, as I told them about my train ride to Bulawayo, my first jobs over there, my first races, my first prizes, I suddenly understood that, from once being the poorest and most underprivileged of them all, I now had a full and rich life, which made all the hardships I had suffered in the past worthwhile.

First Year in Europe

I returned to Cape Town with Paddy and headed to Durban for a big reunion with Marlene. We travelled together to compete in all the races in South Africa and Rhodesia. We were on the continent of Africa for only a few months and the great distance which separated Bulawayo and Cape Town made it impossible for us to set up any kind of home, so we stayed with Marlene's family in Durban and with our very good friends, Norval and Phyllis Smith, in Redhouse near Port Elizabeth, and with other friends all over the country as well. We decided that whatever happened, from now on, Marlene was going wherever I went. Whilst in Bulawayo, I had a long talk with Glen and we decided she would divorce me, which was something we had discussed a few months earlier when Glen made the trip from Rhodesia to see her folks in England. We both knew it was over and our divorce was finalized a few months later. Glen stayed a few more years in Rhodesia and became a school teacher, before deciding to return to England to teach.

5
Life of a Nomad

I sold my two bikes for what I had paid for them, since they were in very good condition and impossible to buy new, as there was a long waiting list, and used the money to pay for the two new ones I had already ordered. Luckily for us, Norton had a policy of giving fulltime riders priority each year in allocating the new bikes.

So I was back to England in 1959 with Marlene for the new racing season. Having Marlene with me made life much more pleasant and, of course, a lot easier. I worked on the bikes, she took care of the caravan, doing all the housework, including helping me clean the bikes when the pressure was on. Without her, I would never have been able to drive all those hours night and day to get to the various circuits on time. After the races, I was so tired sometimes that I literally collapsed on one of the folding beds in the caravan. Marlene did her bit, driving the van so that I could sleep and then drive through the night to the next meeting. It was often very tedious, but nothing on earth could have made us change our life, we loved every part of it. On the circuits, Marlene took care of the blackboard, giving me signals on times and race positions, and becoming very good at all of this. Not once did she try and convince me to stop racing, even when she became pregnant. We loved each other passionately and, even though we didn't have a lot of money, we had the necessities and were happy.

The 1959 season was much the same as the previous one, with one small difference: I had fixed myself a very precise goal: to get a place in an official factory team. Gary Hocking's rise was incredibly rapid and he attracted the attention of the East German MZ factory, which gave him a position in its team in 1959. Gary had just won the Shell Gold Cup ahead of John Surtees, and had been riding so well that, on occasion, he had beaten some of the 250cc MV Agusta riders on his 250cc MZ. Count Agusta, owner of the famous MV Agusta Team, asked to have an interview with him and, on the spot, signed a

Life of a Nomad

contract for the 1960 season. For Gary this was the realization of all his dreams. Of course, the news spread like wildfire through the racing paddock and all the racers knew there was now a place available on the MZ Team. I lost no time in meeting with Walter Kaaden, director of the team, to convince him to hire me. Gary Hocking had already spoken to him about me. However, to my great disappointment, Walter Kaaden refused, saying I was too slow and, above all, too tall and heavy to be able to ride his 125 and 250 MZs.

Marlene's pregnancy was beginning to show. As I was soon to be a father, I asked myself if it wasn't time for me to hang up my helmet, find a permanent job and settle down and live normally like everyone else? I thought about the young racers - around six a year - who were getting killed on the circuits. A lot of them were beginners just arrived from South Africa, Australia or New Zealand, but older, experienced riders were dying too. I considered retiring at the end of the 1959 season and returning to Rhodesia. Things had not worked out at all as I had hoped, in other words, a place in a team. I had been pretty consistent during the season, always placing in the top ten and mostly in the top six, and giving it everything I had with the equipment I had available, but this was not enough. I had no desire to just race on and be one of those independent racers that made up the crowd on the starting lines, with all the hardship, money problems and insecurity that entailed! I was tired. For the moment I had to think about my wife and my child, and about offering them a proper life with a home and a comfortable wage coming in regularly.

Without saying a word to anyone, I gathered all my belongings - everything I owned - and headed for Africa and the racing season there. As I raced around the circuits in South Africa and Rhodesia, seeing all my friends, I realised that, although racing might kill me, I could not live my life not knowing if I could make it in the big time. So, instead of retiring, it was back to Europe again after the African season for one last try for a place in a works team. Maybe this time I'd be lucky ...

Again, I sold my two Nortons for the price I had paid and bought two brand new ones from the Norton factory. I'd decided that the only way to achieve my goal was to have a successful season, and be noticed by a factory team manager and given the opportunity to show what I could do on competitive machinery. I had the whole thing planned in my head, knowing exactly which race meetings I should attend.

For me, the season always began in England in March at Brands Hatch, and then went on to Italy for the first races at Imola and at Cesenatico in April. Next, came the Spanish Grand Prix, then the Austrian Grand Prix in Salzburg in May, immediately followed by St. Wendel for the Saar Grand Prix (Salzburg and Saint Wendel were called GPs even though they did not count toward the World Championship). After this it was the Tourist Trophy on the Isle of Man and Mallory Park for the post-TT meeting. At the end of June, I took off for Assen for the Dutch TT, then on to Spa Francorchamps

Jim Redman

at the beginning of July for the Belgian Grand Prix, followed soon after by the German Grand Prix, which took place either in May or in July. Then I headed for Sachsenring in East Germany and on to the Czechoslovakian Grand Prix in Brno, although, in 1958 and 1959, these last two circuits were not counted as World Championship circuits. After that, we left for Finland, then went again to Italy for the Italian Grand Prix at Monza. Then it was back to England for the last races on the English circuits, which occurred between the end of September and beginning of October. From there, we took the boat to Cape Town for the African season, and then back on the Union Castle ship in March leaving for England to begin again the European circuits. We used to joke about being in a rut, as it was the same routine each year with a few variations. Of course, we said this tongue-in-cheek as it certainly beat fighting the freeway traffic on the way to an office everyday.

My son, Jimmy, was born on 26th December 1959 in Port Elizabeth. I was racing in Johannesburg and Marlene had just been admitted to hospital when she heard on the radio that Paddy had fallen and taken me down with him. You can imagine how she must have felt.

Marlene and I were married immediately after Jimmy was born. We had waited until then because, in those days, it was considered disgraceful if the girl was pregnant during the marriage. During his first 18 months of life, Jimmy visited no less than 36 different countries. We took him to his first race when he was only three weeks old. During the races Marlene used to place his cot under the pit counter, where he used to sleep quite happily. We were known on the circuits as one of the first rider families to travel with a baby. This soon changed as more and more couples decided that if we could cope, so could they, and suddenly the paddock was full of children, which was quite good as they all had friends to play with.

During that era we were real nomads, taking our caravan everywhere and living in it for most of the season. We once asked a doctor how the lack of a home was affecting Jimmy. He told us not to worry as we were Jimmy's anchor and the constant thing in his life.

I rode in a lot of races, always on my Nortons, with a fair amount of success, and had built a certain reputation in the profession. I was perceived as a 'sensible' rider, someone who rode fast but didn't take off on a frantic, suicidal course. I knew for a fact there were a lot of other riders just as capable as I was, which meant I had to be the best private rider if I wanted to get a factory ride. The first two places in Grands Prix were usually taken by works riders, who no-one had a hope of beating. Another thing I was well aware of was that the future would be decided by the Japanese teams in the 125cc and the 250cc classes. This was especially true of Honda which was the first Japanese motorcycle marque to arrive in Europe and one which had the financial resources to make an all out effort to win.

Early in 1960, I won the Spanish GP at Montjuich Park on my 500cc Norton, beating into second place the 500cc MV Agusta of Remo Venturi.

Life of a Nomad

I was over the moon at beating a fully-fledged factory MV with a private Norton as, besides the pride of such an achievement, it was very obvious to everyone that I must have ridden well, even if they did not actually see me ride that day. This could only be done on a circuit such as Montjuich where, by riding 110 per cent, I compensated for the obvious power advantage that the MV had. Of course, even as I was savouring the win, I was hoping the powers-that-be in the various factory teams had noticed my performance. I wanted to be part of a factory team because I knew that it was the only way I could reach the top of my profession. I hoped that my victory at Montjuich Park was going to help me realise this ambition.

Unfortunately, I did not account for the effects of Mick Woollett, a very well-respected English racing reporter, saying in his race report that he had felt so sorry for Venturi, battling his way round on the MV while Redman had it easy on his better-handling Norton. I was so surprised and disappointed as I had expected to get all the kudos for pulling off such a fantastic feat in beating the works bike with my own Norton. I was very upset. However, to my surprise, John Surtees and several other riders, irritated by this race report, took the trouble to write to the magazine and make known their anger at the article, pointing out that, instead of crying over the defeat of a factory rider, Mick Woollett would do better by praising the performance of a young rider who, on his own bike, had beaten a factory machine. The letters were considered important enough for the magazine in question to print a new article, in which it spoke about me in the most glowing terms. Obviously, I couldn't have been happier, because the more the press and radio spoke about me, the more chance I would have of being noticed by the big firms.

I also had to show that I was capable of being the best in the other categories and be considered as someone who could ride in any class on any size of machine. So, the following month, at the Imola circuit, I decided to buy a 125cc Ducati from Ken Kavanagh and make myself known in this category. I knew that if I could do well in this class I would stand a chance of getting noticed by the MZ or Honda teams. The Ducati was an expensive bike, and the Ducati people were so happy I had bought it and was going to ride it that they asked me to call at the Ducati factory after Imola, where they would overhaul the bike completely at no charge to me. This was fantastic news and, early on the Monday morning, Marlene and I arrived at the factory where everyone was so friendly that we stayed a few days, sleeping in our caravan in the factory so they could work on the bike until late at night. I was making myself very late for the Austrian GP at Salzburg but did not mind as I wanted the bike to be in perfect condition. I was keeping in mind the forthcoming Isle of Man Tourist Trophy races, which, in those days, were the most important in the calendar. I knew that for 1960 the Honda Team was going to be there in force.

The TT was, without doubt, the most difficult circuit and the most spectacular race in the Grand Prix calendar, which made it the favourite GP

Jim Redman

of some riders and a very large public. From all over England, people from all walks of life travelled many miles to get there, sleeping on the beaches, in hotels, under tents or in their cars. Whole families hurried there several days in advance, to be certain to get the best spots. Boats filled to the brim arrived at Douglas Bay docks and neither storms nor earthquakes would have dampened the enthusiasm of the race's supporters. The TT gathered together all those who were passionate about bikes and, for a lot of them, it was a chance to closely admire the bikes and mingle with the riders, talk to them and get autographs and also proudly show-off their own machines for others to see. A lot of fans arrived with their own road bikes polished until they shone like a thousand lights, with not so much as a scratch on them. For a lot of people, the TT was definitely The Race of the year.

It was also the most testing of all the races, for rider and machine. Each turn, each bend could be dangerous, and was often misleading. The race meant knowing absolutely every twist and turn, every bump and dip and every manhole cover. The rider had to fight his machine at high speed to make it change direction, and rush through absolutely blind corners, trusting completely his knowledge of the circuit. Concentration had to be total, in wet or dry, and even in mist, as this mountain circuit threw up all kinds of conditions. I make no bones about it; I never really liked racing on this circuit, which contained too many brick walls and curbs, houses and trees ... and nowhere to go if you made a mistake, which could prove fatal. A lot of riders lost their lives here. Although most of the riders were terrified by the idea of racing on this circuit, they would not miss this meeting for anything.

In 1960, the organizers decided to start practice a few days earlier, instead of on the traditional Monday one week before the first race. A lot of riders headed there very early that year, straight after their race on the Sunday, but I was not one of them. Instead, I decided to fit in as many races as I could while so many riders were already on the Isle of Man. These were less important races and, with not much opposition there, I knew I could have a field day, resulting in quite a lot in start and prize money. While all the cats were away, this mouse could play - my racing appetite was insatiable!

In ten days I competed in no fewer than ten races, dashing from country to country. On the Sunday, I was in Finland, where I finished 3rd in the 125cc race and 2nd in the 350cc. Then I left right away for the Karlskoga Circuit in Sweden on the Thursday, where I finished 2nd in the 350cc. We left after the prize-giving in Sweden and drove flat out through the night for Hockenheim in Germany, arriving just in time for the last qualifying practice on Saturday and race on Sunday. I finished 3rd in the 500cc and we then drove all night and raced in Chimay in Belgium on the Monday, where I won the 500cc and was 2nd in the 350cc. Then we dashed through the evening to catch the midnight ferry from Ostend to Dover, managed to get some sleep in the four hour crossing, and I rode at Brands Hatch on the Tuesday, where again I was 2nd in the 350cc and 3rd in the 500cc. These were all good results in a very

Life of a Nomad

short period but it still wasn't over as, straight after Brands, we drove up to Liverpool to catch the midnight ferry to the Isle of Man so that I could be in the Isle of Man for the 5.00am practice session the next morning. On the night ferry which took me from Liverpool to Douglas, I never even thought about my tiredness as I had to change the sprockets on both bikes, from the short circuit gearing for Brands to the high gearing required for the TT.

Generally, we had to change this gearing for nearly every meeting, so I was quite used to it and it had to be done then as I had only Wednesday, Thursday and Friday to prepare for the TT; practice was of the utmost importance, even in my tired state. Wednesday morning found me with the rest of the riders out on the TT course, tired, but happy, with only three days before the race. I had little time in which to familiarize myself with the circuit and came in for a lot of flak from my friends, who said I was mad to do what I had. I smiled to myself as my pockets were full of money whilst they had been spending theirs. For a lot of them, this did not matter, as they were a lot better off than I. But I had come to Europe to fight and was determined to place myself as best I could.

Suddenly, it was race day. I had managed to catch up with some sleep and get the bikes into shape, so here I was on the start line, just the same as the guys who had been there for nearly two weeks already. The atmosphere was electric; the moment of truth not far away. My heart began to beat very quickly and I felt the adrenaline rise, little by little. The faces of the racers were tense with concentration and nervousness. We sat astride our bikes, in our minds running through the first few corners, hypnotized by this road which for the following two and a half hours would either be our friend or most cruel enemy. The clock ticked away the last moments: five minutes, then two minutes, then one. A last look at the gas tap ... take off the goggles ... put them back on again ... fasten the helmet - already fastened ... try out the brakes ... press down on the forks ... check it's in first gear ... advance and then back up the bike. All these checks to ensure everything worked well and that the machine would take off instantly, like a rocket.

It's too dangerous for a mass start, and so riders are sent off in pairs at ten second intervals. Then, as it gets to your turn, you stand next to the bike, ready to push-start it yourself - no helpers are allowed - with eyes glued on the starting flag. At last the 'signal' is given - as always when you least expect it - and the public roars as if with one voice, making the adrenaline rush to your brain. You have to push this bike, which seems to weigh a ton, and pray that the engine starts - a miracle happens. You wedge yourself into the saddle and, without another thought, take off as fast as possible. The butterflies are suddenly gone.

The race is not so much against each other as the clock, with signals from our pits to let us know how we are doing. From here on, everything depends on the rider. In front of him there are 6 laps - 226 miles - and more than 2 hours of racing which will leave him physically wiped out at the end.

Jim Redman

That's what the TT is all about. Even though I managed pretty well during this race, I couldn't win because our Nortons had no chance against the works machines. However, I did manage to beat a lot of my critics who had told me I was mad, which gave me a lot of satisfaction.

Picture Gallery 2

Silverstone. That bloody Hailwood giving me a hard time – with a Benelli this time.

August Balthazar, the organiser of the races at St. Wendel, Saarlandes, and his daughter, Monika, who is, today, married to Mr Shoei the famous German helmet man.

Jim Redman

Ulster Grand Prix 1961. Redman leads Takahashi then Phillis and Hailwood; too big, huh?

Isle of Man 1960/61. Four good privateers, sadly all no longer with us. Bob Anderson (15), Harry Hinton (54), Bob McIntyre (52) and, behind, Alistair King.

Picture Gallery 2

A good shot at taken at Brno, probably in 1962. When will the others learn how to start a bike and get away quickly?

Guess who got away first again?

83

Jim Redman

Another good shot taken at Brno in 1961.

Typical Isle of Man shot taken at the Quarter Bridge in 1962.

Picture Gallery 2

Another Brno shot. 1961.

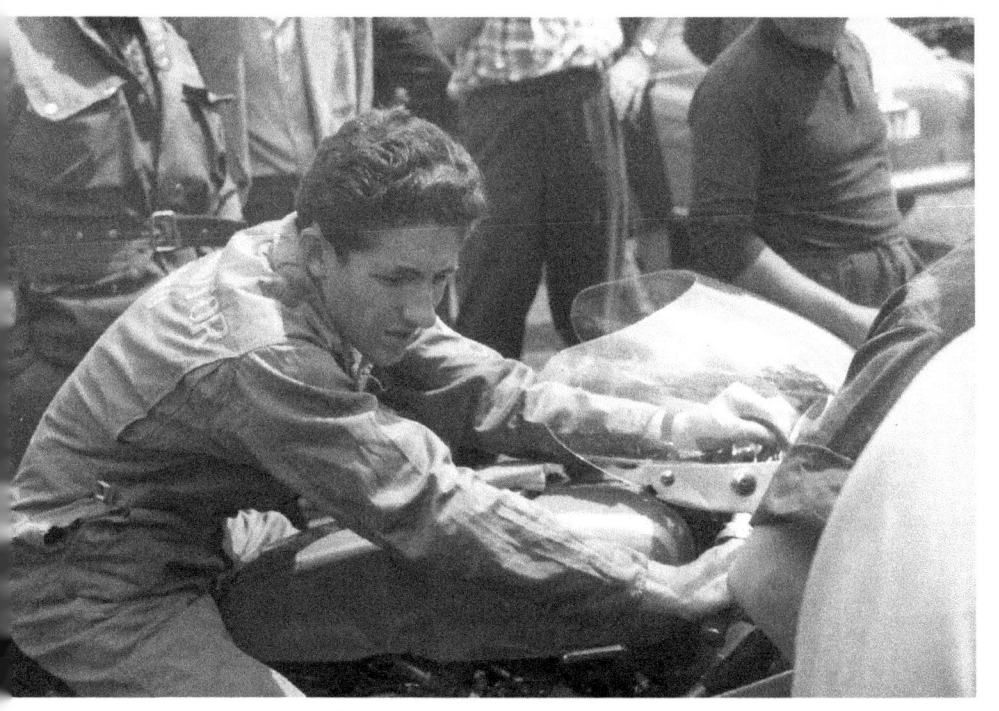

Tom Phillis, a great man and a great rider.

85

Jim Redman

My friend Tom Phillis.

The 'Flying Scotsman.' The great Robert McGregor McIntyre. Another good friend gone.

Picture Gallery 2

Jim in winning mode.

Jim Redman

If Tom had to go Jim, this was the best way ...

88

Picture Gallery 2

Clermont Ferrand, the French Grand Prix 1961. Marlene took 18 months to knit that jersey!

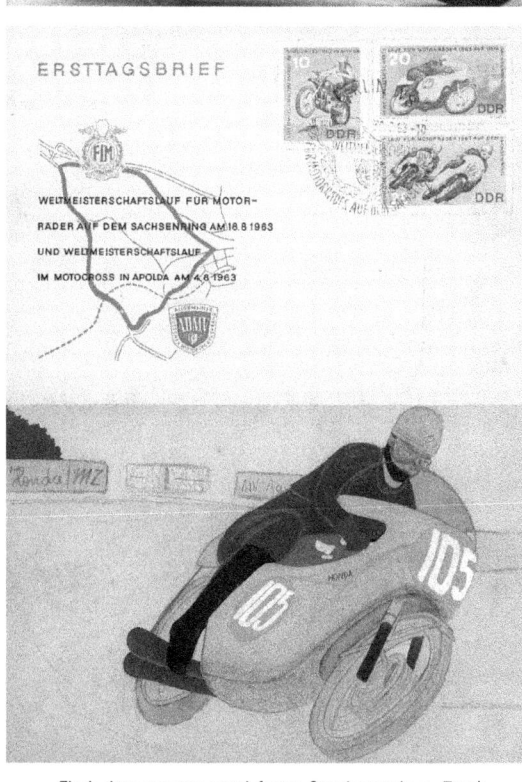

First day cover sent from Sachsenring, East Germany, by a fan and the drawing that was enclosed.

The epic dice between Mike (132) on the MZ and Jim (129) on the Honda at the Sachsenring in 1962 ...

89

Jim Redman

... a nail-biter to the finish!

Picture Gallery 2

Mike 'the bike' Hailwood and Jim 'the car' Clark seen at Zurich airport shortly before Jim was killed at Hockenheim, Germany.

Jim Redman

Solitude, Germany 1962. This is what I call road racing.

Picture Gallery 2

Luigi leads Mike, on 125s this time.

93

Jim Redman

Team talk. Jim with Luigi and Tildy Taveri.

1963 350cc Honda – undressed.

Picture Gallery 2

Jim and Phil (left) before the start at Spa 1964. Which one with butterflies, which one with seagulls? Less than one lap later both narrowly escaped a serious crash.

95

Jim Redman

Jim does the work, Nobby gets the girl. Talking to a French journalist from *Moto Revue*.

"*No*, Mr. Redman, we will *not* pay your team any more start money ..."

6
Some Dreams Come True

The next Grand Prix was held in Assen in Holland, and was a turning point in my career as a grand prix racer.

Tom Phillis - the Australian rider who had been one of the first to believe in Honda - had just had an accident. Some time before, Tom had asked his father if he thought Tom should write to Honda, asking to ride its bikes. His Dad was a man of few words, who said to Tom "Son, they are not going 12,000 miles to lose." Tom wrote to Honda.

The Japanese firm was the object of derision from some individuals in and around GP racing, who thought these little Japanese machines would never be a danger to the big teams of the time, the MVs and MZs. Even though they still needed to be improved, the results obtained by Tom and his teammate, Taniguchi, at the TT were very encouraging. Unfortunately for Tom, he crashed during practice at Assen and broke his collarbone. Taniguchi, too, was in bad shape following a fall, so Honda had problems with two riders out of the race. Having heard the news about Tom, I immediately rushed over to his caravan to find out how he was getting on. He seemed fine apart from the broken collarbone and the main damage was to his pride at doing something as stupid as putting himself out of action by crashing in practice. I knew there would be a lot of riders who would be hanging around, waiting to get Tom's ride and to see who Honda was going to choose to replace him, so I told Tom I was glad he was okay but that I wanted to get in line and try for his ride.

Racing is a dog-eat-dog game and, if you crash, there are always riders lining up to take your place. That's the way it is, no bad feeling, just the law of the game and everyone knew it, including myself and Tom. As I was about to leave, Tom said to me "You know, you are just the right guy to take my place." Tom's confidence in me dated back to the previous year, when we had had a huge dice in the Czechoslovakian GP in Brno. My 500

Jim Redman

Norton was not going well, while Tom's bike was flying. We both knew that his machine was a lot faster than mine, and yet, each time we came to the villages on this long (at that time) circuit (it is much shorter today and all the cobblestones are gone), I would pass him on the slippery cobblestones, then he would steam past me on the next straight and I would pass him again in the next village. This went on for the whole race and I cannot remember who beat who, but I felt real good when Tom came to me after the race and said "Bloody good ride, you would have been a sensation today on a quick bike." A rare compliment from another rider, but Tom knew how to give a compliment when it was deserved. Tom had many good qualities; I don't know of anyone who did not like him.

Luckily for me, this day in Assen he remembered the episode. He asked his wife, Betty, who was at his bedside, to call Mr Kawashima, head of the Honda Team, and ask him to come over to his caravan right away. A few minutes later, he was with us and listened in silence to everything that Tom had to say to him. Tom gave a good recommendation to Mr Kawashima and made it clear that I was the man of the moment, and the right one to race in his place in the 125 race. Mr Kawashima turned to me and asked very casually if this would suit me, adding that he would be very happy if I could ride their 125 machine. I couldn't believe my ears, at last the chance I had been waiting for for so long. I felt like saying "Who do I have to kill to be able to take his place?"

I did not know then just who Mr Kawashima was but found out later that he was one of Mr Honda's first twelve employees, and that Mr Honda held him in high esteem. He had come to direct the team because he enjoyed it, and also had enough responsibility within the Honda company to make important decisions when the need arose. A lot later, when Mr Honda retired, it was Mr Kawashima who replaced him as President of Honda Motor Company. However, back then, he was just a friendly, kind Japanese man who was in charge of the team. Now I had this golden opportunity, I was just so glad that I'd bought the 125 Ducati and had had a bit of time to adapt my riding to ultra-light machines. I felt confident I had a good grip on them and would be able to give a good account of myself the next day on Honda's 125. I knew that I had my future in my hands: if I failed I would have only myself to blame ...

The last of the practice sessions was scheduled for the following day, but I spent the rest of that afternoon with the engineers, getting the bike set up to my liking, knowing that I absolutely had to qualify in a good position. I knew I wouldn't get a second crack at this, it was now or never. It was a good thing I didn't have to practice for the 350 and the 500 classes as I was already qualified, so could concentrate totally on the 125 race. Mr Kawashima took me aside for a moment to tell me that Tom had gone very fast during the previous day's practice and achieved excellent times. He tried to reassure me by saying that he did not expect me to do as well as Tom had, especially

Some Dreams Come True

since it was my first race on a Honda. He said he would be happy if I was able to get close to Tom's times, say, two or three seconds slower.

The next day, after doing a couple of laps on the circuit with the 125, I returned to the pits for a few adjustments. Once that was done, I sat on the bike for five minutes, going over the circuit in my mind and weighing up every curve, every bend, every angle and every turn I was going to come up against. I knew that I usually went better the next day after the first practice, but this was the only chance, maybe, and I was not about to blow it. I was working out where I could scrape off fractions of seconds, and perhaps make the difference between me getting or not getting a permanent place in the Honda Team. At last, the fateful moment arrived. I felt ready to give it a full go, a 110 per cent effort to try for a really fast lap that would please the team.

Strangely enough, all my fears faded away as soon as I set off and suddenly I felt calm and very much at ease. I somehow knew that I was going to do it and I left the pits and rode as fast as possible without thinking anymore about the fact that my future was at stake. When I came in, the whole team was excited: I had lapped a full two seconds faster than Tom's best time, and on the same bike! What was more, I had even managed to beat one of the three MVs which, at that time, dominated the 125 class. This placed me just behind Gary Hocking and Ubbiali on their MVs, and in front of Spaggiari on his. As soon as I pulled in the whole team - including Mr Kawashima, who was over the moon - crowded around to congratulate me on this incredible performance.

When the official times were published, some of the journalists were so surprised by mine that many were convinced the Dutch organization had made a mistake: to them it was unthinkable for a Honda to achieve such a good time. The rumour quickly spread around the paddock that the organizers must have made a mistake, but they insisted they were right. The journalists even came to see me. I told them I had been having a full go but they said did I really think I could get round faster on a Honda than one of the MVs? I was thinking that, even if there had been a mistake, the journalists could have just kept quiet and let me enjoy my place in the sun, it was just what I needed. But, no, they had to cast a doubt. Never mind, I thought, tomorrow we shall see.

I was furious but didn't show it, and asked Mr Kawashima not to take any notice of all this nonsense. He only half-listened to me because he had another problem to take care of (a big one, this time) with his rider in the 250 class, John Hartle. John had been refused permission to ride the 250 Honda because the bike was contracted to Castrol and John to Mobil. The petrol company was uncompromising. Honda found a way out by asking the organizers to let Bob Brown take John's place, because Bob had already ridden on this machine on the Isle of Man and knew it well. But, here again, Honda came up against a wall as the organizers categorically refused this request, as Brown had not practiced at all on a Honda in Assen.

Jim Redman

Mr Kawashima was devastated. The organizers came up with the solution; they said that, according to the rules, the only other rider who could ride the 250 was Jim Redman, as he had qualified on the 125 and the rules said that if you had qualified on a similar machine you could ride (I had just ridden the 125 during practice).

Mr Kawashima was greatly relieved and immediately came to see me to ask if I could race the 250 as well as the 125, knowing that I would not be allowed to have even one lap of practice on the 250. It's relevant to know that, at the time, Honda never signed a contract with a rider and each of us was hired to compete in only one race at a time. That the company was offering me the chance to represent it in two classes was fantastic, but I had never ridden a 250 before: not only that, but this 250 was a four cylinder and I had never ridden a four cylinder of any size! So I was in a quandary. It wasn't that I didn't want to ride - of course I did - but I couldn't see how I could do well without the chance to ride the bike at all and do even one practice lap. In those days, there wasn't even a warm-up lap, it was simply a case of warming up the engine, pushing the bikes to the start line and off we went. My worry - which I voiced to Mr Kawashima - was that, if I didn't do well, I may never again be given the opportunity to race the 250. Mr Kawashima replied, in a fatherly manner, that I should not worry at all about that, and that it would make him very happy if I just managed to finish the race. Touched by his understanding I accepted, whilst at the same time warning him that he should not expect miracles.

The next day, as I was on the starting line of the 125 race, I decided that, once and for all, I would show these reporters, the race organizers and the world what I was capable of. The day before the journalists had tried to demolish my self-esteem and the time had come to set the record straight. My strategy was simple: I would try and stick right behind Gary, Ubbiali and Spaggiari on their MVs in order to to get away from the MZs, since their bikes were, after the MVs, the fastest of the moment. Deep inside I still harboured bad feeling toward the MZ team, which had turned me down because it was thought I was too slow. Well, I would show them!

The first lap was in every way exceptional. I wound up the throttle as far as it would go and pushed the bike and myself to the limit, I braked as late as I possibly could into every corner, taking risks everywhere to get into 3rd position behind the MVs of Gary and Ubbiali, but in front of Spaggiari's MV. I was determined to show the doubting Thomas' and poor Spaggiari, against whom I waged a fierce battle, did not know what had hit him. He would pass me on the straights but, as soon as he braked, I would pass him either on the brakes or in the corners, sometimes inside, sometimes outside. In a straight line he was much faster than I was, but I made up for it by sheer hard riding. Just one lap without crashing was all I was hoping for on that first lap and I almost crashed a dozen times. I knew that I was betting my future and wanted to show Honda it had not been a mistake choosing me to race

Some Dreams Come True

for them and that I really had made the third best time. We passed in front of the stands at the end of the first lap with Hocking first, Ubbiali second, me third and Spaggiari fourth. I smiled quietly to myself; I had done it. A few laps later it was Spaggiari who crashed, and not I, despite the reckless way I had been riding. Because of this I found myself in 3rd place. However, I could not continue to ride at such a deadly speed, and had to just take the edge off a bit if I wanted to finish the race. Then I made a big mistake. Thinking that I was clear of the other competitors, I slowed down a little too much. I soon got the signal from Honda, warning me that the two other MZs were catching up. The MZs were, of course, not as reliable as the Hondas (I had expected that they would probably break down), but they were a lot faster ...

I tried, but there was nothing I could do and found myself being overtaken by the first MZ, although at least managing to hold off the others. At the finish line I was fourth and, knowing that this was the best finishing position ever achieved by a Honda up until then, felt okay about it as at least I had not crashed on that first do or die lap.

At the Honda pits it was total euphoria but, already, the criticism about my size had started. Honda refused outright to listen to the nonsense and I began to believe that I had a chance of becoming part of this team, although still had to prove that I could do well on the 250.

On the starting line, all the riders were standing next to their machines, hands firmly gripping handlebars and eyes fixed on signal lights. The judges watched the riders intently to ensure that none jumped the start, but I knew their attention was on the front of the grid. I was pretty well placed, at the end of the line nearest the pits but on the back row of the grid (as I had not set up any practice times). I had Aika San, the Japanese engineer, as close as he could get next to me, so that when the lights turned to orange - indicating that we had 30 seconds left to go - he would do the count for me, which he did, When he got to 27 I started to push my bike, trying not to be seen, so that when the lights turned green I had already advanced three rows of riders and shot into the lead when the lights went green.

My bike then starved of fuel as I'd warmed it up too much, and I dropped back from first to twelfth. This, however, was lucky for me as I know that if I'd been up with Hocking and Ubbiali going into the first fast bends, I would have crashed for sure as the bike handled so differently to the 125 and was unlike anything I'd ridden before. I must admit I got a huge scare when I went into my first curve, because this bike was not very easy to ride. I sincerely believe that if I had still been up near the front, I would have crashed because of my lack of experience on this bike. Having to overtake a lot of competitors meant I could not ride as fast as those in the lead, which gave me the chance to get used to the bike's handling. I finished the race, not too badly, in eighth position. Tom Phillis was the first to congratulate me and simply saying "Well played" to me as he shook my hand. Tom said he was delighted I had done so well and had justified his confidence in me.

Jim Redman

He had been particularly impressed by my fourth place in the 125 race, at the same time admitting that the eighth place in the 250 event was quite remarkable, considering I had not had any practice. As for Honda, they couldn't believe their eyes, Mr Kawashima came personally to give me long and warm congratulations. Although I was making excuses for a mediocre performance on the 250, he seemed completely happy with my eighth place in the race and said he had not expected such a good result, especially from a rider who had not even had a practice session. Of course, I quickly took advantage of the occasion to tell him that if ever he wanted me to race on his bikes again, I would easily be able to get used to the 250 Honda and achieve better results. He just smiled and did not commit himself.

I still had work to do so it was back to the starting line to compete in the next race, the 350. Despite feeling pretty tired, I managed to finish seventh. I had to drop out of the 500 race because I had reached the maximum mileage allowed for a rider in one day. Honda paid me 100 pounds for each of my two rides, which, added to the start money and the prize money, meant I had my best day ever financially, plus had managed to get my foot in the door with the Honda team, I just hoped I would be asked to ride for them again the following weekend.

Early on in my career I had tried to procure, without much success, an increase in the starting money paid by the organizers. We all knew that the gate money was good; you had only to consider the size of the crowd to know that; but the organizers were reluctant to pay decent start money to the guys putting on the show, the riders. A lot of riders didn't help this situation, as they used to show up at the races without a contract to ride and would grovel for whatever start money they could get, just to keep going. In time, the organizers came to know that they could always fill their fields at the last minute - and very cheaply - from this pool of riders. I made up my own mind, set my own modest standards and would just not go if I was not paid what I considered to be reasonable money.

Factory riders were paid a little better, but because they had to ride in Grands Prix to get the points, some GP organizers were very stingy with them too. Even so, with machines and expenses available from the factory, these riders were always okay. They did not make the huge amounts that riders do today, but this was in the era when the FIM had banned advertising on the bikes and riders, so there was virtually no sponsorship available. This situation always angered and upset me as it was so wrong that the guys who, every weekend risked their lives, often did not have the money to eat properly and maintain their bikes well, and yet the organizers and the FIM all lived and travelled in the lap of luxury. Their attitude was that riders came and went, and were like cannon fodder, very expendable. In fact, about six a year were killed in those days as no-one was concerned with their safety.

The organizers continued to pretend not to hear the protests coming from some of the riders, and didn't give a damn about the problems of the

Some Dreams Come True

private racers. God knows we had plenty; driving all night long in the most unthinkable conditions in order to be on time for the race, having to buy spare parts with so little money (which meant using parts longer than we should), sometimes with the most disastrous and dangerous results, doing our own repairs.

For all these reasons, I decided to fight against what I considered a flagrant injustice, which many others accepted without saying a word. My fight against this injustice gave me, over the years, the reputation of only being interested in the money, which was just not true. There was absolutely no chance in those days that any sane person would get into motorcycle racing for the money as there was no quick way to the top, you had to put in long years of hard work and dedication to get there, living a very modest, to say the least, nomadic life. Conditions that no-one would put up with if they were not madly in love with this violent sport. Despite everything, I was determined and continued to stick up for my rights in the best way I could, knowing that one day I would be in a stronger position.

After Assen the next GP was in Spa Francorchamps in Belgium and, of course, I was hoping that Honda would invite me once again to race for its team. Tom was still convalescing, so I hoped that Honda would choose me to take his place. However, the practice days were getting closer and I heard nothing from Mr Kawashima or Honda. Of course, I made sure that everything I did in those few days before practice took me close to, or past, the Honda camp, just to give them every chance to call me over and invite me to ride. The waiting and hoping was the worst part; if only they'd tell me if they didn't want me I could get on with preparing my own bikes. As it was, all I could do was wait on tenterhooks.

At last, Mr Kawashima came to my caravan and asked, just one day before practice was due to begin, if I would like to ride for Honda. There was no 250 or 350 class at the Belgium GP that year, so I was to ride the 125 for Honda and my Norton in the 500 race. Spa Francorchamps was then held on a longer circuit than is now used, and was just a flat-out blind on a 125. All I could manage was a lowly 9th place on the 125, which gave my critics plenty of ammunition with which to renew their cry for Honda to get a smaller, lighter rider for the 125s and 250s, In all honesty, they were right, but I was so determined that I rode the 125 like a man possessed in order to keep my ride and - luckily for me - Honda was always very pleased with me. The British motorcycle press was pushing for a lightweight English rider to be chosen, so I prayed that no-one at Honda subscribed to these magazines!

After Spa we travelled to Stuttgart for the German GP, which didn't have a 125 class. Bob Brown and I were asked to ride the 250s for Honda, as Tom Phillis was still out of action, although we knew he would be ready for the Ulster GP in Belfast, which was next. Tom, Bob and I sat in Tom's caravan at Solitude and discussed this; we knew there were two bikes but three of us, so someone had to go. We were pretty certain that, as Tom was first to

103

Jim Redman

be invited to ride by Honda, he would be the first choice to stay, so either Bob or I would be dropped. Even though Bob and I were very good friends, each of us, of course, secretly hoped that the other would be the one to go. I, for one, was determined to do as well as possible in Germany to try and hold onto my place. As it happened, fate once again stepped in and made the decision, and in the most radical and horrible manner.

Bob and I were very good friends who greatly respected each other, and his laid-back, pleasant manner meant he was liked by everybody. During the first day of practice, I came round a bend to see one of our Hondas smashed against the Armco barrier, with the rider also crunched into the barrier. At this time in racing, Armco barrier was used everywhere as the organizers were absolutely terrified of spectators getting injured or killed, as had happend at Le Mans. The Armco stopped the cars from ploughing into the crowds but, unfortunately, bounced them back into the path of oncoming cars, creating a domino effect. In the case of motorcycle riders, it meant that quite a few were killed. Of course, no-one cared too much about this as riders were expendable, as one kind race organizer once told me.

I stopped and rushed over to see who it was, expecting it to be one of the Japanese riders in our team as Bob was usually very safe and steady. However, it was Bob, and he was conscious and talking so I asked him if he was okay. He said not too bad but the back of his head was very sore. He still had his helmet on but had loosened the strap, and I could see that the big wads of cotton wool that Bob always put in his ears to dull the noise were red with blood and wondered if I should pull them out or not. Not wanting to do anything to make him worse - and as the ambulance was just arriving - I told Bob I would go back to the pits and tell his wife, Bernadette, that I had spoken to him and send her to the hospital. I pulled into our pits, where everyone was worried as we were both missing, and told Bernadette that Bob had crashed but was not too bad, but that she should go to the hospital. Imagine my shock when, after finishing my practice session, I found out that Bob had died. I just couldn't believe it but the doctors told me that the back of his head, at the base of the helmet, had been smashed in. I told the doctor of my dilemma about the cotton wool, but he reassured me that nothing I could have done would have saved Bob.

This sort of tragedy was quite commonplace and so it did not even cross our minds not to compete in the rest of the meeting, although, of course, we were a very sober team. A few deaths every year were expected, and yet, we still loved this sport. When people said to us that we must be mad to race bikes for a living, we simply replied "You don't have to be mad, it's not compulsory, but it does help." and laughed it off that way, as part of our lives.

Following Bob's accident, I had a talk with Mike Hailwood and we both agreed that, one day, we too, could be killed in the same manner although, deep down, I always felt it wouldn't happen to me, even though I used to joke that I always had a strong desire to retire whilst still alive. I did wonder, though, whether the riders who had lost their lives had felt the same as I did?

Bob's death meant that Honda now didn't have to make a choice, and this thought left me feeling like ice. When I had finished my races - with terrible results - in an effort to get away from the pain, Marlene and I packed our van and caravan and left as soon as possible.

The next race was the Ulster GP in Northern Ireland, where I finished in third place in the 250 race behind Ubbiali on the MV, and Tom, who was now completely recovered. Then on to the last GP of the year at Monza, the Italian GP. Before this, I still had to compete in two other races - the Czechoslovakian GP in Brno and the GP of Finland. Whilst in Brno, I suggested the idea of leaving with another rider, Peter Pawson, to go to Finland and from there flying back to Monza. However, there were a couple of problems associated with this, and they were big ones. Marlene would be left alone with our son Jimmy to drive several hundred miles through Czechoslovakia, Austria and Italy; Czechoslovakia is always more difficult, as it's impossible to understand one word of the language, and Marlene had to be there at Monza to pick me up when I flew in. At the same time, it was important for me to compete in these two meetings for two reasons: the money and to honour the commitment to be there I had made before the ride for Honda came along. Marlene convinced me that I had to go and she would be waiting for me in Monza a week later; she said I shouldn't worry, everything would go well.

However, there was another serious complication. Our son, Jimmy, only two years old, did not have his own passport but was instead added to mine and not Marlene's. I carefully 'added' Jimmy to Marlene's passport myself, hoping that nothing amiss would be noticed at the border. Marlene left first, because the Austrian border is very close to Brno where we were, and Peter and I waited behind for a while in case she 'phoned to say a problem had arisen. Once we were sure she was safely in Austria with Jimmy, we headed north to cross the border into Germany and on to Finland.

We arrived at the Czech border and presented our passports. After a short time the immigration and customs let us through. We had just started to drive under the boom, however, when they called us back. Peter was quick-thinking enough to stop on the other side of the boom and walk back to see what they wanted. Pete came back out of the office and strolled casually over to me, then suddenly jumped into the van and drove away, flat out, across to the West German barrier, which the guards immediately lifted when they heard the Czechs shouting for us to stop. Peter told me the Czechs had wanted to see that Jimmy was with us as he was on my passport, and Peter realised we would be there forever if we tried to explain. However, he told them he would fetch Jimmy but decided, as he walked to the van, that we should just go. We told the whole story to the West Germans, who thought it a huge joke and were much more co-operative, allowing us into their country even before we had shown them our passports.

Jim Redman

For her part, Marlene hadn't run into any difficulty when passing the different borders and, when I arrived back from Finland by plane, she was waiting for me at the airport. Having made the journey by air I was not tired, but fresh and ready, unlike Peter when he arrived much later in his van with my bikes. He was glad of the money I gave him; on such a long trip it was a help to have someone share the expenses as private riders had to make every penny count. Whenever we could help each other out by sharing expenses, we did.

Honda showed its confidence in me and let me ride the 250 again, but I made a very bad start in the race and had to work my way through the field, until I got up to the leading group of Ernst Degner, Takahashi and Ubbiali. On the last lap, I managed to pass Degner and Takahashi and finished in 2nd place, behind Ubbiali, much to the general amazement of everyone. With the second place points I had just notched up, I now found myself in fourth place in the 250 World Championships after having participated in just four races. Mr Kawashima and the rest of the team could not believe it, and were so excited and happy about this unexpected result that they couldn't stop congratulating me on the way in which I had handled the race. Earlier in the day I had made fourth place in the 125 race which, for me at Monza, was very good as there weren't many corners where I could make up in riding what I lost in speed due to my size and weight.

Mr Kawashima told me after Monza that Honda Tokyo wanted to give me a bonus for all my hard work. I asked that, instead of giving me money, I be allowed to borrow a 250 to take back to Southern Africa for the racing there as, for me, that would be a much nicer bonus. At first, they were surprised by such a request and seemed a little suspicious, but I found a way to dispel their doubts by promising Mr Kawashima that I wouldn't strip the motor or try to repair it if it broke down or needed spare parts, but would instead send it immediately to Japan. Somewhat reassured, Mr Kawashima agreed, making me swear to keep the bike under my control at all times and to let no-one have the opportunity to take it apart, or look inside the motor. Of course I kept my word, because I wanted, most of all, to stay with the team and race full time with it.

One niggling problem that just would not go away was that many people kept saying that Tom - and especially me - were far too big and heavy for the 125 and 250. Strangely enough, they did not say much about how well I was doing, given my size and weight, but talked instead about how much better Honda would do with lighter riders. As a result of this, in later years I kept on riding the 125 class much longer than I needed to, as it gave me lots of satisfaction to prove these critics wrong, as my results prove: 4th in the 125 World Championship in 1961, 2nd in 1962, 3rd in 1963 and 2nd again in 1964. In 1962/3/4, I finished one place behind my good friend and team mate, Luigi Taveri, who I was backing up and not trying to beat anyway.

Luckily, the Honda people were concerned only about my results and

Some Dreams Come True

joked about my size, saying that they did not know whether to cut off my legs at the knees, or chop off my private parts. At weigh-in time it wasn't unusual to hear Mr Kawashima tell me, in a resigned tone, to go on a diet or cut off my legs! It's true that, because of extra weight, I was often overtaken when accelerating as I came out of the curves. To catch up meant braking later making up time in the bends, but I was consistently able to do this.

After a few end of season races in England, we left for South Africa with my Honda 250 4, which caused a sensation in South Africa because of its noise and speed, and also because I won all the races I took part in. I sent Honda all the press cuttings about my wins and waited anxiously for news about the following year. Finally, at the end of February came a telegram, inviting me to Japan, with my family, to discuss a contract for 1961.

I contacted Tom and found out he had had the same invitation, so we met up again in Japan. After testing the new bikes and finding them fantastic, we were taken to Mr Kawashima's office to finalise our contracts. You can imagine our despair when we saw letters from all the famous riders asking to ride the Hondas. However, when I mentioned this to Mr Kawashima, he replied that Jim San and Tom San had ridden the Hondas when the bikes were slow, and would now ride them when they were fast. It made us feel good to discover that Honda was so loyal.

Mr Kawashima asked us what retainer we would require and Tom quickly asked if we could think about this overnight, giving us time for a discussion that evening. We decided the very bottom line was that we would ride the bikes for nothing, as we would then not have the expense of buying our own bikes and maintaining them, plus we would receive better starting money on factory bikes. We finally settled on a figure midway between what MV was paying Gary Hocking and John Surtees, which was the only yardstick we had. Mr Kawashima accepted this without any quibble at all.

As we were strolling along a passage in the factory, Mr Kawashima stopped to talk to another Japanese man in working clothes. Turning to us, he said he wanted us to meet Mr Soichiro Honda. We were amazed that the great man responsible for this huge company was such a nice, down-to-earth man, who stood chatting to us in the passage as if we were old friends (Mr Kawashima had to interpret for us, of course). After this, on my frequent trips to Japan I would often meet or see Mr Honda and he was nearly always in working clothes, part of a team of engineers. He seemed to mix with his employees in the most natural way.

7
A Factory Rider

Tom and I knew what a great opportunity we had been given and, upon our return to Europe, were the envy of all the more established riders. This was especially so as rumours were circulating that Honda had improved its bikes so much. We were so grateful - and I still am to this day - to Mr Kawashima for placing his full confidence in us, in preference to riders like Mike Hailwood and Bob McIntyre, for example, who were both keen to ride for Honda.

Stan Hailwood, Mike's dad, was particularly frustrated by this. He owned Kings of Oxford and had around fifty motorcycle shops all over England. He was a multi-millionaire whom we nicknamed "Stan the Wallet." We said Stan's policy was if you can't beat it, buy it. It was so unusual that Mike, who was born with a silver spoon in his mouth, went on to become the greatest motorcycle rider the world has ever known, when normally the son of a rich father who is given everything is useless. Stan did make sure Mike had everything he needed to become successful, and they arrived at each circuit with a big van full of bikes and Stan in his Bentley. They also had their own mechanics and a famous full-time tuner called Bill Lacey, who was brilliant in his day.

Mike had everything he needed to win with no excuses and, contrary to what one may have expected, this poor little rich boy won practically everything he tried for. No wonder Stan was frustrated that Honda chose Tom and me, who had a cheap, second-hand van, only two machines and did our own mechanics, whilst our wives helped with the cleaning, were our pit crew and took their turns at the driving. Now I was a member of the Honda Official Works Team so could hope, at least, to rival Mike, who was a good friend of mine. I was lucky to have Mike as a friend, but unlucky that he was riding when I was as it was always very hard to beat the world's all-time greatest.

Now that Tom and I were in the Honda Team, we asked Honda to send

A Factory Rider

us each a 125 and 250 machine which we could use to compete in the non-Championship International races. The bikes were shipped to Amsterdam, so we headed off there with Tom's van and my station wagon and caravan. Marlene was with me, and Jimmy of course, but Tom was on his own. The ship was delayed, so there we were kicking our heels at the docks waiting for it to arrive - and starting to panic because we were entered for Imola and Cesenatico in Italy and had to get to Imola for practice. We started to worry that my station wagon, towing the caravan, would slow us down, so sent Marlene and Jimmy off on their own in it with instructions to drive across Holland, turn right onto the *autobahn* in Germany, and just keep going as long as she could, and we would catch her up. If she got tired, we told her to pull off into a *Parkplatz* and stop right at the exit end so that we would be able see her as we caught up.

Marlene went off early in the morning while Tom and I waited at the docks, finally getting the bikes late in the afternoon. We loaded all four bikes into Tom's van and set off. We travelled some distance and were beginning to think that we had missed her as she had gone a lot further than we thought possible, but finally saw the outfit in full view at the end of a parking area. We woke Marlene and Jimmy and bundled them half-asleep into the back seat of the station wagon, and off we went again, now with three of us to take turns driving the two vehicles through the night.

It soon became very obvious that, towing the caravan, we were never going to get to Imola in time, so we pulled into the next service station, unhitched the caravan and threw enough clothes and gear into the station wagon for two weeks. I went to tell the owners what we were doing. As I was walking over I thought to myself, how am I going to explain, in my broken German, what it was we wanted to do? I turned on my heel, got behind the wheel and said, let's go. As we pulled off, Marlene asked if the owners had said it was all right. When I told her what I had done she burst out laughing and said that they would get a shock. We had parked the caravan close to the office, so felt sure it would be safe; anyway, if we wanted to race at Imola there was nothing else we could do. We soon caught up with Tom, who had pressed on in the van knowing that, without the caravan, I would be faster than him, and we drove all night, arriving at Imola in the morning in time for practice.

Our troubles were not over, however, as Honda had sent us four of last year's machines, which had not been serviced and checked since the previous year, and we had all kinds of problems sorting them out and getting them running properly. While we were struggling to get the bikes ready, we were befriended by two Italian guys who helped us tremendously by pushing the bikes with us to get them started, and doing all sorts of running around jobs which saved us a lot of time. They helped us all weekend and one of them, Elvio Marconi, said that, at the next race at Cesenatico the following weekend, we should stay with him as he had a big house in the nearby town of Bellaria.

Jim Redman

Well, we arrived in Cesenatico after Imola but did not fancy staying in the home of someone that we did not know very well, so found a small *pensione* in Cesenatico and made ourselves comfortable there.

Having plenty of spare days, we drove through to Bellaria to try and find Elvio. We had no problem following his directions and found his "big house:" it was called "Hotel Marconi" and was the biggest hotel in Bellaria. Such are the little misunderstandings that occur with limited language! However, this turned out to be the start of a long and beautiful friendship, which lasted for years.

From Italy we headed to Barcelona in Spain for the first GP of the season at Montjuich Park, the scene of my epic battle with Venturi the previous year on the 500. This was our first GP of the season and also our first GP as full members of the Honda team, so you can imagine how proud and excited we were. Tom managed to win the 125 with me third, and then Tom was second in the 250, with me fourth. Not bad results, especially for Tom who did much better than I had done.

On to Salzburg in Austria. On the way we had to pick up the caravan which we had left at a service station. As we drove in, I was thinking "This is going to take quite a bit of explaining, but here goes." and I backed up to the caravan, hitched it to the station wagon and turned to go in and face the music. As I started to walk towards the office, I realized that no-one was taking any notice of me at all, so I took the easy way out, got back behind the wheel and drove off! I signalled to Tom to pull in at the next parking area and we killed ourselves laughing, thinking about the surprise the owners would get when they realised the caravan had gone just as mysteriously as it had arrived. We looked inside the caravan. One of the windows had been forced open and it was obvious that someone had made a thorough search, but nothing had been stolen and there was plenty that could have been. We decided that it had probably been the police who broke in, to check there were no dead bodies or drugs, or whatever.

1961 was the year of my first victories in GPs on the 250 - first at Spa and then at Monza, the two fastest circuits - that counted toward the World Championship. It was also the year that Tom and I fought our hardest battles against independent riders on Hondas, as some riders borrowed bikes from Honda England, especially Mike, with Stan's help. It was, above all, a phenomenal year for the company: Tom Phillis won the 125 World Championship on the factory 125, and Mike Hailwood won the 250 on his private Honda. Whether the bikes were factory or private made no difference, as they all had the same technical specifications and - remarkably - the same speed and all-round performance and endurance.

This was the great difference between Hondas and the MVs and MZs, for example, where the best engines were often given to the top riders, or the rider that was the flavour of the month, or even, according to some rumours, the rider that bribed the mechanics the most. I have no first-hand knowledge

A Factory Rider

of this as there was never a hint of that kind of thing in the Honda team, but I do know that in other, non-Japanese, teams there was often a huge disparity between the bikes, even with the same rider on board. Honda was the very first team in GP racing which produced a whole batch of bikes that all offered exactly the same performance. To think that in 1960 the other motocycle firms didn't take the Honda team seriously ...

By 1961 the Hondas had changed a lot, having undergone a complete redesign, and the results of this were already being felt as the all-important wins started to come. After Tom's 125 win at the Spanish GP, Takahashi won the 250 German GP at Hockenheim just in front of me, to give Japan its first Japanese GP winner. The writing was on the wall; from then on, Hondas dominated the 125 and 250 classes, so much so that after winning the 250 Spanish GP, Gary Hocking persuaded Count Agusta to let him drop out of competing in the 250 class and take over the 350 and 500 classes from the now-retired John Surtees. (John had felt a chill breeze when Gary Hocking joined the MV team. He knew that Gary was very talented and very, very determined, and would never be happy playing second fiddle to Surtees the way that John Hartle had for the past three years. John retired while he was still on top.) Gary knew that the MVs were getting old and he would have no chance in the 250 class against the Hondas, unless MV made the effort to build a completely new 250, which would take time. Even then, there was no guarantee it would be good enough to beat the Hondas. He also wanted the added prestige and personal satisfaction of winning the bigger classes, as the 500 event has always been the most prestigious. He felt he could win the bigger classes easily as he would have only the private riders on their Norton and Matchless machines to beat.

It was general knowledge, too, that starting with the French GP in Clermont Ferrand, Hailwood would be contesting the 125 and 250 Championships on his private Hondas. In fact, after finishing second behind Tom in Clermont, Mike went on to win both the 125 and 250 races at the TT on the Isle of Man, and finished the season by winning the 250 World Championship. Two short years after its first tentative appearance at the TT, Honda was crowned World Champion in two categories.

For me, it had been a mixed year. I had managed to finish in the top four positions in every GP of the season in both classes, except for the 125 German GP where I crashed in spectacular fashion (but still managed to get back on and finish seventh) and the 250 French GP, where I crashed but finished sixth. I had ridden in a total of 22 GPs and scored points for finishing in the top 6 in 21 out of the 22. I had amassed enough points to finish fourth in the 125 Championship and third in the 250, but was disapointed as my goal had been, and still was, to win a World Championship.

Next year. Maybe ...

I owed Bob McIntyre a favour after the 250 race at Monza that year, as I needed to win at Monza and in Sweden in order to still have a chance at

111

Jim Redman

the World Championship. Bob was not yet part of the Honda team, but was riding a Honda borrowed through the Irish sponsor, Reg Armstrong, and racing against me. There was also John Hartle on another Honda, borrowed from Bill Smith, and, of course, Mike Hailwood on the machine his father had organized for him. I went to Honda to complain, not understanding why the company let so many independent racers ride its bikes. I told them frankly that I could win the title for Honda, but that my fiercest rivals were on the same bikes as me. I was told that this was Honda's marketing policy and that, if I was to win the World Championship, I would have to beat the other Honda-mounted riders. It was as simple as that.

This was when Bob came to see me and said "What is your position in the World Championship?" I told him I had to beat Mike, both here and in Sweden, to win the title. To my great amazement Bob said "I'm going to try and help you to beat them. If you're in front of Mike I won't try to pass you, but will stay behind and try to give you a hand." (Bob had the fastest bike, mine was second fastest and the others were more or less equal.) I couldn't believe my ears and had no idea why Bob wanted to do this.

From the start of the race Bob and I were in the lead, with him in front of me, but I thought he was going too slowly and passed him in one of the bends. Mike, Tom and John Hartle were all there, a few metres behind us, but it seemed that Bob and I could just keep them at bay. I could see Bob was trying to help me but then he crashed badly at exactly the same spot that John Hartle had crashed on the previous lap. Despite this, I managed to keep the lead and win the 250cc race. Afterwards, I went to see Bob at the hospital. The first thing he asked was "So, how did it go?" I replied that I had beaten Mike by just the length of the bike. His face broke into a huge smile and he said "After watching the way you rode in this race, you've proved to me that you're a better rider than I ever thought you were!" Bob was not one to hand out compliments too freely so, coming from him, it meant a lot.

At the Swedish GP in Kristianstad, I learned of a touching and exciting sequence of events which, apparently, had been planned for months. Ernst Degner, the most successful of the MZ team riders (who all lived in the Eastern bloc), told me that a friend of his had gone to East Germany to smuggle Ernst's wife and children out. Ernst said he was going frantic, waiting for the 'phone call to say they were safely out so that he, too, could make his escape. (At that time, the whole team was given visas to leave East Germany to compete in races all over the world, but could not take their wives and children with them in case they did not go back.) I was horrified that Ernst had taken me into his confidence, only because, as I told him, he was mad to talk to anyone, even me. I might have been the sort to go and tell his team, and perhaps get some financial reward for doing so. Ernst said he was feeling the pressure so much that, despite all his efforts, he was unable to keep it to himself any longer. A good friend of his - and what a good friend this man must have been to drive behind the Iron Curtain and bring Ernst's family out - had had

A Factory Rider

his car modified to accommodate a secret place between the back seat and the boot, so that Ernst's wife, Gerda, and his two children, baby Boris and four year old Olaf, could be smuggled out. This was the only way they could get out of East Germany and escape forever its Communist grip. Ernst was beside himself with anxiety and needed to share the burden by letting some of us in on his secret. We did not know what we could do to help him, but knew how risky it was just talking about it.

Eventually, Ernst received the news that his wife and family were safely out of East Germany. Mad with happiness, he ran up to his room to pack his bags and left immediately to join them somewhere in Germany. Of course, he had to be careful as all Eastern bloc sports teams contained individuals whose job it was to stop defectors, so very few people knew why he had left so suddenly and everybody was looking for him. I pretended not to know anything and feigned surprise. A few weeks later we found out the whole story. Ernst's friend had arranged that he would collect Gerda from her house in East Germany. Once the friend arrived, the children were injected with something that would make them sleep through the whole journey, and settled into the secret compartment, where Gerda joined them. A tube from the secret compartment ensured the fugitives could breathe. Squashed in the small space, scared to death, Gerda sat holding her children.

They drove to the East German checkpoint where to Gerda the time spent at a standstill, waiting to pass through customs, must have seemed like an eternity. They had only the clothing they were wearing, no money, and had left everything they owned behind. But they were free! Ernst found his family safe in West Germany, where they settled immediately, but not before one last scare when the smallest child would not wake up as the injection given to make him sleep had been too big. Thankfully, by the time that Ernst arrived, the child was fine.

By not competing in the Swedish GP, Ernst, at that time first in the classifications, lost the title to Tom Phillis. Ernst was later hired to ride factory Suzukis, and the money he was paid and won allowed him to get back on his feet. Of course, there was no question of him ever returning home to East Germany where he had been a national hero, even to race. In later years, when Ernst participated in the Finnish GP, he was worried that as Finland was so close to Russia, the Russians might capture him and take him back to East Germany to face the music. Throughout the entire race he was accompanied by two friends, who acted as bodyguards. Wherever he went they followed, and never let him out of their sight. One of them was even armed in case events turned nasty.

I found this whole episode both exciting and very sad. There should never be this type of restriction for sporting events and sportsmen, but it seems that we live in a world where the most elementary values are sometimes violated.

Fortunately for us, we were free to enjoy ourselves where and whenever it pleased us, and I can assure you that it did not take much to get us going. One of the best parts of the whole European circuit was the after-race parties, some of which were fantastic, although, as usual, the best parties always happened spontaneously. There was one memorable time at Hockenheim, though I forget which year, when the prize-giving was held in an old, castle-like building and, as each rider was called to collect his prizes, he was accompanied by a fanfare of trumpets played by chaps stationed in alcoves in the walls.

This made the event seem so exciting, especially after some of the more mundane ones, that everyone got into the real party spirit, helped along by the Martini company giving a magnum of the stuff to each winner. The party went crazy and at one stage Gary Hocking - who did not usually drink at all - was lying on the floor close to our table so that we could tilt his magnum from the table and pour it straight, more or less, into his mouth. It is always hard to explain a good party, as when the booze is flowing the smallest, silliest thing can seem so funny. If you were asked the next day why you did things you would probably say "It seemed like a good idea at the time, Your Honour." It was one of the best parties I had ever been to and the crowd that had come to the prize-giving joined in and stayed to transform a simple little party into a real earthquake. With the fanfare and all the pomp, it felt as if we were back in the Middle Ages at King Arthur's court. The magnums of Martini emptied in the shortest space of time ...

The podium was magnificent, richly decorated with lots of superb green plants. When Ernst Degner had to collect his prize he went to get MZ boss, Walter Kaaden, so that he, too, could celebrate his victory on the 125. Going up to Walter, Ernst said "Walter, you deserve a special prize for your efforts ..." and, without warning, grabbed a plant from its pot and put it in Walter's lap. Then things got hectic as Hailwood, Degner, Frank Perris and Frantisek Stastny began to throw plants at each other to the great displeasure of the authorities and the great pleasure of the crowd. In just a few seconds the whole floor was covered with plants, earth and Martini.

The band continued playing while the hostesses brought everyone more to drink. This went on till midnight when the band wanted to go, but we convinced them to stay until one o'clock in the morning. At one o'clock, our cries and protests made them decide to stay with us until two. Finally, they left and then only because someone very drunk had thrust a flower into one of the trombones. Everyone - waitresses, riders mechanics and musicians - agreed it had been a magnificent party.

Another good party was at Assen in Holland, where, again, we had a really good time. It was a little bit wild, but no-one seemed disturbed by this. All around the reception hall everyone had taken off their shoes and thrown them over the balcony, in order to dance in socks only. Tom Phillis had come to Europe with a very good Australian friend as his mechanic. Bob Lewis was his name, but he was nicknamed "Blue." Towards the end of the

A Factory Rider

evening, as people started leaving, Blue, completely drunk, unhooked a fire hydrant and though not really intending to joked that he was going to wash us all down a bit. However, Rex Avery, the EMC rider, found a way to open the tap and nobody was more surprised than Blue when the water started gushing out of the hose. Lots of people had the most memorable shower. One of the waiters tried to stop Blue, but was arrested on the spot by the incredible force of the water jet against his chest. It took quite a few people to bring Blue down and the waiters were obviously appalled, not understanding any of the explanations offered by Blue in his Australian drawl.

Tom Phillis and I left, having escaped a soaking, and returned home. Luckily for Blue, he found someone who took him back to his hotel on a bike. When he arrived, making enough noise to wake the dead, the manager tried to calm him down, panicking and saying "Shush, you will wake Mr Hailwood," meaning Mike's father, Stan. Blue answered by shouting out "Hey, Stan the wallet - are you awake?" It's not known whether Stan Hailwood did wake up that night to pay Blue back ...

The journalists covering the races were mostly British, and they jingoistically praised Mike Hailwood's and Bob McIntyre's every victory over the official Honda riders like myself and Tom Phillis, never missing an opportunity to emphasise the fact that both Hailwood and McIntyre were racing private Hondas. They did not know - or turned a blind eye - to the fact that all of the Honda motors were the same technically, and that nothing distinguished a private Honda from an 'official' Honda. For them, it was a excuse to say that the English riders were, in every way, superior to their Australian and Rhodesian counterparts. This prejudice was very often difficult to live with, but more important for us was to maintain Honda's confidence in us. Tom and me sometimes wondered if the company listened to all this gossip, and if it would influence its decision to re-engage us for the 1962 season? In this sport, like in any other, it was necessary to fight with everything one had to keep a position. It was a constant battle, with terrific tension - something we could have done without. Tom and I had to compete against all the other riders on the circuit, and also contend with a press that was intolerant toward colonial riders. At the same time, we had to counteract Stan Hailwood's ambitions for his son. Stan was untiring in his efforts to get the best possible for Mike, trying as hard as possible to get him into the Honda team. With Mike's talent, there was good reason for us to be worried ...

Even though well established with Honda, I continued living in my caravan and not hotel rooms like most of the factory riders. Marlene and I found it easier, especially with Jimmy still a baby, as it was more practical for Marlene to look after him in this way. Later on, a lot of factory riders copied us by buying their own caravans, most notably Mike Hailwood. He and I used to joke about it, saying that hotels were for those factory riders who couldn't afford to buy their own caravans. This started out as a joke but, little-by-little, we began to see more and more caravans appear with, of course, the factory riders in a group of their own. This little enclave soon became known as "Nob Hill," especially by some of the less lucky privateers who still had to sleep in their vans. This feeling of envy, or jealousy, was quite human and natural; I had felt exactly the same in the past watching John Surtees and John Hartle having life so good with MV Agusta, while I was battling along in my van. Most of the independent riders spent their whole careers without ever enjoying the limelight, only to find themselves at the end financially poorer than they were at the start.

Yet, it was still a good life. Take Jack Ahearn, for example, he used to say "This sure beats working for a living." Jack was a character that Marlene and I loved having around. He got into the habit of always parking near our caravan because he knew that Marlene would invite him to eat with us because we greatly enjoyed his company. He was always good for a laugh as he had a great sense of humour.

Even though we factory riders maintained reasonably good relations amongst ourselves, the only thing that mattered was winning. So, there were certain questions that we did not ask, and we took great care not to reveal any of our secrets. In general, the atmosphere remained friendly between us; more so, it seems, than in today's world. The rivalry between us was always tempered by respect and friendship. I prayed for everything to stay just as it was as life was good. The Honda team was not only one of the most successful on the circuits, but also one of the happiest as all of us got on well and worked perfectly together, not prone to the big arguments or tensions that seemed rife in some of the other teams.

During 1961, a rumour began that Honda was going to increase the size of some 250cc bikes to 285cc, in order for us to compete in the 350 category. Tom and I had submitted this proposal in order to race in another class yet, in one way, it was not a good thing for us because it gave Mike Hailwood and other well-known riders a chance to get into the Honda team. However, it also opened up more opportunities for us and everyone else, and riding 350s the press could no longer complain that we were too big for our machines. During the year I had won 20 international races in Europe and Southern Africa which, added to my GP results, meant I had had quite a good year. But no World Championship yet, so this was my all-consuming goal.

8
Tears of Blood

By 1962 our team had grown with the addition of Bob McIntyre as a fully-fledged team member, and Honda had added a bigger bike in order for us to compete in the 350 class as well. Honda had also produced a new bike for the 50cc class and, in consultation with Honda, we decided our strategy for the year would be that Tom Phillis was to win the world title in the 50cc category, Kunimitsu Takahashi would win the 125cc, with help from me and Luigi Taveri, I would win the 250cc with Bob McIntyre backing me up, and Bob would win the 350cc with me backing him up. Of course, everything could change depending on our results as the season went on. Nevertheless, our plan was to go out and win four World Championships that year - two of which we had never competed in before - and we thought we had a good chance of doing it.

Honda also badly wanted a Japanese rider to win a World Championship for the first time and on a Honda. From the two or three Japanese riders who had always competed with us, Kunimitsu Takahashi was chosen as the most talented and most capable of achieving it. Bear in mind that there was a sharp learning curve for all the Japanese riders, as they had no history of racing and were having to learn circuits which the rest of us knew well from previous years. Honda asked all of us if we could help Tak San win the 125 Championship and, of course, we were only too happy to do so. We all liked Tak San and Honda's wish was our command, although it must be said Honda always *asked* us to help rather than gave orders, which generated a good team spirit.

Not everyone liked our plans and, because of a small incident which occurred at the first GP at Montjuich Park in Barcelona, our team was violently criticized by the press. For a large part of the race, Luigi and I were up front, riding hard to beat the riders of another team - I think it was MZ - and Tak San was a bit further back. Near to the end of the race the opposition dropped out

Jim Redman

and Luigi and I were left with a big lead over Takahashi, so we slowed right down and let him pass us to win. Luigi and I tried to dead heat for second but they gave it to me. Honda was delighted and thanked us profusely and we were happy for Tak San, who was in seventh heaven. Our team strategy was working! However, the press howled and headlines trumpeted "Please Mr Honda, let the winners win."

It was nice, therefore, that just as these headlines appeared, the following GP at Clermont-Ferrand worked out totally differently. It was raining for the start of the 125 race and Tak San passed us all fair and square and pulled away, riding brilliantly that day in the wet and winning the race by more than half a minute. There was nothing any of us could have done to stop him, even if we had wanted to. It was satisfying that Takahashi got his revenge on the press, and so quickly too. Unfortunately for him, in the TT on the Isle of Man, Takahashi fell at Union Mills, just a few miles out on the first lap, and hurt himself so badly that he had to stop racing for the rest of the season and was in fact lucky to survive.

This meant that Luigi, who won the TT fair and square, was chosen as our main contender to win the 125 World Championship, a decision which we were all happy about as Luigi was a very well-liked member of our team. The TT, by the way, was always treated differently to the other rounds in the World Championship. There were no team orders, it was every man for himself, and may the best man win. The reason for this policy was the prestige associated with winning the TT, as it was such a difficult race and so dangerous. So Honda's hopes were pinned on Luigi Taveri winning the title, starting with the GP at Assen in Holland. Luigi more than justified Honda's faith in him as, not only did he win that race, but the title that year as well.

At the TT, I was supposed to back up Bob McIntyre on the 350, but Tom Phillis asked me to let him have my machine since there were only two 350s available, and he knew that I didn't like riding in the TT as much as he did. This was not my class and, as I was intent on winning the 250 title and only being back-up for Bob in the 350, the points did not matter and I was happy to let Tom take over my ride, which he dearly wanted to do.

I never, ever forgot the importance of human relationships and the strength of friendship. On the circuit it was every man for himself, but afterwards we liked to relax together with a beer on the rare times that our tight schedule allowed. Tom and I became particularly good friends, which I guess helped him get me a place in the Honda team; he was a very likeable guy.

One day a rider would be there, the next day perhaps not. The death of a healthy, young man is always a terrible waste, but when it touches someone close to you, this injustice becomes almost unbearable. For this reason, 1962 was one of the best years of my whole life because I won the 250 and 350 titles, and one of the worst in other ways. Three of my best friends died that year.

First, it was Tom Phillis, one of the best racers in the world. He was

Tears of Blood

also a best friend and, as far as the team went, one of the easiest guys to get along with and the best team mate a rider could have. I cannot ever remember hearing a bad thing said about him. Even with his typical Australian laid-back attitude, his particular sense of humour and his very slow way of moving through life, everybody liked, admired and respected him. As soon as he mounted his bike, though, he became a different person: first and foremost a great champion who was very hard to beat.

He had an incredible desire to win, but one trait that worried me; he would ride beyond his natural ability if someone passed him. I tried to tell him to be more careful, but his attitude was the faster the opposition, the better he liked it. Tom and I were very close and often shared a hotel room when without our wives. We spent a lot of time together, competing against each other in many races but during that year fate decided that the sport which had brought us together, would tear us violently apart. When Tom was killed in the Isle of Man TT, the shock was so terrible that I thought seriously about quitting racing. I was heartbroken and completely lost. At Tom's death I cried: me, nicknamed "The Iron Man;" me, whom many said was incapable of emotion; me, the so-called calculator, interested only in the money and the honours.

In the racing business at that time, the fact is that sudden death was a part of the profession: we all knew this and tried to prepare for it. Each time that one of us fell, the others tried not to show their feelings and, above all, not to talk too much about it. We all knew that the sword was hanging just above our own heads.

Strangely enough, on this ominous day, by rights, Tom should not have been riding. Bob McIntyre and I had been chosen to ride the new 285cc bikes, but Tom begged me to let him ride mine. We were out to beat the Italian MVs ridden by Mike Hailwood and Gary Hocking (who had won this race four years running). Tom, as usual, was ready to take up the challenge and, even though we both had to compete in the 125 and 250 races, he so wanted to have a shot at beating the MVs. I agreed as I knew that Tom loved the TT while I hated it and he knew the circuit as well, or better, than any of us, so he took my position on the starting grid. I went to watch the start of the race with Tom's wife, Betty, and his young son Brad. Tom's daughter, Debbie, was in nursery school with my son, Jimmy. After the start we left Betty at the finishing line and Marlene and me went to watch the race from the bottom of Bray Hill.

Right from the start it was a tight race. Gary Hocking led, followed by Mike Hailwood and Tom. After the first lap, the three were still very close, one right behind the other, but I could see that Tom was riding too hard against two of the best riders the world has ever seen. It seemed impossible that he could keep up such a pace, but he managed to hold on to them by taking more risks. At the bottom of Bray Hill, the MVs passed through smoothly with Tom just behind, jumping and wriggling on the Honda.

Jim Redman

About a third of the way round on the second lap (the race was 6 laps of 37-plus miles), we stopped hearing Tom's name being mentioned over the loud speakers by the commentators. This was a very bad sign, and I knew it. Usually if a rider drops out for any reason, to reassure the crowd the commentator would say something like "The rider has just retired from the race because of a technical problem" or "The rider has had an incident, but he's all right." But for Tom there was nothing ... My heart started to beat very quickly because, somehow, I just knew he had crashed and was dead. I waited, praying for a word about Tom, yet knowing, deep down, that it was hopeless.

I said to Marlene, without mentioning my fears, "Now that Tom is out, let's go and get Debbie and Jimmy from the nursery school and go back to the pits." We collected the children and as I looked at young Debbie, I was thinking that she would not now really get to know her father. This certainty I had that Tom was dead was the strangest thing, and the first time anything like this had happened to me: I knew, but didn't know how I did.

We drove into the paddock. One of the Avon tyre boys walked over to me as I was stopping the car and before he could speak I said "He's dead, right?" and he nodded. I went right away to see our team manager, Reg Armstrong, who told me that, trying to keep up with Hocking and Hailwood, Tom had smashed into the wall at Laurel Bank, one of the trickiest and most dangerous parts of the circuit. He was just 28 years old.

The news crushed me. Betty, Tom's wife, never got over his death, but she knew Tom would never have stopped racing because it was his life and, like him, she accepted the joys and the risks. Tom was not what you'd call a dare-devil, but he loved pushing his bike to the limit. How many times had I seen him take the curves so wide and banked right over at an incredible angle, that I thought he would never be able to lift himself up again, but each time he did.

In 1961 Tom had competed in phenomenal races with Ernst Degner's bike in the classical 125 races. Ernst's MZ was a lot faster than the Honda and Tom seemed to be glued to it. At the time I remember suggesting he should slow down, or at least be more careful. His only reply was "The faster my rivals go, the more I enjoy the race. I'd much rather quit racing than slow down ..." That's how he was; an exceptional human being with an incredible desire to win.

After Tom's death, Honda ensured that Betty didn't suffer financially, even the mechanics had a collection to help her. Afterward, people from around the world donated to a foundation set up to financially help families bereaved in this way. I was shattered and, for a while, could not stand the bike racing world with its continual tension and absurd competition. I was cynical and hard towards the others, talking to practically no-one and becoming withdrawn and morose.

This was when Bob McIntyre took me under his wing and did his best

Tears of Blood

to perk me up. This strong, serious Scotsman was straightforward in his discussions and didn't like to waste his time with subtleties. He was a man's man, tough and uncompromising. Bob had joined the Honda team in 1962 and before this, although I didn't know him very well, I knew of his incredible exploits. "The Flying Scotsman," as Bob was affectionately called, had been one of the best TT riders ever, and was known as the finest rider never to have won a World Championship. We now came to know and appreciate each other better, and I discovered that hiding behind this impassive mask was a very considerate, warm and humorous individual who was however not a man to mess with. Tom's death drew us together and reinforced our friendship. When I wanted to abandon everything, he kept telling me that, whatever I thought or did, nothing would bring Tom back. So for Tom's sake, Bob told me to pull myself together and continue with my career and, little-by-little, I found the heart to do as he said.

Gary Hocking decided on more decisive action as he said it was crazy to go so fast on such dangerous tracks with practically no safety measures. It upset him that even though we were all such good friends, so many of us were getting killed because of the way we were pushing each other, always trying for a little more. He said if we went on like this there would be none of us left, so he packed up the bikes after the TT and drove straight back to the MV factory. There in an interview with Count Dominico Agusta, Gary asked to be released from his contract. The Count respected Gary's point of view and released him so that Gary could retire and go home to Rhodesia. I know that it was a very difficult decision for Gary, especially as he had just now reached the summit. He told a journalist in an interview that he had had enough of seeing young riders killed on the race track, and the fact that some of them were close friends had made him realize to what degree he was risking his own life. The bike racing world was still a fabulous one where the danger was part of the game, but he could no longer handle it. Gary was both a great racer and a perfectionist. I remember when he started racing he would not race until he had tuned his Tiger 110 to perfection as he was determined to win his very first race. He would have done so, too, if it were not for a small technical problem.

Gary had so much confidence in himself that when he found out that I was second in my first meeting at Brands Hatch, he immediately sold everything he owned to jump on the first plane leaving for England. He figured that he could do a lot better than me, even though he didn't even have a bike. Gary - whose nickname was "Sox," though I don't know why, though it may have been because he hardly ever wore them - was a mixture of gentleness, reserve and tenacity and loved life more than anything. He was also very religious, reading a passage from the Bible every night before going to bed. He said that he put himself in the Lord's hands. When he started car racing, he was so gifted that the champions of the time predicted he would have a outstanding career.

Jim Redman

Unfortunately for Gary, he never had time to do all the great and wonderful things predicted for him. He was killed on the Westmead Circuit near Durban, at the wheel of a Lotus Climax V8 that Stirling Moss was supposed to have driven. Moss had to withdraw from the race following an accident he had at Goodwood. His death was another huge blow especially as he had been telling me, the very weekend he was killed, that car racing was so much easier than bike racing; in fact, he said, the real danger was that it was so easy you were lulled into a false sense of security.

In the meantime, Bob, me and the rest went on after the TT to Assen for the Dutch TT where I won my 250 race with Bob second, and then I won the 350 race when Bob had problems. This was the first time I had had a real wheel-to-wheel dice with Bob on my favourite circuit, and I was very proud to discover that I could quite comfortably beat the great Scotsman!

Bob won the 250 race the following week at Francorchamps in Belgium, with me limping home in second place due to a mechanical problem on the last lap. I was leading and as we went through the very fast Stavelot turn at the bottom of the track, my engine locked solid. I managed to grab the clutch and correct the slide; as I straightened up Bob came alongside and looked at me questioningly, so I waved him on to win (remember, this was the 250 race which it was my job to win). As Bob pulled away I thought to myself, I wonder if this bike will start again and get me home second? I stood up high on the footrests and thudded down on the seat, simultaneously dropping the clutch to start the engine. The back wheel skidded, but I was still going very fast and suddenly the engine started to turn over and slowly picked up on three cylinders. As I rode slowly on I could feel bits of engine hitting my left leg as the motor slowly broke apart, but it kept going. The mechanically-minded will know what a great piece of engineering this little motor was to take this abuse. As I limped up to *La Source* hairpin, that last corner before the finish, Luigi came screaming alongside. Our team spirit was such though, that he braked madly and followed me round the corner and over the line to let me get second place points. Of course, I thanked him profusely afterwards as, at that stage, every point counted towards my title.

I went next to an international race on the continent and Bob returned to England for a race at Oulton Park. His Norton skidded and ran off the racetrack, hitting a bridge or trees or some such, when he was riding at high speed, and Bob was flung like a rag doll from his bike. For nine days he clung to life, with his wife, Joyce - who nine days previously had given birth to their first child - there supporting him. Then his heart just gave up the fight and this lion of a man, who had seemed indestructible, died. I just could not believe this was happening; in the blink of an eye another of us was gone and this time it was Bob, who had seemed invincible. First Tom and now Bob - the man who had helped me get over Tom's death - was dead himself just two months later. As before, I felt totally crushed but the season was not yet over and so the show had to go on.

Tears of Blood

Strangely enough, despite the horrible pain of Bob's death, I had no thoughts of quitting: to do so now seemed like running away. With Bob's help I had come to terms with Tom's death, in a strange way Bob's words helped me to accept his own death.

Despite everything, I still had this strong belief that I would survive, that I would not die, that whatever happened I would survive. As always, my appetite for life got me through this very difficult period.

When I think now of the many friends who died violently at a young age - people like Tom, Bob, Gary, Bob Brown, Dave Chadwick, Harry Hinton, John Hartle, Keith Campbell, Des Woolf, Richard Fay, Bob Anderson, Ralph Rensen, Dickie Dale, Bill Ivy, Alistair King, Peter Ferbache, Florian Camathias, Fritz Scheidegger and many more - I consider myself incredibly lucky to still be alive today. At the same time, I often feel very nostalgic about that era. In 1962 we started the season with the five of us (Tom, Mike Hailwood, Bob, Gary and myself) racing for the 350 World Championship; at the end of the year, I had won - with Mike second - but the other three were dead. Young guys, all in their twenties, cut down in the prime of life. Compare that to today's racing where there are much better safety measures. You can imagine my feelings when, after surviving all his bike and car racing accidents - 16 in one year was his highest score - Mike Hailwood was killed in a stupid road accident.

I am very proud to be one of the last survivors of this period, even if I manage only to keep alive the memory of these great riders who were racing in what has turned out to be the greatest era in the sport's history.

9
The Ultimate Dream Realised

Now I was on my own on the bigger Hondas, given the job of trying to win two World Championships, the 250 and 350.

At the East German GP in Sachsenring I had a terrific battle with Mike Hailwood, who was riding an MZ. Mike and I had agreed at the start that we would ride together for the first part of the race, and then actually race for the last five laps. This arrangement was made on the start line when Mike flung a flippant "What do you want, last five to count?" at me; (we had had this arrangement before, but more so at international races than GPs). I replied "OK" and the contract was made. Some of the other riders were annoyed with this arrangement, but Mike said "If you don't like it, pass us ..." Of course, this strategy was only possible when we were certain we could walk off with first and second places.

At Sachsenring we rode together for most of the race, passing and re-passing each other to the great delight of the 250,000 fans. Most of them were East Germans so, I guess, wanted Mike to win on the East German MZ. At the start of the last five laps Mike pulled alongside, looked at me and nodded: the race was on. From the spectators' viewpoint nothing changed; we had been so close all through the race, continually passing each other. But now we were racing and giving it 105 per cent: for us it had become deadly serious. We raced on, shoulder to shoulder, and, on the last lap coming down the hill with the finishing line in sight, I was leading as we approached the last sharp corner. I had to choose: should I brake down the outside on the proper GP line knowing that Mike would come down the inside, or should I go down the middle of the road and try and block him? Decisions ... decisions ... In the end I decided to stay on line, as with Mike on the outside, I would be beaten because he was so good out wide. As I braked, I watched out of the corner of my eye under my left arm for his front wheel, and suddenly saw him coming. I did the only thing I could and peeled in early for the corner.

The Ultimate Dream Realised

Mike could not stop quickly enough and the nose of his bike's fairing crashed against the side of mine, which knocked me into a slide as he wobbled; I was quickest to recover and as I had skidded out wide, was able to turn on the power quickly enough and head for the line.

The Honda - being a four stroke - had to be ridden at a higher cornering speed than did the two strokes which had such superior acceleration, so I *had* to get on the gas first. I just made the line first (see photo) and Mike passed me just after, but I'd won the race. As we stood with our team around us we looked at each other and laughed. Later, though, on the winners' podium, we admitted that our legs were trembling from the collision a few minutes beforehand. Mike whispered in my ear on the podium "I'm bloody glad that we only had to race like that for five laps, I couldn't have kept that up the whole race." Even though we'd only really turned it on hard for five laps, we finished over one and a half minutes in front of the field.

The next year a picture of Mike and me racing appeared on a postage stamp and I was able to get a first day cover, also pictured here. At that time I thought only royalty and presidents got their pictures on postage stamps ...

As incredible as it may seem, during the GPs, riders had to deal with a lot of problems with the police. Sometimes it turned really nasty as at Monza, where the Italian GP is held, one year: the Monza police are notoriously vindictive. Each year an argument broke out between the riders - who wanted only to do their work as professionally as possible - and the police. But the way we were treated by the police at Monza always caused problems, and the race organizers could do nothing to stop it.

One year Eric Hinton and me arrived at the entrance to the riders' paddock, each in our own vans. The police at the entrance gates refused to let us in on the pretext that our bikes were not in the vans. We immediately showed them our correct passes and windscreen stickers which were all in order, but nothing worked. They were adamant: no bikes in our vans, therefore no authorization to enter. We tried every way we could to explain to them that we had left our bikes at the garage the previous day after the trial sessions, but they didn't want to know. Then they let another rider enter who had only a bike frame inside his van! This injustice sent us overboard and we started to act as stupidly as they. We decided to block the entrance, shouting at the police that, if we could not get in, then nobody else would! Their reaction was aggressive and immediate, swearing and even taking out their guns as if we were dangerous criminals. One of them pointed his gun at my head through the window of my van. Strangely enough, I was not worried too much, knowing full well that he wouldn't shoot just because I was blocking the entrance, so I pretended not to see him which made him even madder. I don't think he had ever been ignored in his life, and he was shaking with rage.

Then the situation became even more absurd. The police called in reinforcements which arrived accompanied by a breakdown van. I watched in amazement as they hooked up my van and began pulling. I stood hard on the brakes, but this didn't do much and I was dragged a hundred yards from the entrance with my wheels locked. I remember now that this was in 1959 because of the van I was driving. At that particular moment everyone was looking at me, so Eric managed to move his van even more and completely block the entrance gates. When the police saw what he had done they were really furious and went to hook up into the side of his van, as if they wanted to tear it apart. Eric had to give in and move the van as the situation was getting completely out of hand.

The father of one of the German riders, who had witnessed the scene, showed us another gate through which we could enter. This had no guards controlling the entrance for the simple reason that it was locked; however, our new friend simply cut off the padlocks and let us in. Unfortunately, we were seen by two policemen who arrested the German and then Eric. I had taken off my distinctive blue jacket so that I wouldn't be so easily recognizable and a few seconds later saw some poor man (in a jacket very similar to the one I had been wearing) walking between two policemen and shouting about his innocence. The three men were taken to the local prison.

Dickie Dale, who spoke a few words of Italian immediately went to look for the organizers to tell them of our ordeal, and warn them that if these three men were not released immediately, not one English-speaking rider would race! Despite this, the police didn't want to know and said that we would all go to prison. We quickly called a meeting and right away agreed that none of us would compete in the race. The organizers then took our threat a little more seriously and went immediately to the chief of police to have the three men released. Eventually the race took place ...

Another time Luigi Taveri, wearing his racing leathers and helmet, was strolling in front of the stands having just finished a practice session. As he stopped to talk to his mechanics about a persistent problem with his bike a man, not in uniform, spoke to him, and told him to move along. Luigi pretended not to hear. What a bad idea! The individual seized him violently by the arm and started shaking him. Luigi fought back and nearly punched the chap in the face, then three policemen arrived and arrested Luigi. Of course he was taken to prison, all the while cursing about the man's insolence and aggressiveness. He understood later that the man in question was the Chief of Police. Once again we threatened to go on strike if Luigi was not immediately released and, once again, the ploy worked beautifully.

Italy was the country where I met a delightful and charming man, Elvio Marconi, who became a very dear friend. As I have mentioned earlier, I made his acquaintance at the races in Imola. One of the most regular and enthusiastic spectators I knew, Elvio was always at the races and always ready to lend a helping hand. His hotel, the Hotel Marconi on the Adriatic Coast in Bellaria, became a regular place for us to visit and unwind every year before Monza.

The Ultimate Dream Realised

I introduced him to Mike Hailwood who also enjoyed his flamboyant and dynamic personality. We got into the habit - at the beginning of each season in April and in September after the Czechoslovakian GP and before the Italian GP in Monza - of going to Elvio's hotel for a well-deserved rest.

Since signing with Honda money was no longer a problem for me, because at last I had a contract which allowed me to live comfortably and not worry about the next day. However, we could have made even more money if our team manager, Reg Armstrong, who was supposed to look after our interests had done his job better. He was a good guy who knew how to link the different elements of the team, but his problem was that he also had very good relationships with the organizers of the races who took advantage of his kind and obliging nature.

Reg got into the habit of dining with the organizers. Being such a nice fellow he never tried to get our starting money upgraded and just accepted the organizers' first offer without negotiating at all. Reg was "a gentleman" who naively imagined that racing was a "gentleman's" sport. We told him that he had to be stronger and more demanding concerning our interests. But nothing changed and I was furious as I had absolutely no sympathy for the men who pocketed huge fortunes whilst we took all the risks.

At the end of the 1962 season I was at last crowned double World Champion in the 250 and 350 categories - the dream had become a reality after so much hard work and dedication. The victories tasted a little bitter however as I had that year lost three of my best friends. I would gladly have exchanged my two titles for the lives of Tom Phillis, Bob McIntyre, and Gary Hocking.

I felt so much resentment about the injustices in life, and towards the organizers who got rich whilst most of the riders went hungry. I promised myself that, as soon as I was in a position of strength, I would make them pay dearly and at the same time improve the lot of the racers. I became colder and more distant, to the extent that even the journalists noticed the change and nicknamed me "Iron Man."

In October 1962 after the GP season had ended, the first ever Japanese GP was organized on the brand new Suzuka circuit. This race did not count towards the World Championships because before being approved by the FIM for a GP, it first had to be tested to see if it met security and organizational standards, although we knew this was just a formality and the following year it was bound to get GP status.

The circuit had just been built this same year, and belonged to the Honda factory and its employees, which was an incredible thing at the time, the employees holding shares. This was one of the most difficult circuits that I had ever ridden on, but it was imperative for Honda - who wanted to win every class - that we win here. The Suzuka circuit opening day was a huge event for Japan, a great number of journalists were present and the stands were packed to capacity with spectators.

Jim Redman

All that year our team manager, Mr Sekiguchi, or "Poppa San," as he was known, would come to me on the start line and say "OK, Jim San, be careful." Just those five words. At Suzuka he came to me and said "OK, Jim San, be careful - but win." He wanted the win in Japan so badly that he just had to say it. I pulled his leg by saying "Which one do you want, Poppa San, be careful or win? I can't do both" He was flustered by this and said "No, no, no, be careful, be careful." I know it scared him when I just laughed.

I had a wonderful debut in Japan winning the 250 and 350 races, which made everyone very happy. Mr Honda was, of course, present and came to congratulate me personally, which was obviously a great honour for me. He had on other occasions previously visited us on the circuits in Europe to see how we got on. He was a man of great humbleness and incredible courtesy who was always very friendly and never pressurised us. Seeing that we were doing very well during the races, he didn't interfere, apart from giving us some helpful suggestions. However, he was always very interested to know how his motors were reacting during the race, since he was a great technician. He made a point of shaking hands with the whole team, from the lowliest engineer to the most important, and you could tell from their faces how they admired and respected him.

Marlene had returned to South Africa after deciding to let me go alone on the long journeys. Luigi Taveri and I were treated like kings in Japan: whatever we wanted to do, wherever we wanted to go, the Honda people obliged and nothing was too much trouble. They loved having us visit the factory and to show us around, but were also delighted to take us wherever we wanted to go, even those places which were, let's say, far removed from the motorcycle world, places where we could relax and improve our Japanese in the most agreeable way possible ...

After Suzuka the team managers of Honda and I found ourselves around the table in order to re-negotiate the next season's contract. With two World Championships under my belt I was in a strong position as I knew they really wanted me to remain with the company. I was ready to stay but before saying "Yes," wanted to know who would be team manager for 1963. "Reg Armstrong," they said; "in which case," I said, "I'm going elsewhere." They were completely taken aback but I told them that I did not want him as manager of the team as he was costing us a fortune in lost start money. "There is no-one else," they said, but I was ready for this and immediately replied "Yes, there is ... Me, I'll do the job!" Once I had assured them that it would not interfere with my riding, it was agreed and I became the new team manager of the Honda team.

I looked after the interests of the riders and Aika San and Poppa San decided which engineers worked on which bikes, and matters like that. I enjoyed myself immensely when negotiating the starting money with organizers as I was inflexible and hard with the difficult ones. My appointment as team manager was well received by my fellow riders who knew I

Continued on page 145

Picture Gallery 3

Jim in victory lane – with Jimmy Junior. It took a lot to impress him then!

Jim Redman

One of racing's real characters – the evergreen, ever-popular Jack Ahearn.

Jim tucked away on a 125 (16) trying not to look too big!

Picture Gallery 3

Rare! A comfortable lead over Mike – Creg-ny-baa, Isle of Man.

131

Jim Redman

A wave to famous photographer Volker Rauch. Assen, Holland, 1964.

Jim in team manager mode.

132

Picture Gallery 3

Caught with its pants down, the 6 undressed. Sorry about the poor quality of the picture.

A typical Isle of Man shot of Jim in action and showing how the spectators were able to enjoy the racing close-up.

Jim Redman

Yes, you can see 1-2-3-4-5-6 cylinders. Jim and Aika San with a nosey official.

Picture Gallery 3

Jim on the 6, showing the concentration of a man at work at Hockenheim in 1965.

The infamous Hotel Marconi: if Elvio sees this, please will he contact me?

Jim Redman

250 start at Francorchamps, Belgium. From left: Frank Perris (2) Suzuki; Phil Read (22) Yamaha; Mike Duff (28) Yamaha; Jim (6) Honda.

Picture Gallery 3

Jim on the Isle of Man again — note the 'soft' stone wall.

137

Jim Redman

Having a full go on the 6, Assen 1965.

Luigi and Ralph discuss a problem, perhaps how to get the engineer to stop smoking ...

Picture Gallery 3

1965/66. Bill Ivy 'the tiny strong man' who tried to pack so much into his short life.

Jim leads Phil at La Source hairpin Spa Francorchamps, 1965.

Jim Redman

Back at Sachsenring, same number – 129 – but this time in 1965 so the cobblestones have all gone. The 6 would have been very tricky in the wet on cobblestones!

Jim leads Alan Shepherd and Ernst Degner at the hairpin during an Ulster Grand Prix.

Picture Gallery 3

Two Swiss Champions, Luigi Taveri and Florian Camathias, shortly before Florian was killed in a crash at Brands Hatch in 1965.

Derek Minter at Spa 1965, perhaps thinking – "why no factory ride for me?"

141

Jim Redman

Put the kettle on for tea, I won't be long winning this. Solitude 1962.

Picture Gallery 3

Jim and Mike dice at Assen 1966.

Newspaper picture shows me trying hard on the 6 at Assen in 1965.

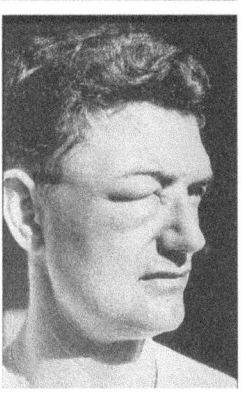

Prize fighter or the Grand Prix World Champion? The bee sting. Suzuka, 1965.

143

Jim Redman

Where are the rest? Jim winning – first time out on the new 500 Honda – at Hockenheim 1966.

They don't look much – but try beating them ... The feared Honda team of 1966: from the left Jim, Ralph, Luigi and Mike.

The Ultimate Dream Realised

would do a better job than Reg had and would not be going to dinners which would lose us a fortune. I took good care with signing riders and made sure the team ran smoothly with the right atmosphere. In short, it was an important responsibility and sometimes very difficult, but I did it to the best of my ability, with the rider's interests always foremost, and tried to be fair to all.

However, I recently heard that a member of the team had suggested that I took a percentage of each rider's money. This is simply not true and I received the same as the others for each start. In retrospect, I think I did a very good job on the start money side and, perhaps, deserved a percentage; maybe I should call them all and work something out ... ?

Once I became World Champion I received an enormous number of telegrams and congratulations from my family in Rhodesia, the Minister of Foreign Affairs of Rhodesia and the Minister of Tourism, Rhodesia. In fact Gary and me were national heroes in Rhodesia. This stream of good wishes and friendship from so many people warmed my heart and touched me.

When the season finished, I returned as usual to South Africa and Rhodesia, where I competed in a few more races on Hondas lent to me by the factory. The welcome that I received in South Africa was incredible - from the press, my friends, the fans and also the Natal Motocycle and Car Club, of which I was an active member. Also, not forgetting of course the general public, who became ever more numerous at each race in which I participated and who gave me a wonderful welcome home. I was filled with pride and emotion. Afterwards, I went on to Rhodesia, to Bulawayo my home town, for the GP, where once again the welcome from the crowds was so very enthusiastic, in part thanks to the Matabeleland Motorcycle Club which was so proud that one of its members was doing so well.

At the Rhodesian GP, bare to the waist and wearing just shorts because of the heat, I was working on my bike and all hot and sweaty, when I heard someone say "Jim Redman?" I turned to see where the voice was coming from and saw a man wearing a large smile standing in front of me; it was none other than Mr Clifford Dupond, then Deputy Prime Minister of Rhodesia. He approached me very assuredly and energetically shook my hand, his face very jovial. Personally, I was a little embarrassed because of my bare chest, dishevelled state and filthy hands. When I asked him why he had not warned me that he would be coming over so I could have cleaned up and changed my clothes, he told me that, on the contrary, he wasn't at all embarrassed! In his eyes, I had done so much for Rhodesia and dirty hands and perspiration were only to be expected considering the work I did. Mr Dupond had wanted to personally shake my hand and thank me for keeping the Rhodesian flag proudly flying all over the world. I was so happy and proud to be the recipient of all these accolades, at a time like that you forget all the bad moments. My cup was truly running over.

10
Expensive Victories

In 1963 Honda decided to mothball the 50 despite all the research, investment and energy that had gone into it and, for the time being, concentrate on the 125, 250 and 350.

It was this year that I had enormous battles with Tarquinio Provini and his 250 Morini single cylinder, and with Mike Hailwood and his 350 MV Agusta. I managed, however, to win these two World Championships again, even though the 250 was not decided until the last race of the season at the Japanese GP at Suzuka circuit. At the Argentinian GP - the last but one of the season - I had to finish in first or second place on the 250 in order to keep alive my chances of being World Champion at Suzuka.

I can now say I am very glad that the circuit in Argentina isn't a part of the racing calendar any more. It was by far the most dangerous and the most badly organized of all the circuits. Even before arriving in South America, I already had many problems. I had to leave a deposit of £2000 at the RAC office in London in order for them to complete the documents giving me authorization to take the bikes into Argentina. Once there, I had to wait five hours for the bikes to clear customs. The police didn't give a royal damn that I had just spent thirty hours in airplanes and was dead tired. As it was, I had more luck than did Tarquinio Provini (my principal adversary in this race) who had to wait four days for his bikes to be released from customs.

We experienced a lot of problems with the bus which was supposed to take us every day from the hotel to the Autodrome. Either the bus didn't show up, left sooner than it was supposed to, or it was full up with passengers picked up along the way. Because of this we never got to take the bus, instead finding our own way, usually by taking a taxi. As it was a long journey, the cost of this practically ruined us.

The training sessions were supposed to be at 9am, but never began before 11.30am, with only one organizer present who stood in front of the

Expensive Victories

starting line and waved to the riders with his flag. It was sad.

On one occassion, Mike Hailwood, Luigi Taveri, Alan Shepherd and me went behind the stands to watch the 50cc practice from another angle, and arrived just in time to see Hans-Georg Anscheidt crash with his Kreidler. Since there were no marshals or first aid people around to help Hans, we had to do it. Alan jumped on to the racetrack and ran back in the opposite direction to draw the attention of the other racers and get them to slow down, meantime Mike, Luigi and me ran to give some help to Hans. Quickly, we got him up on his feet and took him back to his team, where he was given medical care from the emergency kit the Kreidler team had brought with it. Immediately after, Hans was transported to the nearest hospital where after an X-ray it was discovered that he had a broken shoulder.

Mad with anger, we asked the interpreter where in hell was the first aid team of ambulances and doctors? He only shrugged his shoulders and pretended to know nothing. This was the last straw and we refused to train on the circuit as long as the emergency services were not present. We also demanded to see the race organizers but were told quite nonchalantly, that they were not available that day, the first day of practice: what a joke of a GP. Finally, after we'd finished our practice sessions, the organizers appeared. We told them it was totally unacceptable not to have a full medical team present every day and that we would submit a full report to the FIM on our return to Europe. We knew the FIM was just as useless, but they didn't and this threat forced them to take action.

We returned to our garage after the training session still wound up, and were enfuriated to find that one of the window panes had been smashed. Someone had got into the garage while we were on the circuit and had stolen all our watches and money - about £400. Were we mad!

Even then the nightmare wasn't over. During practice it was found that one section of corner number two was covered with dust, so we asked for it to be swept clean. This needed to be done before the first race as it was very dangerous and would cause problems. We were thanked for bringing this to the organizers' attention and assured it would be cleaned up immediately. Of course it wasn't done and on the first lap I almost crashed because of it, at a time when I was only a few centimetres behind Provini (in this type of duel every centimetre counts).

Throughout the race this area was very slippery and without a doubt something was bound to happen, which, eventually, it did. Provini was leading when suddenly he headed straight off the track. Miraculously, he regained control of his bike and got back onto the track, but now in second place, behind me, because of this incident. My delight was shortlived as, two laps later, it was my turn to slide at exactly the same spot. I had less luck than Provini and lost it completely and crashed. I picked up myself and the bike but had to stop at my pit in order to repair the footrest and gearlever, letting Provini back into the lead.

Jim Redman

Luigi Taveri, who had just retired from the race almost got into a fight, simply because he wanted to signal my position to me. He was told by the marshals, who had no idea what they were supposed to do, to leave the area immediately as he was not supposed to be in the pit lane. It was ironic; here was an experienced rider, still in his leathers, wanting to signal his team mate, being told he should not be there, when all the time the Coca Cola and coffee merchants strolled up and down vending their wares. In the meantime, things were not going well for me. The engineers couldn't repair my footrest and gearlever, and I heard on the loudspeakers that Umberto Masetti on the other Morini was about to take second place - my position. As I heard this I jumped back on my bike to defend my second place as best I could, even though my footrest kept slipping out of its socket. Every time it slipped out I would have to ride one-handed and reach down and shove it back in again, then put my foot on it and try and slide it inwards towards the frame to try and stop it falling out again. Again and again I had to replace the damned footrest; I would pull away a bit from Massetti, the footrest would slip and whilst I was struggling with it he would close in again. Although this went on for the rest of the race I did manage to hold on to my second place behind Provini. This meant we would go to the last round of the World Championship at Suzuka in Japan, where it would be a case of whoever won the race, won the Championship too.

We riders had trouble getting our start and prize money and Mike Hailwood had to fight like mad to get his trophies. It also took an incredible amount of time for the organizers to find our return tickets for the flight home. In the bus which took us back to our hotel all that the Italian riders and mechanics could talk about was the 250 race, all the while cursing me. Luigi Taveri, normally the calmest of people, got up and defended me, pointing out that I had ridden superbly despite my problem with the footrest and gearlever, and had ridden even better than Provini. Masetti tried in vain to utter a few remarks but, very authoritatively, Luigi ordered him to shut up, saying that as Masetti had been so slow during this race he was not qualified to speak.

I kept asking Luigi what was being said (the argument was in Italian) as I was only getting the general drift. Afterwards, Luigi told me he had been on such good form that he thought he spoke better than a trial lawyer, and said I did not have to worry my head about it as he had really put the record straight. We all had only one wish, to leave this sordid place as soon as possible and put the whole thing behind us.

On returning home I wrote a long letter of complaint about this GP to Mr Ken Shierson, secretary of the ACU (Auto Cycle Union.) Luigi Taveri, Mike Hailwood and Alan Shepherd backed me up on this, with Luigi sending his own complaint to the Swiss Federation. We were hoping to have the Argentinian circuit removed from the list of events that made up the World Championships and stressed that the organizers did not know how to run

Expensive Victories

a GP and appeared totally disinterested. We emphasized that riders were obliged to go there against their will to get points towards the championships. Lots of us, like me, had to go or lose the title I had battled for the whole year. Thank God, the following year the Argentinian GP was removed and lost its status as a World Championship event - news that everyone received with a very big sigh of relief.

The Isle of Man TT of 1963 was a very important event for me. It was one of my greatest ambitions to win a TT. During the hot afternoon of June 10th, 1963, I knew I had to win my first TT. On the starting line it was going through my mind that I had never liked racing in the TT, but I knew I had to put those thoughts aside and concentrate, focusing completely on the job in hand. Conquering my dislike of the dangers of the TT course to earn my victory this day remains one of the most incredible and exciting victories of my entire career. Since 1958 I had participated in this race, but had never really sparkled on the circuit. Strangely, the idea of winning here in 1963, and again in the future, became an obsession.

But before this could happen I had to first learn how to live with this circuit and it took me some time. Don't get me wrong; I love riding around the Isle of Man circuit in a race as it's most exciting for a rider and the challenge is awesome. As a privateer with no responsibilities I enjoyed my races there and just swished around, winning silver replicas each time and not getting into any trouble. Many riders do that for years and have a lovely time.

What I did not like about racing at the TT was the heavy responsibility of being Honda Team Captain, and knowing that Honda was looking to me to win. For this reason, the 250 race remains, without a doubt, one of my dearest memories. It was called by the press "The Slip and Slide TT" as the hot, sunny day had transformed the circuit into a sea of bubbles and melted tar and areas of it had become dangerously slippery. I knew what conditions would be like from the state of the road from my hotel to the starting area, and we were all warned by a board at the start line which said " Melting Tar."

Despite these difficulties, I was excited by this real chance to win here on the Isle of Man, even though I did not like the circuit. I took things relatively easy from the start, knowing there would be lots of patches of melting tar. I could feel the sweat running down inside my leathers; it felt as if I was in a Turkish bath, but this did not worry me as I was used to this kind of heat in Africa. What did concern me was how the Isle of Man roads would bear up as they were not used to this kind of heat. I tried to handle things as serenely as possible and, at the same time, evaluate my chances of success once things settled down.

Things soon began to happen and I knew that my wait-and-see tactics were going to pay off. All over the circuit riders were dropping like flies because of the melting tar. Altogether, 26 riders had quit the race, some because they'd gone off the track, others because their bikes had failed them. In some of the curves one could see fallen bikes, or the tyre marks of

Jim Redman

those that had slammed on the brakes before shooting off the track. It was inevitable that given the state of the track someone was going to be seriously hurt, which is what happened to Tony Godfrey.

Tony, a well known rider of the time, was sponsored by Lord Montagu of Beaulieu, a car and bike enthusiast with a great interest in the TT. Before the start, Tony - who was riding an incredibly fast Yamaha - had thrown down the challenge "The last one home buys the beers" to Dan Shorey. However, on the third lap when Tony was in third place following close behind Fumio Ito and me, he crashed at 120mph on a very dangerous bend close to Ramsey, and his bike threw him against a garden wall resulting in severe head injuries. The immediate diagnosis was a fracture of the skull. He's lucky to be alive, thanks in part to the Shell petrol company, which arranged for an emergency helicopter with flying doctors to be present during the whole week of racing. Tony was transported to hospital in no time.

I was having problems with the engine of my motocycle, which was heating up terrifically because of the tropical heat and burning my legs right through the leathers: it felt as though I was sitting with my shins against hot coals. However, I had to push to the limit; the only important thing right now was not to lose precious seconds as I could feel my Honda slowing on each lap. I couldn't understand what was happening - there was nothing broken - and figured it was losing power simply because of the intense heat. When I stopped on the third lap for fuel, the engineers asked me if I wanted them to look at the problem, but I thought it would cost us too much time and wanted to get back on the circuit as quickly as possible and not lose my position in the race. I just had time to take a mouthful of ice cold coke and then shot off knowing full well that Ito, riding a Yamaha, was only a few seconds from overtaking me.

For the time being at least I was in the lead, and very determined not to be passed, so it was a case of riding as fast as possible and staying focused. The next three laps were a mixture of extreme suffering (because of the heat that was burning the front of my legs) and anxiety and fear that the bike might suddenly break down and cost me the race. On and on I went with the bike slowing in a very worrying manner. My teammates, Luigi Taveri and Kunimitsu Takahashi, had been forced to abandon the race because of problems, so now there were only two of us to defend Honda's colours, Tommy Rob and me.

Tommy was in fifth position which was no help to me. I had to be careful with the motor and avoid a fall on the tar, all the while trying to go as fast as possible to ensure that no-one could catch me. Never had I ridden so hard on the Isle of Man, digging deep into my inner strength to regain the time that the slowing engine was costing me each lap. I did not signal my problems to the Honda pit as I passed in front of the stands at the end of each lap for the simple reason that I did not want my adversaries to know I was in difficulty.

Expensive Victories

The fifth and sixth laps were much the same, though a few times I felt my Honda had reached the end of the road. Given the conditions, it's understandable that when I saw the flag as I reached the finishing line - after 226 miles of superhuman effort and intolerable tension - I felt like singing and crying at the same time. I didn't have to worry any more, I had succeeded - I had won! I could hardly believe it but, yes, it was really true, the crowds were applauding, their hands raised in victory, handkerchiefs waving in the air. When we got to the area reserved for the winners, Marlene was waiting for me with an army of journalists and cameramen. I couldn't feel my back anymore from all the slaps on my shoulder from happy well-wishers congratulating me. Marlene was both overwhelmed and radiant and took me into her arms and kissed me. She was happy that the race was over and relieved that I was still safe and well and had survived the conditions. For me, it was a dream that had become reality, but which could easily have turned into a nightmare ...

Racing in such conditions on the Isle of Man was at the very least a harrowing experience, and I was going to try and do it again two days later. During this hot Monday evening in June 1963, with the huge TT Trophy standing in the hall of the hotel, conversations were very animated and exclusively about the race. Not only mine, of course, as each rider told of his own problems and his view of the race which, for many, was the bike event of the year. I loved listening to these stories; the magnificent and incredible accounts of each one, and seeing the riders getting fired up as they relived the race. I had trouble believing that I had actually won the TT and now my name appeared on the trophy next to those great riders from the history of motocycle racing who had won before me, and filled my dreams since I was a kid.

On the Wednesday we were on the starting line for the Junior TT 350 race. The conditions were terrible at the start but during the race became appalling, making it the worst I had ever competed in. Following a boiling hot Monday, the following Wednesday turned out to be wet and icy cold, with some of the circuit covered by a thick mist. Despite the weather, I still had to compete against some of the best riders in the world, Phil Read and John Hartle, both of whom Geoff Duke was running in the World Championships on factory Gileras. Also racing were Mike Hailwood, Champion and great TT expert on his MV, Alan Shepherd and the Czech, Franky Stastny. Rivalry between Gilera, MV and Honda teams was very great and I was in the middle of it. For sure, this was not a day for the faint-hearted ...

In the morning, New Zealander, Hugh Anderson, had won the 125 race in which I managed only sixth place, but it did give me the advantage of knowing where all the bad parts of every corner and curve of the circuit were. The weather conditions were particularly abominable on the mountain, and all those who had participated in the 125 race had had some difficult moments. Hugh Anderson admitted after the race that he had almost left

151

Jim Redman

the track at least twice. We finished the 125 race and all the riders who had returned were literally soaked to the skin and visibly exhausted, but most were now able to relax and thaw out, knowing they were finished for the day. Not many riders competed in both the 125 and the 350, but we could already hear the throbbing of the 350 motors which had started warming-up.

I was in no rush to go out there again and race, and win if I could. Marlene had attached my Number 1 for the 350 race under my number for the 125 and, while I tried to warm up with hot chocolate, she was taking off my old number. My rest was very short. In less than 15 minutes I found myself back again on the starting line, with the prospect of another six gruelling laps of this unforgiving circuit. It's funny, but in moments like this I asked myself what had made me decide to become a professional racer...

Before the 350 race, Mike Hailwood and I knew that, barring problems, one of us was going to win. Everyone thought that Mike would have the advantage in the rain because he knew the Island and all its peculiarities so well, and was such a good rider in the wet.

To determine how they will be placed on the starting grid, the names of the twenty best racers are drawn from a hat. I got the Number 1 spot next to my fiercest rival Mike Hailwood, who was drawn Number 2. Everyone was saying how well the organizers had arranged this as it was impossible to believe that the two main contenders could be drawn out as numbers 1 and 2 from 20. The organizers knew Mike and I were going to put on a show and wanted it to be as exciting as possible for the spectators.

As usual, I was thinking about a strategy, wondering if I should follow Mike to see how he was going, and then use the superior acceleration of the Honda to overtake him later on in the race. It was obvious that the Honda had its limits in the handling department, especially in the wet, due to the fact that it was a lot lighter and livelier than the MV and a lot harder to ride. Before the race, the 350 riders were anxiously watching the weather, hoping it would clear up later. Unfortunately, this did not happen, though it was slightly better at the start than during the 125 race.

It had been a long time since I had seen so many serious and grim-looking faces on the starting grid. I think we would all have much preferred to go back to a nice warm home if by a stroke of luck the organizers had decided to put back the race till later. In the stands the people were shivering with cold and wearing thick coats when only two days before they'd been in Tee-shirts under a blazing sun. This was typical of Isle of Man weather, which would change completely in a couple of hours. No-one could ever be certain of the next day's weather, but when it was bad, it was very, very bad.

The flag came down and away the two of us went with the rest following, all of us filled with trepidation and freezing cold. I got away quicker than Mike and rushed down Bray Hill, determined to go as fast as possible to try and shake him off. Behind us, Alan Shepherd had to stop because of a problem with his motor. "That's one less" I said to myself, but it still left Hailwood,

Expensive Victories

Hartle and Read. I was expecting that Mike might try and overtake me, but kept my head down without ever looking behind, concentrating on what was ahead. Nobody was more surprised than I when, at Ramsey, my crew signalled I had a ten second lead on Mike. As I was going up the mountain, I saw that the fog had come down again just like it had in the 125 race. If there's one thing I hated when I raced it was to have my visibility reduced. This did not seem to be a problem for Mike because as I came out of the mist into the clear again dropping down to the Creg, driving with one hand and using the other to wipe my goggles like a windscreen wiper, I was stupefied to see Mike coming up next to me. Through four miles of fog he had managed to make up the ten seconds - incredible! He gave a little wave of his hand and passed me. I wasn't going to have that so overtook him again, but he slipped in front of me just as I put on the brakes for the Nook. Then once again I overtook him, and both of us thundered down the Glencrutchery road almost as one.

We raced each other for two more laps, with Mike behind hounding me all the way, pushing me as hard as he could and hoping to force me into making that one mistake that can cost the race. Luckily for me my normal race strategy was to lead, so I was used to being pushed like this and did not mind the pressure. One rule I forced myself to stick to was not to look back; I knew Mike was there, so what was the point of looking over my shoulder? I was very strong with myself about this because I knew how I felt when I was following someone who kept looking back at me. As they turned to look back I would mentally say to them: "Yes, I'm still here, and I know I have you worried" - a thought which gave me a good solid feeling of confidence.

During these two laps I did not let Mike through anywhere, although I was aware of him breathing down my neck all the way. When we arrived on the mountain there was absolutely no fog, and on this lap I was leading by about 100 metres. At the end of the third round, we both had a routine pit stop to fill up our tanks. I always meticulously prepared for these pit stops, hoping to squeeze a few seconds' advantage over my rivals. Aika San had on this occasion, calculated the amount of petrol consumed during practice and cutting it to the minimum was able to reduce refuelling time by four seconds, which allowed me to take off that much sooner. A few other small time-savers helped: having the petrol cap open before I stopped; backing up the bike a few centimetres in my alloted space so that I would be ready to take off immediately; a new pair of goggles placed on an engineer's head; getting the bike moving again before refuelling was completely finished and as another engineer called out the seconds from his stopwatch, so that I knew exactly when to start moving. The last second or so I was already moving as the last drops of fuel were going in, and the pit mechanic snapped the fuel tank closed with his left hand as he pulled out the nozzle with his right.

My stop at the pits was one of the quickest, allowing me to gain a couple more seconds on Mike (who was very casual about his refuelling) giving me

Jim Redman

a 23 second lead. As he passed the Honda pit Mike pulled a face and stuck his tongue out which was typical Hailwood humour, joking in the heat of battle. Soon after this his bike decided it had had enough; I think he was pushing it really hard to try and catch me up before I got too far ahead. He retired and cruised slowly back to his pit, where he was able to get dry and warm whilst I was still slugging it out. "Two down," I said to myself, really relieved to be free of my greatest rival. Now I was alone and far ahead of everybody. Geoff Duke saw his chances improve but Phil Read had to stop because of a problem with the motor, and John Hartle, then in second place, was slowing down due to 3rd gear problems. Behind him, Frank Stastny was in third place on his Jawa.

There were now great distances separating the first three riders and I knew all I had to do to win this race was stay in the saddle and not do anything stupid. The weather got worse and worse, and I spent the rest of the race hoping the organizers would stop it, even though I was leading. As I passed the start at the end of the 4th and 5th laps I sat up and shut off, expecting the race to be stopped. I even signalled the organizers to do this as I felt it was suicidal to let the race go on, but they didn't. I had plenty of 'moments' on the next two laps but on the last lap it was really bad. There were crashes happening everywhere and I had the fright of my life when, arriving in Glen Helen on the last lap, I found a small river flowing across the track. Luckily for me, as I had such a good lead I had decided to change down one extra gear for each corner to try and make the last lap very safe, and this saved me. As I came out of the Laurel Bank section towards Glen Helen, I managed to pick the bike up in time as I hit the water. My bike aqua-planed across the stream with me trying to balance and keep it upright and on its wheels, but it was touch and go until the tyres found grip on the other side of the stream. As this happened, the bike shook its head a bit and we carried on. (At the prizegiving that evening, one of the fans who saw the whole incident said to me "You must have had a big fright there, I don't know how you stayed on." I replied "Neither do I!"

The track had become a real skating rink, rain was pouring down and visibility was practically nil, and several times I came close to having a very serious accident. Arriving on the mountain, my goggles were so misted up and full of water that I could not see through them and I pulled them down to be able to see. This only made it worse as the wind and stinging rain made me want to close my eyes and I had to force them open, although they felt glued together. I felt like singing as I crossed the finishing line; I was so cold and my muscles hurt so much from being so tense. I stopped my bike near the marshalls as I was not sure I could hold it up. I had to be helped off as I was numb with cold, my fingers were glued to the handlebars and my back so bent that I couldn't straighten up. I couldn't feel my legs and was totally incapable of speech. I finished first, six minutes in front of Hartle who had to fight hard against Stastny to keep his second place position. The other riders

Expensive Victories

came trickling in long after us.

In the early stages of the race, when Mike was pushing me, I lapped at about 101mph. My last lap was closer to 70mph - and even then I was minutes quicker than John Hartle, who was second - this gives some idea of how conditions deteriorated. The happiness that should have been mine after this victory was spoilt by the deplorable conditions in which this race had taken place and the thought of all of the riders who had crashed. Even so, I left the Isle of Man that year with two prestigious trophies, a lot of money and a head filled with marvellous memories ...

At the last GP, at Suzuka circuit in Japan, I just had to win - whatever the cost. I knew my opposition was Provini and Yamaha's new rider, Phil Read on a brand new machine. Actually, Fumio Ito, also on the new Yamaha, came the closest to beating me, but I was able to overtake on the outside on the last bend and win by a hair's breadth.

A little while before I had been crowned World Champion in the 350 category and now had defended my title in the 250 race. Another fantastic year for me, which was both very difficult and very successful.

For its first year in competition, Yamaha had an amazing debut. At Spa, Ito and Sunako won the double, and Ito made second place in the GP at Hockenheim and at the TT on the Isle of Man. But all that was behind us and all I could think of was that I was double World Champion once again.

Late in 1963 an American friend of mine, Henk Vorse, who lived in Finland, advised me that the organizers of Finnish motorcycle racing wanted to hold a GP in their country, a GP which would count towards the world title. The event then currently held in Finland was classed only as an international race. Knowing the circuit quite well, I said I thought that this aim was impossible as this circuit was too dangerous: trees were literally growing in the tarmac at the edge of the road.

Despite this, authorization to proceed with the Grand Prix was received from the FIM. I asked Henk how the organizers had managed to get the circuit approved and he told me that he and the organizers had taken the FIM representative under their wing and wined and dined him lavishly at the best restaurants, where he ate and drank as much as he wanted to, and was lodged in the best hotels.

My fears about this circuit were confirmed much quicker than I imagined and by Mike Hailwood, who had a very bad fall on the MV. You can imagine what a terrible feeling it is to see a good friend hurtling at high speed through the trees, knowing if he hit one it could be curtains for him. Today, that circuit would be considered too dangerous as an approach road to a circuit, never mind as a circuit. Furious, I gave the press the whole story, spiced with plenty of harsh words about the FIM for allowing its use.

After the Japanese GP I raced in Australia up until Christmas and then went on to New Zealand for the after-Christmas races. Whilst in NZ, I contacted Bill France at Daytona, USA, the venue for the first GP of 1964, to

155

Jim Redman

start negotiations for the Honda Team to go to Daytona. Bill told me he had arranged a charter flight from the UK and that our team should all come on that. This was okay for Ralph and Luigi, who were both in Europe, but the bikes were in Japan and I was in New Zealand. I told Bill that it would cost more for me and the bikes to go to the UK than it would to go straight to Daytona, but he was adamant he was only prepared to fly us on the charter flight from the UK. We could take it or leave it, he said, but he knew we'd take it as there were World Championship points at stake.

Before I had chance to reply to this, Honda contacted me to say that the new bikes would not be ready for the beginning of the 1964 season and how would I feel if we missed the meeting at Daytona, as that was what Honda preferred to do? Was this a big disappointment to me, not to go to the GP in the USA, they asked. I couldn't have been happier and immediately sent a telegram to Bill, in which I asked him for a very large sum of money if he wanted to see the Honda Team at his circuit. Of course, he gave me a flat refusal, repeating that he knew we would be there for the points, so I was very pleased to tell him that our team would not be coming. If Bill France had accepted my proposal, the money would have been enough for me to have found a way to go to Daytona with last year's bikes. Later on this incident allowed me to extract more starting money for our team from other organizers, starting at the next GP, the Spanish in Barcelona. It gave me a great deal of satisfaction to write to Bill France and say what a pity it was that a poor country like America could not afford to pay for the Honda team to come to its circuit ...

My racing tour of Australia was reasonably successful, but it was in New Zealand that I achieved one of my greatest feats by winning all fourteen races in which I was entered! We had just arrived there, when we met Mr Smiley, the representative for Castrol New Zealand, who told me that he had received a telex from Castrol England telling him he should award me quite substantial bonuses for each victory. He understood that I was to participate in five meetings and explained that if I won all five he would not have enough money to pay me. I had to explain to Mr Smiley that as I was competing in at least two or three races per meeting, I would be riding in fourteen races in total. Growing more and more uneasy, poor Mr Smiley asked how many races I thought I would win and I replied "I think we will be all right." meaning I thought I would win all of them. (Before I left England I had arranged with Castrol to be paid for wins only, with nothing for second or third positions. This way, I got a much larger amount for the wins, as Castrol gambled that I could not win them all, but would be even happier if I did) Mr Smiley immediately telephoned England to ask Castrol what he should do and was told that he should pay me whatever he could, and the rest I would pick up from Castrol UK on my return to England.

I had heard from Mr Smiley that Hugh Anderson, the New Zealand rider and 125 World Champion, was going to race in the 350 and 500 classes

Expensive Victories

on his Nortons and that his main objective was to beat me. I won the 250 and 350 raves quite easily but during the first 500 race, which was held on a small circuit (at the most 2 kilometers) right in town, I really had to fight hard against him, while overtaking the slower riders in whole groups. On the second lap I saw Anderson fall, which happened when he was trying to overtake a whole bunch of lappers. With him out, I won the race easily. Sadly, the meeting was marred by the death of a side-car competitor and his passenger, who had been flung right through the window of one of the shops that lined the circuit.

I won all of the other races in which I participated and arrived at the last meeting at Pukekoe, near Auckland, for the New Zealand GP with eleven wins to my credit. I then won both the 250 and 350 races quite comfortably but knew that as Hugh was still looking for a first victory, he would give me a hard time in the 500 race. I managed a good start and after one lap was already 3 seconds in the lead and trying to go even faster. On every lap after that I was signalled, 'plus 3 Hugh' and ended up the winner by just those 3 seconds!

I had been in New Zealand a short while staying with my old friend, John Hempleman, when I received a letter in a plain envelope. It was from Buckingham Palace and marked for the personal attention of Mr Jim Redman only - private and confidential. I immediately opened the envelope and found inside another, smaller envelope also addressed to me. Inside, was a letter, which read: "If The Queen, in her graciousness, were to make me a Member of the British Empire, would I accept?" Of course, I replied I would be very honoured to accept. I was told I would be contacted later and given a date to come to Buckingham palace to receive the actual MBE medal, but it would be announced in the 1964 New Year's Honours Lists. What an honour; I felt particularly proud to have been chosen from amongst the thousands of possible personalities. On January 1, 1964, we turned on the radio and heard that I had been decorated with the MBE award. A little while later it was the Beatles' turn to be so honoured, but they later famously returned their decorations!

Whilst still in New Zealand, I was contacted by the FIM and ordered to appear at its head office in Geneva for a court of enquiry into the damaging declarations I had made regarding the GP in Finland. I was accused of conduct prejudicial to the FIM and the sport. I asked to be allowed to come once all my races were finished in New Zealand (they weren't to know they'd finished already!) This reply was not well-received and the FIM demanded I come immediately, adding that if I did not my licence would be taken away. They certainly didn't beat around the bush! Also at this time I got a call from Castrol UK asking me to stop over in London before going on to Geneva.

On arrival in London, Castrol told me the FIM had been notified that I was the only rider Castrol was prepared to sponsor in 1964 in all and any mechanical sports. Castrol further explained to the FIM that if it persisted in

Jim Redman

its intention to take away my licence, then Castrol would not be making its usual annual donation to the FIM of £100,000 at the beginning of the season. As if by magic, the FIM decided it was not necessary for me to go to Geneva and all I had to do was write a letter of apology and the file would be closed. Not particularly pleased about having rushed back from New Zealand for nothing, I wrote a long letter to the President of the FIM in which I explained everything that had happened and ended by saying that if, after reading my letter, he thought I should apologize, I would be prepared to do so. I received a one-line reply to say my apology had been accepted.

In the meantime, *Motor Cycle News* had two photos of me on the front page, one in which I was smiling and one in which I was looking sour. The caption was: "The two faces of Jim - Jim The Saint and Jim The Sinner. Who is right: the Queen or the FIM? On the one hand he is awarded the MBE for service to sport and, on the other, the FIM is threatening to take away his licence."

The Bill France incident about start money helped me at the Spanish GP at the beginning of 1964 as I had spent a long time negotiating with the organizers for more starting money for our team, but on arrival at Montjuich Park for the meeting had still not reached agreement, and negotiations continued right up to the moment that practice started. The organizers told me that the money I had requested for our team was three times more than they were paying any of the other Japanese teams, to which I replied that that was okay as we were four times better than them! When I explained to them that this was the reason we did not ride at Daytona they capitulated and paid us.

1964 saw the arrival of a new Honda four-cylinder 125cc model, and later in the season the famous Honda 250cc six-cylinder. Also during 1964, motorcycle racing underwent a phenomenal revolution; for the first time all the attention and interest focused on the 250cc class and not the 500. The 250cc class was the one the public most wanted to see and the promoters were quick to exploit this by holding the 250 race at the end of the day, when excitement would be at its peak.

Spectators had become tired of seeing Mike Hailwood - without any serious competition - cruising to yet another win in the 500 race. There was no-one with a bike good enough to even give him a run for his money, never mind stand a chance of beating him on his MV. It wasn't Mike's fault, of course. I'm sure he would have relished some serious opposition, but as it was he raced against the clock and tried to set new records if he felt in the mood, or just cruised to an easy win. In 1963 the Geoff Duke Gilera Team had made an effort to compete, but it was a half-hearted attempt with basically unchanged bikes and an unhappy, unco-ordinated team.

For a long time the lightweights had been left in the shadows, but now with the quality of competition in the 250 races it was fitting that they take their rightful place as the main event of the day.

Expensive Victories

For 1964, we knew the competition was going to come from Yamaha and Phil Read. Phil Read had been chosen by Yamaha to lead the team and they were definitely the fastest 250cc machines at that time.(I discovered just how fast they were only much later in my life when I rode one in South Africa against Mike on the Honda 6, and found this Yamaha twin was quick enough to give even the 6 a run for its money on a short, twisty circuit.)

In the end the 250 races that year became private duels between Phil and myself, and culminated in Phil stealing my crown - the 250 title. The stakes for me were so high and the pressure unbearable. For Phil Read it was the same. The tension between us was tangible, and each race was a war of nerves, complete with extreme excitement, disappointment, broken hopes and dreams and torture both physical and mental. I don't think anyone could complain about the show we put on each time we competed. We were so close together on the tracks that we seemed like one rider; in fact, one article said it looked as though we were riding a tandem. Throughout the races we swopped positions, tried to break away from - or overtake - each other, be the best at braking in order to accelerate first and grab the lead. We used every trick in the book in an effort to oust the other from the top slot on the podium. Unfortunately for me, I spent a major part of the year tucked into Phil's slipstream as my bike did not have the power or speed to get by. Watching this sort of racing was a real treat for the spectators, but for us riders it was unrelenting. I knew that losing even one hundredth of a second could ruin my chances of winning the title, so I concentrated on this goal and was drained and exhausted from the effort at the end of each race.

Our fight started during the first European GP of the season, on the difficult circuit of Montjuich in Barcelona. Phil and I were both desperate to win the Spanish GP and notch up some points for the World Championships, but were beaten by Tarquinio Provini riding his 4-cylinder Benelli. I led the race but Provini overtook me and went on to victory. I was second, far ahead of Phil.

Next, was Clermont-Ferrand. Phil and I fought it out for first place, smashing the lap record in the process. Then I went out with ignition problems, leaving Phil to claim his first victory of the season.

The following round was the most dangerous and most exhausting of them all - the TT on the Isle of Man. Both of us had triumphed on this circuit in previous years but I figured I had reliability and a better chance of finishing than Phil. We both knew the circuit perfectly: all of the bumps, curves, bends, turns, manhole covers and telegraph poles of this legendary track. Few people really believed that I had a chance of winning the 250 race, simply because the Yamahas were much faster than the Hondas that year. Everyone was predicting a win for Phil, which did not bother me particularly as it's never over until the fat lady sings, and I had no intention going down without testing him and his bike to the limit. I was number 1, Phil number 16.

So 80 seconds separated us at the starting line, with the advantage

159

Jim Redman

to Phil, as it's easier to try and catch your opposition than to avoid being caught. Phil had been faster during the trials but, as a reporter noted, "Just how much was this cunning Jim Redman holding in reserve?" This reporter asked me about being slower, to which I replied "How much cash and how many points do you get for winning the practice?"

I knew that this race would be very bitterly fought. Phil and I took turns leading but then he had to stop at his pit to change sparkplugs which meant he was immobilized for more than a minute. It happened again and Phil jumped off at Quarter Bridge and tried in vain to rectify the fault. Eventually, he grabbed the sparkplugs and threw them to the ground in disgust. Alan Shepherd was hanging on to second place, but I was more concerned about my bike which had sprung an oil leak, making my foot slip on the brake pedal and oiling the back tyre. This caused me a couple of nasty moments when the back wheel slid out on corners, but I managed to keep control of my machine and win the race, even beating the lap record. This was my first victory of the season and I felt I richly deserved it!

Two days later I was on the starting line in the 350 class. From the start I went into the lead, averaging over 100 miles an hour. However, when I refuelled on the third lap, one of the spectators called out "Don't forget the boys and their silver replicas, Jim." (Each rider in the TT who finishes behind the winner within a certain time receives a silver replica of the winner's trophy and, more importantly, extra cash bonuses.) I must admit I hadn't thought of this so slowed right down to give more of them a chance, but still won the race easily.

The earlier 125 race had been something else completely, and I was beaten by my team mate, Luigi Taveri, by just three seconds. Our plan was to beat the Suzukis ridden by Hugh Anderson and Frank Perris. Right from the start I had trouble as my Honda would only run on three cylinders initially, and it took me some time to coax it to run on four. After several miles it cleared and was going on all four cylinders. I looked round and saw Ralph Bryans and Frank Perris catching me up, despite the fact that they had both left ten seconds after me; I'd lost a lot of time trying to coax that fourth cylinder. Despite this, I felt as aggressive as ever: if they wanted to beat me, they'd have to pass me! After pushing my bike to the limits for a some miles, I looked back and was pleased to see no-one behind me. I managed to lead for the first lap and pressed on as fast as I could in the second.

Frank Perris and Hugh Anderson both went out with engine problems, and I was pressing on so well that I was pulling away from Luigi and Ralph. Luigi had been given the task by Honda of winning the 125 Championship that year, but the TT was a free-for-all, as it always was in our team, which meant I could try for three victories in a week. Then, halfway round on the last lap my twist grip came loose on the handle bars, which made life very difficult for the last 20 miles of the race. Luigi closed in on me relentlessly as I struggled as best I could to hold him off, difficult at the best of times. His

Expensive Victories

light weight would give him a tremendous advantage when climbing up the mountain: I just prayed I could hold him off.

We crossed the finishing line and had to wait for the timekeepers to announce the winner. I started to wonder if maybe I could win three TTs in a week and equal the record set by Mike Hailwood. Murray Walker, the well-known sports commentator, came over right away to interview us, and asked Luigi to say a few words to the BBC viewers. Luigi's words were "First of all, I would like to know who won, Jim or me? When Murray told us that Luigi had won by three seconds my heart sank; three lousy seconds and that loose throttle had cost me half a minute at least. My only consolation was that if anyone had to beat me I was glad it was Luigi.

This TT week left me very tired, but content; in fact, it was probably one of the most satisfying weeks of my entire life! I was very happy to have won the 250, as the experts had not given me a chance. The 350 race was easier as Mike Hailwood was not able to participate because of sickness. Of course, I was sorry not to have achieved the triple, but that's life. Other races were waiting for me, other challenges would present themselves, and it was this that was important. Aika San had told me that a brand new 250 six-cylinder was in preparation in the Honda factories, which would be ready before the end of the season. All I had to do was simply wait for this revolutionary bike ...

The following GP, at Assen in Holland, was even more trying but full of magic ... and probably the best race of my life! The heat was unbearable and once again Phil and I fought over first place in the 250 on a surface judged by many - me included - as the best in the world, even though it had deteriorated in the heat with all the rubber from the practice sessions. The tyres of our bikes were almost boiling and were shedding bits of rubber every lap as we raced each other, neither one giving an inch. We had to be exceptionally careful because of the rubber and oil on the track, but this did not prevent the lap record from being broken again and again.

We raced like demons, banging knees at more than 130 miles an hour as we braked, side-by-side, going into the corners. For most of the race I had to sit behind, as I was well down on power and 15km an hour slower on the straight. On the last lap half lap, I outbraked Phil over and over, but he simply accelerated past me again. Then, as we approached a fast kink I decided that if I could get through it without lifting my chin off the tank, it would give me enough to win. It was a mistake as the extra speed caused the back wheel to step out in a big slide and Phil went past again as I fought for control of the bike. I cursed my stupidity. As we approached the second last corner I made up my mind that wherever Phil braked, I would go down the inside and pass him. I had to change down an extra gear to try and stop for the corner and when I cracked open the throttle the bike surged forward, with the rev counter needle two or three thousand revs over the limit.

When I saw how well this had worked I did exactly the same on the last

Jim Redman

corner. As we approached the finishing line, I saw Phil creeping up alongside and knew that if I changed gear I would lose the race. I decided not to change gear and let the engine rev its heart out: if it burst I lost, and if I changed gear I lost, so I hung on. The engine responded magnificently. No-one will ever know what figure it revved to as the needle was hard against the 18,000 revs stop, and this a bike I had never pushed over 15,000 revs before! What a little beauty that motor was. Aika San stripped it after the race and found nothing wrong, but still replaced everything as every part must have been unmercifully stressed.

On seeing our two bikes hurtling towards him, the man with the chequered flag took an involuntary step back while Nobby, who was quick-thinking, rushed up to the finishing line and took a picture in case of dispute. During this last lap, Phil and I passed and re-passed each other no less than twelve times. We were way ahead of all the others, lapping the entire field, except for the rider in third place who was nearly 3 minutes behind. The lap and race records for this race were well and truly smashed!

Once off my machine my legs felt like plastic and I could hardly stand up; I was like a sailor who had just spent a very long and very rough time at sea. People were slapping me on the back, there were congratulations and smiles, the crowd was yelling: it all seemed so faraway from me at that moment. I wanted only one thing - to collapse and be alone ... When I arrived on the winners' rostrum I was met with a standing ovation, the press called it the race of the century, just as they had a week before in the Isle of Man. Nobby said to me "This is getting real rough, a race of the century every weekend." In the shade of the pits I sank down to the cool concrete floor. My face was radiant with the satisfaction of having ridden the race of my life, despite my bike being so down on power. I took down the top of my leathers and washed my face with Eau de Cologne, all the while thinking "I'm too old for this type of race. I don't ever want to have to ride like that again."

However, just an hour-and-a-half later I had to be on the starting line for the 125 race, again with Phil and the rest as opponents and I knew I could expect another very difficult race. Personally, I would never have participated in the 125 race if it was not for Luigi. He'd crashed in practice and so asked if I wasn't too tired from the 250 race if I would try to keep the others from winning in the 125 to keep alive his chance of winning the World Championship.

The crowds were still talking about the 250 race whilst waiting impatiently for the 125 to begin. I knew Phil was just as exhausted and weary as I was, although I had also won the 350 race from Mike Hailwood earlier in the day. I heard Phil was lying on his camp bed, a cigarette between his lips, and I bet he was wishing just as I was that the race was already over.

We walked slowly to the start line again as our bikes were brought out for the 125 race. For the public it was going to be an incredible race, full of suspense, but for us riders it was going to be a job that had to be done.

Expensive Victories

However, very quickly excitement had the adrenaline pumping: I didn't feel tired any more and gone were the aches and pains. In their place now was the fire and determination to be victorious again!

Phil Read took the lead as I made a terrible start - almost last away - but was so keyed up from the 250 race that I just carved my way through the field. I caught up and passed Hugh Anderson who had made a good start on a tricky right-hand bend that normally I would have had more respect for, and pulling away as I went after Phil. Once I caught Phil, I just sat behind him. Phil maintained a good rhythm, and in no time we'd left the others far behind. This time I had the extra speed and so waited for the right moment at which to overtake.

With three laps to go to the finishing line, I saw a chance to go ahead; we'd just reached a slower group of riders and I shot past Phil and overtook them. Phil pulled out all the stops, taking all kinds of risks to try and overtake me, but I knew it was too late for him: from now on he would not be able to do it. I was very determined to win and did not want a repeat of the 250 race - that had been too close for comfort and I had taken too many risks. I knew Phil wanted revenge, but I had the speed advantage so I just opened the accelerator all the way, put my head down and took off as fast as my two wheels could go. I finished six seconds ahead of Phil, at the same time beating the lap record, with all of the first six racers beating Hugh Anderson's old record. The latter was thanks in part to Phil and me who, due to our frantic speed, had carried the field along with us. Hugh Anderson, not known for throwing compliments around too readily, shook my hand warmly, saying "Brilliant, bloody brilliant!" His praise meant a lot to me since it came from an individual I respected.

The 125 race was the third of the day and it completed my 'hat trick.' At the end of the day I was exhausted, but so satisfied; I had won three races and beaten six records. As I wearily made my way to the rostrum to stand again on the top rung, I knew I had achieved something that no man had ever done before: three GPs in one day for a man too big for a 250 or 125! The crowd was wonderful and went crazy; you can imagine my feelings as I looked out over it, wondering could anything be better than this? Lots of riders would like to win three GPs in a lifetime and I had done it in one day! In 1995 when I attended the Dutch TT once more - in the capacity of demonstrator rather than racer - Kevin Schwantz said to me, having heard this story, that he was lucky to win three GPs in a year, never mind one day! Everyone should experience the euphoria of victory at least once in their life.

However, the road to victory is often hard and rocky. For example, on certain parts of the TT circuit, going at almost 140 miles an hour, the track feels like aluminium roofing. The bike bounces up and down incessantly, your wrists are hurting and you're praying for it to stop just for a moment. It's like being in a marathon, and every muscle aches. The ears are constantly cocked, listening for the slightest suspicious noise which could come from the

Jim Redman

engine; the eyes are fixed on the rev counter and the track, which is changing all the time. The flies stick to your goggles and you don't have time to rub them off, even if it means driving half blinded, and the burning sun pierces your eyes.

However, I can tell you that the party which was held that night at Assen was quite exceptional. I was now four points ahead of Phil Read for the title, but still had to fight hard if I wanted to hang on to my lead.

At the GP in Belgium a week after Holland, I had one of the biggest scares of my life, and which made me lose precious points for the championships. I had made a good start, going as fast as I could, knowing that Phil was chasing. With his greater speed he would catch up pretty quickly.

Suddenly, he was there, sweeping past me like the wind: I had to get into his slipstream and try to stick with him as best I could. I stayed a bit on the side, hoping that his two stroke motor would break down as it often did. I saw that Phil had his hand on the clutch, waiting for the first warning signs of this problem. As we were approaching one of the fastest left-right kinks on the circuit, I saw a puff of smoke from his exhaust pipes and knew instantly that his motor was going to seize (to this day I don't know *how* I knew, as the puff of smoke was not something that had happened before). I flung my bike to the left out of Phil's slipstream and just missed him as his bike seized solid, but this meant I was right off-line in the bends and had to throw the bike frantically to the right to get through the bend. Even so, I could not keep it on the road and went off into the dirt on the side at a speed of about 140 miles an hour. I managed to keep control of my Honda - or should I say hang on to it - but couldn't get off the grass. As I was trying to master the machine, I almost ran into a telephone pole and then into the wall of a house. I just hung on, my face streaming with sweat. Eventually - and luckily - I regained control of my Honda and carried on with the race behind Mike Duff and Alan Shepherd, who had passed me whilst I was fighting my bike as if it were a bronco in a rodeo! To tell the truth, throughout this incident I didn't have time to be afraid as everything happened so fast, but when I got back on to the track my stomach went into knots: I knew I had come close to death.

I caught up with and overtook Alan Shepherd, but couldn't get near Mike Duff, whose bike was too fast and he was just too far ahead. He finished first, at the same time breaking the record, with me second. Phil had abandoned the race. Afterward, Alan and Bert Schneider told me they had seen me go off the track and were convinced I was living my last moments on earth. Alan admitted he thought he would have to pick up the scattered pieces of my body from all over the track.

I must say I was relieved to know I didn't have to race again that day. I also knew that had I not instinctively swerved out from behind Phil in the way I had, and instead waited for him to straighten up having realized that his motor was dead, then I would have smashed straight into him at 140

Expensive Victories

miles an hour; it wouldn't have been a nice thing to see ... People asked me if I'd had a fright - of course I had! The man whose never been scared won't survive for very long because he won't see and accept danger. Generally though, whatever risks I took were always calculated, until something like this happens and then its just instinct, reflexes and luck that gets you through.

My lead over Phil in the World Championships was now 10 points: I had 28 to his 18. The battle continued on the Solitude Circuit in Germany. It was the first time that Phil had raced there, but this did not stop him from breaking the records. I knew this circuit and Phil decided to use my knowledge to his advantage.

This time, it was Phil's turn to play the waiting game. My strategy was simple; take the lead from the start and try to drop him off, which is just what I did but Phil clung to me like a shadow the whole time. I tried to make him overtake me, but he did not fall into my trap; he just sat behind me and followed my every move until he had the circuit taped. Then he came out of my slipstream and used all the extra speed of his Yamaha to pull clear. I tried to hold on to him as I had at Assen, but it was a waste of time - there weren't enough corners. It was at this moment that I understood just how much faster the Yamaha was than my Honda. Crossing the finishing line, Phil set a new track record of 99.37 miles an hour on a circuit he'd never raced on before. All the honours were his. After the race he came to see me and admitted he had stuck behind me only to learn the layout of the circuit, if he'd wanted to he could have overtaken me at any time he'd wanted to.

I won the 350 race very easily; it was more like a stroll in the park than a race as there was no other bike that could shake Honda's supremacy. My bike was perfect and I set a new lap record, faster than that of Mike Hailwood on the 500, and I was not pushed. The 350 Championship was going to be mine but, on the other hand, my anxiety was growing progressively as I saw Phil get closer to the 250 title. I now had 34 points and he had 26 ...

The following GP took place at Sachsenring, in East Germany. Racing on this circuit was always a magnificent experience. The number of spectators reached a record 300,000 and included people who had come from all over the country, all fanatics about the sport of motorcycle racing. They spent hours queueing the night before the race to get better places and be closer to the riders. A lot of them didn't even have any transport and hitch-hiked from all over the country. Some brought with them their own portable 'grandstands,' something I have never seen outside of East Germany. Try to imagine the huge mast of a ship, with its high pole and cross spar, driven into the ground with stays to hold it up. There, fans spent the day, perched some thirty or forty feet above the ground.

The money won at Solitude never amounted to much as the exchange rate was terrible. Anyway, it was illegal then to import or export East German money and I'm sure Customs took great delight in confiscating any found. For these reasons, we got into the habit of spending our winnings during our stay there. Marlene loved walking around the city and looking in the shops. I estimated how much money I was going to get at the end of the races and Marlene reserved the goods in the various shops. In 1960, for example, I had spent all my money before I had even ridden a race! I knew that I had a good chance of winning the 350 race, but was not certain of having the same success in the 500, so had based my calculations on fourth place in this category. As hoped, I was first in the 350 but, in the 500 race, dropped from second place to seventh when my bike developed a mysterious misfire. Luckily it disappeared near the end of the race and I was able to snatch back second place. To my great relief I now had enough money to go and pick up all that Marlene had reserved and paid a deposit for.

This time, the 250 race was going to be particularly hard, as Mike Hailwood was racing an MZ and was ready to do anything to beat Phil and me. In the morning I had won the 350 race which gave me a chance to make a good evaluation of the circuit. Mike Hailwood was favourite to win the 250 race, encouraged by a crowd that was completely with him. The MZs were known to be strong when they raced 'at home,' especially when one of them was ridden by Mike. Phil and I needed the points to win the championships and didn't want another rider getting in the way.

On the first lap Mike caught Phil and overtook him, while I managed to catch up Phil, but could not pass him. Mike was in front of us and going like a rocket, beating his old track record of 102.06 miles an hour. However, misfortune befell him as he accelerated too much and too early, coming off his bike as we swept through the village of Hohenstein-Ernstthal. Phil, who was right behind Mike, just managed to avoid him, but we both saw Mike's head hit the road hard, his unconscious body rolling on the track. Phil and I both looked back for a moment and could see him lying prone and still: he looked lifeless. Mike was rushed to hospital where he was rapidly diagnosed with concussion and possibly a fractured skull, several bruises and a serious tear in the shoulder muscle.

So, again, it was just Phil and I battling away far in front of the others; most of them were over a lap behind us. Three laps before the finishing line Phil took the advantage and, from then on, I could not get past him. As we went into the last bend we were almost neck-and-neck, but his acceleration was too good for me and Phil beat me by one length.

We went immediately to see Mike in hospital; he still had his incredible sense of humour, despite the seriousness of his accident. The whole time we were with him he didn't stop joking. Phil commented, ironically, that Mike would have to sharpen up if he wanted to join the fast boys, instead of strolling around as if he was on his 500. Mike just laughed.

Phil had another advantage over me as after Belgium, Aika San and all the engineers went back to Japan to try and get the 6 ready as soon as possible (I think they sort of gave up trying to win with the old 4-cylinder), leaving Nobby and me to soldier on as best we could. It was a frustrating time for

Expensive Victories

me as I knew that with the 6 I could win the championship,. whereas the old 4 was just too slow.

The battle moved on to the Ulster GP in Northern Ireland. As usual, I won the 350 race (for the third time); now my only hope was that the 250 race would be just as easy to win.

The weather conditions were appalling during the 250 race and got even worse as a real storm arrived. Water soaked into our leathers through our waterproofs and visibility was nil; the roads were covered with water and in some places there were actually huge puddles the size of small lakes. Up until the last minute we felt sure the organizers would cancel the race, but the flag went down and we headed straight into the storm. Tommy Robb led for half a lap on his Yamaha and I was right behind him, followed closely by Bruce Beale and Phil. I overtook Tommy quite quickly, but then Phil passed all of us and took first place. As he overtook me I went through a puddle on the track and started to aqua-plane like never before. The same thing happened again a little bit later and I almost fell. I don't know how I regained control of my bike, but I did and stayed in the race even though I had lost some time.

Now Phil was far ahead of me. I kept cleaning my goggles, trying to press on and catch up with Phil, but I was riding very badly and I never saw him again. At the finishing line he took the race, beating me by a full minute. I was beside myself with anger: we'd raced in exactly the same conditions but I'd raced like an idiot, it was one of my worst rides for a long time. On returning to the pits Nobby asked me what had gone wrong with the bike, to which I replied "It's the rider that's the problem." When I judged that I had ridden badly, I always told Honda in a straightforward fashion and it was always accepted; they knew that nobody could be in top shape *all* the time.

11
The Honda 6

During the GP at Imatra in Finland, I received the news I had been waiting so long for: at last, the brand new Honda 6 was ready to be tested and I had to go to Japan as soon as possible after the race in Finland.

Immediately after the 350 race (which I won, by the way), and without having time to pick up my trophy, I went straight to the airport. I was unable to get a seat on a plane going to Japan via Anchorage in the USA, which was the shortest route, because they were all fully booked due to the Olympic games being held in Tokyo. Consequently, I had to go right around the southern route, which meant a lot of stops.

On arrival on a Tuesday morning I was driven straight to the Suzuka circuit where I had the honour of doing the first tests of the new Honda 6. These were very exciting but tiring as well, especially due to my long trip and the effects of jet lag. I could not change to Japanese time as I wanted to be sharp at the weekend when I got back to Monza. Each time the engineers had to make adjustments I went upstairs to the lap scoring room which was air conditioned as the heat was oppressive and napped on the table: as far as my body was concerned, it was the middle of the night. We worked all day long trying to get the handling right, and some of the engineers worked all that night as well in order to make a new swinging arm. We did more tests and more modifications the next day and agreed that although the bike was not yet perfect, it was the best we could do in the time available. We really needed to change the frame, but there was no time for that and I assured them that I would be able to manage at Monza as there were not too many corners, unlike Suzuka where it would have been impossible to cope.

Aika San had worked very hard to get it together and did not seem too sure about racing the bike in this condition. This man who, throughout the 1960s, had been Chief Technician of the Honda team, had worked day and night to get this far, but was worried about the danger to me of riding

The Honda 6

a bike that really was not ready. On the different circuits around the world he directed a team of close to 30 engineers and commanded great respect and liking. He was a very important person within the Honda organization, assuring good liaison between the teams of engineers working in Japan and the engineers with the bikes in Europe. He was someone with a phenomenal capacity to resolve any of the problems we might come up against during the races and always found a solution. After considering all the options, Aika San agreed that, if we wanted to win the coveted 250 title, perhaps it was worth the risk of running the new 6.

It had become obvious that the Yamahas were much too fast for the Honda 4s and that the GP in Monza was going to be decisive. I had to win there and in Japan to take the title, and had already decided that I was prepared to struggle with the handling of the 6 just for the chance of winning the race and the championship. The bike was so fast in a straight line I knew nothing could catch it.

The airline company warned that if we shipped the 6 by freight it could not guarantee that it would arrive on time for the GP in Monza. Consequently we decided to buy five passenger tickets, one each for Aika San and me and three for the 6. Today, of course, it would be impossible to travel with a motorbike in a passenger plane, but the stakes were so high that nothing was going to stand in our way. To disguise the fact that it was a 6 we took off the outside two exhaust pipes and carburetors, which made it look like just another Honda 4. We thought we would give the opposition a bigger shock this way when we started it up and they heard it was a 6.

We did everything possible to keep the 6 a secret right up to the last moment before the first practice. Honda wanted it that way and, frankly, we enjoyed refusing to tell anyone the truth about the new bike and driving them all crazy with curiosity. Because we had taken off the two outside exhaust pipes and carburetors the bike looked like a four cylinder, so word went out that Redman was back with just another new 4. You can imagine how I felt pushing this new bike down off the plane when we arrived in Milan. We wouldn't let anyone else touch it but, of course, had all the usual problems with the customs authorities, although, this being Italy at Italian GP time, they were very helpful. Every Italian is racing mad and, because it was known who we were, they were more interested in looking at the bike and getting a few autographed pictures than anything else.

In a closed garage, Honda engineers were busy putting the extra exhaust pipes and carburetors back on and giving the bike a thorough check to ensure everything was ready for the big moment. What a debut it was: we started up the bike in the garage in our closed-off area, and it was a case of down tools for all the other teams as they came running to see the source of the fantastic noise. To digress for a moment: when I did a few demonstration laps at the Dutch TT in 1995, the same thing happened with the mechanics there. For some time now because of noise pollution, the bikes have had to

Jim Redman

run with silencers on and every time we want to do a demonstration on the 6 we have to apply to the noise abatement people for permission as the bike makes about treble the allowable noise. This has been a major contributor to the drop-off in crowds at the current GPs and I cannot understand why the motorcycle fraternity has let itself be bullied into silencing modern GP bikes, while the Formula 1 cars still sound beautiful and still attract the crowds. Try watching F1 on TV with the volume off, and you'll get my point.

Luigi Taveri was entered for the 250 class at Monza so he took the 4 I had been riding, which was the best we had, and we went out to practice together to compare the speeds of the two bikes. It was crazy how much faster the 6 was; I was able to draw up alongside Luigi, who was flat out, grin and then wind up the throttle and pull away from him with ease. And this at Monza, where the speeds are so high that a slightly slower bike or car can tuck into the slipstream of a faster one and get 'towed' along in the vacuum that the faster machine creates. We pulled into our pits and collapsed laughing, Luigi shook my hand, saying "Congratulations, you have won the 250 World Championship this year for sure. When you passed me I felt like I was riding a 125 not a 250, nothing can beat this bike on the track." I felt the same way, even though the bike's handling left a lot to be desired. I was confident I could manage at Monza, which is a true horse-power circuit.

Aika San and I had already discussed the modifications we would make for the Japanese GP at Suzuka circuit, the last race of the season after Monza, because with the 6 at this stage of its development I could never have won at Suzuka, but Monza was different. As soon as I pulled into the pits, the Honda boys had the bike covered, almost before I had stopped and quickly took it away with the circuit still resounding to that magnificent exhaust note. In later years a fan told me he thought that Honda first designed the sound and then created a bike to make the sound!

Phil Read had been told we had a new bike but that it was just a new 4. He did not believe that, however, and guessed I was preparing something very special. I was in seventh heaven, which caused me to make one of the biggest mistakes of my career. Each practice session I went out with Luigi and although I blasted the bike to maximum for short stretches, I slowed and waited for Luigi so that I could judge how fast to go in order not to make too fast a qualifying lap, when I should have been testing the bike to its limits. During practice the weather was quite overcast, without the usual Monza heatwave and this tricked me as well as it meant that the bike was running nice and cool with everything just perfect.

Race day dawned with a clear blue sky and by the time that racing started it was a real scorcher - this was real Monza weather. We still had no qualms though, as nothing seemed amiss. I got my usual good start and blasted off into the distance, pulling away from the field with ease, which was wonderful after my season-long battles with Phil where I had been down on acceleration and speed every race. The moment of truth had arrived and

The Honda 6

here I was, sitting in the pound seats and cruising away from the field. The motor was starting to get dangerously hot but was still running perfectly: this was a brand new bike so I had no experience to call on and in any case could do nothing but keep on keeping on. Things were perfect for some laps, I forget how many, and then suddenly, on full throttle, the motor cut out completely. My heart lurched as I closed the throttle and it picked up again, then as I opened up it cut again! I found that it would run okay at three-quarter throttle, but as soon I opened up a bit too much it would cut out completely and I would have to shut off and bring it up slowly again. I was not happy at all as I watched my lead slowly dwindle away with the field closing in on me. It was so hard to find the perfect position at which to hold the throttle; all my racing instincts told me to open it more as the field caught up, but would do this too much and the motor would cut, forcing me to shut off completely and start again. Even disabled as I was, it still took Phil a long time to catch and pass me.

By now the motor was so hot that my legs were getting severely burnt. I was juggling with the throttle and had to watch Phil go by. I fought back as best I could and we diced wheel-to-wheel as he battled to pass me and I tried to hold him off, but it was hopeless and all I could do was hope against hope that some miracle would happen and the bike would right itself for the last few laps giving me the chance to pass Phil again. Miracles were in short supply that day though, and Phil went on to win by 10 seconds. Just before the finishing line Mike Duff went past to beat me by 0.3 of a second. This didn't really matter as the championship went with Phil's win.

An interesting aside was that the young, almost unknown rider who finished in 4th place only 13 seconds behind me had also ridden his heart out on a single cylinder Morini to beat the faster MZs. Of course, I did not notice him as I was concerned only with what was happening in front of me. Maybe I should have though, as the following year he was a force to contend with. His name? Giacomo Agostini, he who gave me such a hard time on the 350 in 1965 when he was given the ride on an MV.

After the race Aika San said "Sorry, Jim San." but I told him it was probably more my fault than his. The old story of if only, if only. If only I had ridden harder in practice, if only the weather had been hot in practice, if only the weather had stayed cool for the race ... When I thought of Aika San working flat-out night and day the three weeks before Monza in order to get the bike finished I felt sad and angry. Then there was my frantic trip to Japan to try the bike, sleeping at the track between test sessions while the engineers modified it. When I first arrived in Japan and took the bike out it was almost unrideable so we made stacks of modifications, the kind of things that always need doing but usually over a period of weeks, not hours. This first 6 was tiny, not much bigger than our 125s (against modern bikes it looks really tiny). In Japan during testing, overnight the engineers made a new rear swinging arm to make the bike longer and handle better. But all that effort went up in

171

Jim Redman

smoke when I made the fatal error of not pushing the bike harder; it was a heavy price to pay. I was exhausted as I had been to bed only three nights in the last seven, and was ready to just crawl into a hole and sleep.

I made up for this six weeks later at the Japanese GP as, by then, we had put oil coolers on the bike and modified the frame. In front of Honda's home crowd I blasted off to win by the proverbial mile (or in fact 40 seconds). This was small consolation for losing the championship after all the hard work of Aika San and his team of engineers, and my hard riding on a slower bike earlier in the year. That four cylinder bike, the one I won with at Assen, was given to me by Honda and it still has pride of place at my home as the bike I rode some of my greatest races on. For a rider it is often in the race that he didn't win that he gave his all, and although that 250 race at Assen was one of my greatest wins, I rode my heart out in others that year, only to be beaten by the sheer speed of the Yamaha.

So, the 1964 season ended with disappointment, but I'd still had a good year, taking the 350cc World Championship by winning every single round, an accomplishment not many have equalled, and finishing runner-up in the 250 and 125. It's amazing how your goals change very quickly; just a couple of years before I would have been delighted with those results but, after winning a couple of times, just what is second place but first of the losers ...

There is quite a good story attached to my winning every round. When we got to the German GP we realised it was possible for me to win every round of the championship. During the two days of practice, where I was on pole and easily the quickest, I kept telling Aika San that the motor had a very slight vibration. He made some adjustments but as the vibration persisted after the last practice, decided to strip the motor completely, which I knew meant another night with no sleep for him. I tried to convince him it would be all right for the race as I was confident I could win, but he insisted. He knew that if I said there was something wrong with the bike then there was, unlike some riders who blamed the bike if they were slow, but the engineers soon had them sussed out. Aika San had to strip the whole engine as he found right inside the motor that a small clamp had broken at one end and would have let me down in the race.

We were all very pleased that Luigi won the 125 race at Monza and had taken back from Hugh Anderson the 125 World Championship that Hugh had taken from Luigi in 1963. Luigi is a very good friend and an excellent rider, especially in the 125 class. He was good in all classes and rode in them all from 50cc to 500cc, but the 125 was the one he liked and where he had his most success.

Luigi was professional at all times, as in 1961 when in a do-or-die finish when braking into the last corner, his handlebar snapped clean off: a totally unexpected thing to have happen which would probably have meant a lesser rider crashing, especially as he was dicing on the limit. Luigi wobbled out of control for a moment and then was quick-thinking enough to shoot up the

The Honda 6

slip road and swing around. Rejoining the circuit, and riding with only one handlebar, he got the bike across the finishing line, losing only one place, except to the guy he had been racing. The race organizers in their wisdom had the gall to disqualify him for not rejoining the circuit exactly where he left it, so he lost his 3rd place finish.

12
Two Wheels, or Four?

During the 1964 season we all knew that Honda was building a Formula 1 racing car. Having won five World Championships for Honda, I was starting to look for a new challenge. I was 33, the oldest of the top riders, and felt that perhaps the time had come to follow in the footsteps of others who had made the transition from bikes to cars. Gary Hocking, Jack Brabham and John Surtees - to name but a few - had all given a good account of themselves in cars and Mike Hailwood had become involved with cars as well. My thinking was that if I did want to make the switch, then this was the perfect time to do it as my shares were very high with Honda and I could grow with the car team as I had with the bike team.

I broached the subject with Honda and, after some testing sessions in the car, was told I could make the change to cars - and could have the number two car - as long as I found my own replacement on the bike team. I immediately suggested Mike Hailwood but Honda said no and from there I really had to put my thinking cap on to find the right rider. Previously, I had suggested Ralph Bryans for the 50 and 125 classes and Honda was very pleased with him, so I wanted to find exactly the right person in order to keep up my good record. I tried to persuade the Honda people to reconsider Mike, telling them "If you have Mike, not only do you have him but you don't have to beat him." They weren't convinced, however, and so I had to look again.

As a matter of interest, recently I discovered that Derek Minter, an English rider, had been telling everyone who'd listen that if he had been in the Honda team I would never have won a race. Quite strong talk for a guy known as a short circuit scratcher, who was also good in the Isle of Man and the Ulster. Derek blames me for keeping him out of the Honda team, but I told him when we met at the Classic Bike Show last year that this was not the case. He was never considered as it was widely known that he loved to live at home and do as much as possible of his racing in one day meetings

Two Wheels, or Four?

in England. This love of home comforts kept him from being considered as, even though he sometimes popped over for the Dutch and Belgium GPs, he was not as good on these circuits as the ones he knew so well at home. Derek looked very thoughtful when I explained this to him and told him how, sometimes in my early days, I felt quite envious of him going home to a warm home while we lived in our caravan in the pits. But then, my goal was the World Championship, not home comforts ...

After making a lot of suggestions to Mr Sekiguchi, or 'Poppa San,' as he was affectionately known due to him being a lot older than the rest of us, I asked him who it was he would like to have. The lump in my throat when he said "Another Jim San," felt huge! What a compliment, and coming from him it was like winning another world title. We finally settled on Alan Shepherd who had proved a good, solid runner on an MZ and on his own 350 and 500; it was arranged that he would join me in the team for the last race, the Japanese GP at Suzuka, and then take my place for 1965 while I went off to Formula 1.

After Monza I went to Japan very early and had all the bikes ready with still ten days to go before practice, so I decided to pop to Durban and surprise Marlene and Jimmy, who I'd put on a ship at Southampton bound for Durban in the expectation of not seeing them again until after Suzuka.

When I got back to Japan I was horrified to hear that Alan Shepherd had crashed very badly and sustained a fractured skull and was expected to be in hospital for a long time. When I asked Nobby Clark about the accident, he said that Alan was going well with good times, but had asked Nobby what had been my quickest lap? Nobby told him, adding that I never went that fast here in practice as it is a very hard circuit, even though one I knew well. We think Alan was just trying too hard too soon on new-to-him bikes on a circuit he did not know that well.

The Japanese GP was good to me again that year as I won both the 250 and 350 races, the third year I'd managed this double. I was very proud of the huge scoreboard of results - which took up a whole wall - and had "1st Jim Redman, Rhodesia, Honda" each year for three years for the two classes. I hope it's still there, but maybe it's too long ago now.

Nothing more was said to me about F1 racing until after the GP, when I was told "Meeting with Mr Honda tomorrow, Jim San." At the meeting, Mr Honda told me he now had a big problem with no-one to ride the bikes as all the worthwhile riders had already signed up for the new season. He asked me if I would ride the bikes one more year and race the car in-between when the car meetings did not clash with bike events. It was very hard to say no to a man like Mr Soichiro Honda, but I explained I was anxious that if I did agree to his request something would happen during the year and I would find that my car had been given to someone else. He reassured me on this point, promising that no-one but me would drive my car, even if it meant it did not get used the whole year. He said that the bikes were of paramount

175

Jim Redman

importance to him and please would I do him this favour? What else could I do but put on a brave face and agree? The look on his face and the thanks I got were reward enough; I knew I had made a very powerful friend.

Mr Honda promised I could finish racing bikes at the end of 1965, which would give us ample time to find my replacement and, starting in 1966, I could begin a full-time career in Formula 1 racing. Best of all though, he gave me his absolute word that never, under any circumstances, would anyone else drive my car without my permission!

I had already had a few tests on the Suzuka circuit with Jack Brabham. Jack did not ever race for Honda, but had been invited along with others like Richie Ginther to test Honda's cars and help with the chassis set-up, as Honda had no experience with this aspect of building cars. During tests I was much faster than Jack, who kept telling me to slow down as the handling was not very good. Despite Jack's good advice, I managed to spin the car in a fast curve going at about 150 miles an hour. The back of the car slid out, which meant I was pointed at the barrier and I bumped into the Armco, shortening the car by about a foot. I finished up going backwards, still at over 100mph, but in the right direction. I managed to get the car going the right way and pulled into the pits, which were just around the corner, without losing much time at all. And all this, luckily, with no serious consequences for me, but the front-end of the car was crunched and looked a bit of a mess. The mechanics were all smiles as I pulled in as I had been lapping quite fast, but their faces changed immediately when they saw the state of the car.

The following day, while the engineers and technicians were repairing the car, Honda told me they wanted me to test bikes in all the categories for the Japanese GP, which would take place on the same circuit some weeks later. Jack Brabham said "Off you go and work, while I loaf at the hotel," but I told him "No! I helped you with the car, now you can help me with the bikes". (Few people know that, before becoming World Champion in Formula 1, Jack had had a short career as a motocycle rider in Australia.) So off we both went to the circuit. Jack said he'd start by riding the 50cc but I explained that the smaller the bikes the harder they were to ride. For example, he would not even get the 50 or the 125 off the start line, and might not be able to keep them running because they were so ticklish to ride. The 250 6 was not easy either, and I really did battle to ride the 50, so could not really test it properly. In the end Jack rode only the 350.

As soon as I'd told some of the guys I was retiring from bikes and switching to Formula I, Jack Ahearn asked me to re-form the then defunct and ill-fated Riders Union (my reputation for negotiating was widespread) but I refused, explaining that I have never worked well on a committee as the long-winded discussions and procrastination associated with them frustrated me. However, I did suggest that I take over as manager for, say, the top 50 riders in the world because as such I could negotiate a good deal for all.

We discussed this in great detail and worked out that I could use the

Continued on page 193

Picture Gallery 4

Phil leads Mike and Jim at Hockenheim 1966 on the 250s.

Flashback to Spain — and Jim Redman in a far unhappier position that he found himself in at Hockenheim! In the picture below Jim is sliding down the road having dropped his 250 cc 'six' while leading on the first lap. Team-mate Hailwood snatches a quick look as he speeds past. Above: The Honda has burst into flames but the Spanish firemen are already getting to work with an extinguisher and in moments they had the blaze under control.

Cutting from *Motorcycle News* of the 1966 crash on the 6 at Montjuich Park, Barcelona.

177

Jim Redman

Winning first time out on the 500 Honda – 1966 German Grand Prix at Hockenheim. A first for Honda, and a first for me.

Mike the winner from Jim and Ago. 350 race, Clermont Ferrand 1966.

Picture Gallery 4

The team. Jim and Aika San working on the brakes during practice for the 1965 Isle of Man TT.

Mike leaning on me again ... Hockenheim 1966.

179

Jim Redman

Mike the Bike – "I still don't like the handling." 1966.

Ago leads Jim and Mike during practice at Spa 1966.

Picture Gallery 4

The very popular Nanou with Jack Findlay at Spa 1966.

"What else do I have to do to beat Agostini?" Assen, 1966, 'The 500 Monster.'

Powerboats or motorcycles? Flashback to the very wet Ulster GP of 1964.

181

Jim Redman

1971. Finally getting the MBE at a function in Durban seven years after it had been awarded. Well, I'd been busy!

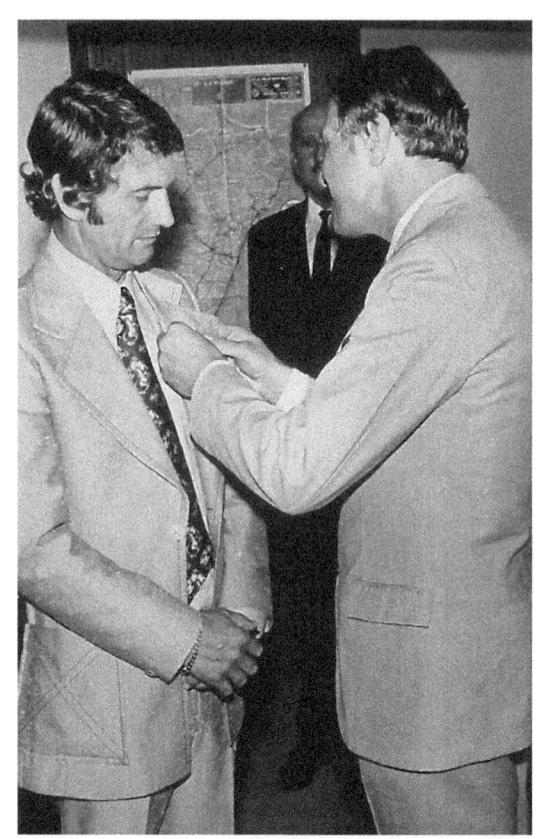

1966. Stuart Graham on the 6 getting the fright of his life, or so he later told me.

182

Picture Gallery 4

Late 1960s. Jim and friend, Pat Clarence, set off from Durban in the State Presidents air race in Jim's Mooney. Marlene was the starter that day.

Jim and Ago share a joke at Daytona in 1996.

183

Jim Redman

Our wedding, May Day 1994.

From left – Dave Roper, Kwezi, Jim, Rob Iannucci with business partner Sonya, Phil, Wendy and Aldo at Clermont Ferrand 1997.

Picture Gallery 4

DJ Andy Kershaw tried the 6 for size. He made his race bike debut on a 1000cc Yamaha a year, or so, later.

"Nearly deafened" Andy Kershaw, famous DJ and motorcycle columnist, pushes Jim off at Scarborough, 1996.

185

Jim Redman

Mobbed by fans at Sachsenring in 1997.

Picture Gallery 4

187

Jim Redman

From left – Stephan Elisat, Kwezi, Jim, Christoph Pietsch and Aldo. Sachsenring 1997.

With Ago and our friend Arnaldo ('Aldo') Wittemberg at Sachsenring 1997.

Picture Gallery 4

Brett grandstanding for his pals and pointing at them.

Brett, many time South African Champion 125, 250 & 500, flying high.

189

Jim Redman

Brett helping his Dad, Jim, at Scarborough 1995.

Picture Gallery 4

Brett with Liane and Jim's grandson, Travis in June 1997.

Jimmy emulating his dad at Welkom, South Africa, in the 1980s.

Jim Redman

Team Obsolete owner Rob Iannucci with (from right) partner Sonia Ewers, Giacomo Agostini, Mick Grant and Jim. Scarborough 1996.

Two Wheels, or Four?

following formula. Each rider would tell me a figure to ask for, and a figure which was the very least he would accept. (If the second figure was too low, I would insist that he raise it in order not to undercut riders of similar ability). I would then present this list of higher figures to the organizers, and let them choose which riders they wanted, whilst knowing from the lower figures how much leeway I had in which to negotiate. During these discussions, Phil Read asked me - in front of a few riders - what I would want to make out of this. I explained that, as I felt I had done well out of racing, I would be happy to take, say, 5 per cent from each of them to cover my travel and communication expenses, as my main motivation was not the money but to try and raise the standard for those riders at the bottom end of the scale. Such riders had no real bargaining power as there were so many of them of similar ability that the organizers could pick and choose. It annoyed me that with the hundreds of thousands of spectators who paid to attend the meetings, the FIM officials and the organizers - who by and large were one and the same - were living off the fat of the land whilst a lot of riders endured terrible conditions and did not even eat properly. Phil's question made me realize that if I did manage the top 50 riders, they would include Phil and a few others who were quite impossible to reason with in those days. We were all - including myself - young, hot-headed and impatient. I told them to forget it: I was tired of travelling and thought I would give myself loads of problems and aggravation if I took on this responsibility. Who knows, but had I done it I might have finished up the motorcycle equivalent of F1's Bernie Ecclestone.

At the end of 1964, Marlene and I had decided it was time for us, with Jimmy then five years old, to have a house of our own for the first time in our lives. We found a modest house in Westville, a very attractive suburb of Durban and from then on Marlene stayed at home when I was competing. As soon as there was a spare weekend, I jumped on the first flight home to Durban for a week or ten days. During school holidays, Marlene used to join me in Europe for a few weeks which was great, but most of the time I travelled alone.

In 1964, the fact that we were now settled in our own home encouraged us to consider a second child. Before this it had been impossible for us to even think about it as travelling full-time with one child is bad enough. Two would have been impossible and my career had to come first: I had invested too much time and effort getting where I was to take my eye off the ball now. Brett was born on May 2nd 1965. At the time he was born I was away racing (in Italy this time for the first meetings of the 1965 season, so we were all at Elvio's). By coincidence, on this particular evening for no reason at all a phenomenal party had developed which ended late that night. Mike Hailwood, Frank Perris, Elvio Marconi and myself were in a pitiful state the next day. We all drank much too much and had huge hangovers when a telegram arrived from Marlene in which she said "Jimmy has a brother."

Jim Redman

I phoned to congratulate her and find out how she was, as well as how the baby was, and she said "I guess you boys will wet the baby's head tonight in traditional fashion." I told her that by a sheer fluke we had done so the night before, right on the day he was born, and that none of us were in any state to party again that night. We named our son Gary Brett Redman, in memory of Gary Hocking, but always used his second name of Brett.

During this same period, when we were in Imola for the international meeting, Mike Hailwood and I had a very friendly discussion with Giacomo Agostini. We felt that, having more experience than him, we should give him some advice about handling his future career, which appeared very promising; it was obvious that soon his name would be there with ours at the top of the billboards and it was important to us that he should be paid properly, if only to safeguard the status we had worked so hard to acquire. With his big Italian grin, Agostini told us he had been very well paid for the Imola race and how much it was. When he saw the expressions on our faces he asked, vaguely worried "It's not enough?" It came as a big shock to him when told that Mike and I had each received more than seven times the amount he had. He let fly a few choice Italian words that did not need an interpreter to understand and vowed he would never be short-changed again. Agostini was a good pupil as he quickly learned how to defend his own interests and to ask for more money from the organizers. Much later on, when he was at the top of his profession, he came to visit us in South Africa and admitted he'd had a few easy years once Mike and I had retired. I asked about the money and, with a smile, he said he now received the equivalent of Mike's, mine and his own, and thanked me warmly for having shown him the way.

Later on during the TT races, Mike and I had taught Giacomo a few elementary words of English, so that he could at least speak to all the girls who hung around him. He asked us how he could start up a conversation with the girls; just a couple of simple sentences to say good morning/evening, how are you, etc. We told him that the most elegant way to introduce oneself in English, was to say "Would you come to bed with me?" He learnt this sentence by heart, then asked us what he should say next when the girl replied. Mike told him, with a straight face, that the best reply - which would be a suitable response to anything the girls said - was "Fuck my old boots," and so off he went to practice his command of the English language. Last year he and I gave after-dinner talks at a few meetings at which I told this story. However, Giacomo had the last laugh as he was able to tell the listeners that, in fact, many of the girls he asked had said "Yes" ...

Before the 1965 season had even started, Honda engineers had doubled their efforts during the winter to ensure supremacy of the 6. The bike had been completely revamped and like the previous year was shrouded in secrecy. It was not, however, the only bike to attract attention as the 350 had also been completely updated in the constant quest for more power and speed. We have to pay tribute to the Honda engineers who worked relentlessly to

Two Wheels, or Four?

make the bikes capable of outstanding performance: it was a real team effort. Few really appreciate the time, self-sacrifice and devotion that goes into this work; it was nothing to spend 10 to 16 hours a day preparing and improving the machines, and then going over them yet again. Throughout my career I never ever saw or heard an engineer complain; I believe they knew better than anyone that they were right at the heart of a fabulous adventure. Most nights, once the job was over, the men were so bushed that they went directly to bed, or sometimes directly to breakfast and back to work again for a new day! But they always had the same smile, the same concentration and the same enthusiasm, day after day. It's these men that made Honda such a powerful force in the world of racing.

You can imagine the conversations that went on with riders and engineers of all nationalities; Japanese, English, Swiss, Irish - don't ask me how everyone managed to understand each other! All I know is that the marvellous, magical atmosphere meant that everyone got on very well. The only minor difficulty was trying to follow Ralph Bryans' very broad Irish accent - I often found it harder to understand Ralph than Aika San.

Nobody outside of team members - and especially not a member of a competitor's factory team - was allowed into the workshops or pits to see what was going on. Too many secrets could be discovered and stolen, and when the bikes were in pieces the workshop was often transformed into a real bunker. Only people we knew had access. The security guards were ordered to keep their eyes open and keep out any intruders, especially during the night when the engineers allowed themselves a few hours' sleep. If someone did manage to get past the security and into the workshops where the engineers were working, the machines were immediately covered with sheets, especially if the intruder was carrying a camera.

I believe it is because of the engineers' devotion to duty that I was able to achieve so many good results and win so many titles. I was always confident when I took off in a race knowing nothing had been left to chance; even technical problems were rectified in perfect calm and co-ordination. When I looked at my bikes I was gripped by an incredible feeling of confidence, pride and satisfaction. Who wouldn't have been? They were always so reliable, clean and perfectly turned out for the job they were asked to do. It's not difficult to understand now why Honda is among the greatest constructors in the world. I knew that my machine was the best and when I took it out for training I had a good feel for the slightest imperfection, which the Honda engineers would be sure to find and fix.

I had just won three World Championships in the 350 category one after the other, and was expected to do it again this year. This was without taking into account a certain young Italian - incredibly gifted, with a promising future - who had already shown what he was capable of the previous year on a 250. Giacomo Agostini, with his Morini, had just robbed Tarquinio Provini of his national 250 title, and at the end of the 1964 season had distinguished

Jim Redman

himself by twice finishing in fourth place in the German and Italian GPs. Ago was a fearless young man, with the good looks and charm of a film star, very 'Italian' in his manner and just 23 years old. He possessed a mixture of charm and seductiveness that made every woman fall in love with him, and he was full of life.

As soon as Ago started to 'shine,' Count Domenica Agusta, the MV factory boss, took a particular interest in him and watched him closely. The Count was always looking for an Italian rider to represent his MV company, and thereby end the supremacy of the Anglo-Saxon riders. At the end of the 1964 season, he decided to sign up Agostini for the 1965 season, all the while quietly preparing a new 350 machine in order that his new prodigy had the means to achieve his ambitions. Agostini became Mike Hailwood's new team mate. During this season, Count Agusta preferred to let the Italian race the new three-cylinder, so Hailwood raced it only on rare occasions. The fight between MV and Honda was going to be merciless ...

The first round of the 1965 Formula 1 Car World Championship was held at the Nürburgring circuit in Germany, I travelled up from the Spanish GP and arrived the day before official practice was due to start. As I was travelling up through Germany the weather became worse and worse and I thought to myself "What a start to my F1 career, the long circuit at the Nürburgring in appalling weather." Talk about in at the deep end; I'd never driven a racing car in a race in my life and could not have picked a worse debut venue. Not only was it pouring with rain, it was bitingly cold and the rain was falling as ice or sleet. No sooner had I arrived than the Honda Racing Car Team Manager asked if he could speak with me. He explained that Ronnie Bucknum, Honda's other Formula 1 driver, had had an accident during unofficial practice the day before and his car had been completely destroyed. The Team Manager had phoned Honda in Japan to get permission to use my car so that Ronnie could continue to race at Nürburgring, as he had already accumulated points for the World Championships. Honda in Tokyo said that Ronnie Bucknum would have to get permission from Mr Honda, since he had promised the car to me. Ronnie spoke next to Mr Honda, who told him he had promised me that nobody else would drive my car. Mr Honda, the Team Manager declared, left the decision to me but had said that whatever it was he would support it. So, either I lent my car to Ronnie, which meant he would have a chance to gain some more points for the title, or raced myself and started my career in Formula 1. What a decision. I said I needed to think about it for a few minutes. I weighed up the pros and cons: the car was not yet completely competitive, the weather was terrible (it was still raining and bitterly cold), and this circuit was one of the most difficult in the world. I could not see how I would achieve good results under these conditions, and it was very important to me to have the best possible debut as lots of eyes would be on me. Graham Hill had already said he'd heard I was coming over to cars to show him and his fellow drivers how to drive. I

Two Wheels, or Four?

protested that it was the other way around, I was coming to learn from him and the other top drivers, but we all know what the press do to make a story ... Added to this, I was not sure what Mr Honda really wanted me to do. In the end I decided to give my car to Ronnie, and for the rest of the year kept my eye on his progress in Formula 1 racing. When I saw his disappointing results for the rest of the season and the problems with the car, I decided once and for all that I would stay with the bikes where I had a good chance of winning. I found it quite extraordinary that someone like Mr Honda, with all his prestige and power, would let me make the final decision, but he proved he was a man of honour and a man of his word. He had the same respect for me as I for him.

Mr Honda was a genuine and modest person. To see him working, in his overalls, in the midst of his engineers, you'd never imagine he was the 'big boss.' He was the personal inventor and owner of an incredible number of patents and was never happier than when he had solved a problem with his team of engineers, or when he found a way to beat his rivals in the races. He had started out in life with nothing, but knew how to instill in all his employees his love for a job well done and his sense of loyalty. He and his team took enormous pride in everything they did and his employees would have worked an eight-day week and twenty-five hour day if he'd asked them.

Later on Mr Honda was awarded the Blue Ribbon Medal for his exceptional contribution to the Japanese economy. Bestowed by the Emperor, this was the ultimate Japanese honour. When a member of the Japanese government advised him of the protocol of the ceremony and told him it was necessary to wear a morning suit, Mr Honda at first said that if a normal two-piece suite was not good enough he would not go. He later relented, realizing he had gone a little too far, and wore the ceremonial dress of the day which he hired or borrowed.

As the money from motorcycle sales around the world started pouring in, Mr Honda continued his quest for perfection. To achieve this dream he spent money unstintingly, setting up a Research and Development Centre with over 600 engineers and scientists in an immense complex which occupied 17 acres of land close to Tokyo. (I believe that today Honda has more than one of these R & D centres with a staff of over 5000.) A new factory was built at Suzuka which was capable of constructing one 50cc motocycle every fourteen seconds on each of two production lines, creating a finished machine every seven seconds. In 1996 Kwezi and I went back to this factory, which now produces about 2200 cars a day.

But Mr Honda wasn't going to stop there. Already the biggest motocycle constructor in the world, he also wanted to do something to boost the sport of racing in Japan. As mentioned previously, he undertook construction of one of the best circuits in the world: Suzuka, which was - and still is - one of the best looking and best organized circuits I've seen. Ten per cent of the finance came from Honda, the rest from Honda suppliers and employees.

Jim Redman

When the Japanese first started motorcycle racing, even though Japanese bikes were widely available throughout the world, Japanese riders had no experience of international motorcycle racing and were not quite good enough against the strong competition found in World Championships. There were exceptions to this rule - riders such as Kunimitsu Takahashi and Fumio Ito, for example. But, although fast, they did not have the experience that the rest of us did and the result was bad accidents caused by going too fast, too soon. The new Suzuka circuit meant that up-and-coming younger riders could train more often and improve enough to have a chance at some of the top positions in World Championships.

My attention that year was focused on the 250cc category as I was fairly confident of once again winning my 350 title, as there had been nothing to touch me for the last three years. More than anything, I wanted to win back my 250 title, especially as I had discovered that Phil Read had won the 250 race easily in the American GP at Daytona, finishing in front of his team mate Mike Duff. This was the famous race I had obstinately refused to attend the year before and we did not go in 1965 either, so my first race against Phil was at the Nürburgring in Germany.

However, before the 250 race I first had to get the 350 event out of the way, and here I was facing a new challenge from Agostini, who had beaten me for pole position in practice. This did not worry me unduly as I made a habit of not practicing too hard and knew I had lots of reserve for the race. What I didn't know, of course, was that this man and his new MV was going to harass me in this race and throughout the year.

I led for the first few laps with Giacomo right behind me, and was feeling quite confident whilst sizing up the various wet patches under the trees that were still around this early in the day. At the uphill part of the circuit I pulled a big slide on a wet patch and before I could recover had slid right across the road nearly into the hedge and was hitting the hedge alongside the road with my shoulder. I was clinging on as best I could, trying to regain control of the bike before the road twisted even more to the left getting me into even more trouble, but to no avail. Through the hedge I went, luckily, without breaking any bones, but I did suffer some pretty severe bruising. I was carted off to hospital as I had hurt my arm pretty badly, to the extent that it could have been fractured, but it was only badly bruised. There was consternation in the Honda camp: Agostini had claimed his first GP victory and I had to withdraw from the following race, the 250, to the great delight of Phil Read and the Yamaha Team, who went on to win it with team mate Mike Duff closely behind, thereby re-enacting their victory at Daytona.

The following GP race was to be held on one of my best circuits, Montjuich Park in Barcelona, where there wasn't a 350 race. Because of my injured arm I had decided not to ride in the 125 race and concentrate my efforts on the 250.

The first day of practice was absolutely catastrophic for me. By the

Two Wheels, or Four?

end of the session I was furious with myself as I just could not manage the 6 on such a tight, twisty rider's circuit and nurse my injured arm at the same time, it just was not on. I phoned Japan and spent two hours talking to Hisakazu Sekigushi, Poppa San, head of the Racing Department, explaining my problem. It was no good my going out and settling for just a podium position, I had to go out and try and win, but felt that by so doing there was a high risk of my crashing again as my arm was not strong enough. Should I risk putting myself out for the season if I crashed again, or should I give Barcelona a miss and get my arm better for the French GP which was the following weekend? Poppa San had no doubts, he was all for me not riding, but then his first concern was always for his rider's safety; winning was important but safety was the number one concern to him. He'd seen too many riders killed and did not want any more deaths in our team, so he urged me not to ride. I knew that was the sensible thing to do even though I just wanted to ride and win. In the end he made me see sense and not ride, a choice made somewhat easier by the atrocious pain in my arm (we didn't have the painkillers available today.) My absence from the race was, of course, a big help to Phil Read, for whom winning this event was becoming a mere formality. The results of these first three GP races of the season were of great concern to myself and Honda: out of the three 250 races in which he had competed, Phil had won all three and I had yet to score a single point for the championships. In fact, I'd still not competed in a single 250 race.

This situation would have to change drastically, and soon, if I was to have any chance of winning the title. It was now imperative that I not only ride in the French GP, but win it too.

Things started off well in France as I was quickest in the first practice session: was this an encouraging sign from fate signifying a change of luck? During the rest of the trials the 6 made the best time and, when the race started, I went to the front right away and soon had a comfortable lead. Once again, my joy was short-lived as my gearbox let me down in the middle of the race and I was obliged to retire. The only redeeming feature was that at least I had started in my first race that year and had led it. I felt under so much tension and strain as Phil continued his incredible climb towards the title and won his fourth consecutive victory. His lead over me was at that time enormous: 32 points to nil as we set off to the Isle of Man.

The TT - the most difficult circuit of the whole season - which both fascinated and frightened me was definitely not my best circuit. All the experts predicted another win for Phil of course, as most of them were English too. However, with the TT, I knew that it's never over until it's over as it is such a long race, often with changing weather conditions. To have even the barest chance of winning such a difficult race it's necessary to pace yourself, so that you're still there at the end. I had the added worry of wondering if the 6 would run reliably, but I knew Phil and the Yamaha camp had the same worry with their machines. Phil liked the Isle of Man and was quite hard on

199

Jim Redman

his machines there, which had worked in my favour before.

It began as everyone expected; Phil had the best time in practise but my Honda had the fastest top speed (as I had been practising in my usual conservative fashion, I knew it left plenty of scope for a surprise). From the start of the race I went as hard as I could and was in the lead on the road as my starting number was 2. At the end of the first lap, in spite of a speed of over 100mph, Phil - who had started 20 seconds later - was now close behind me. He overtook me on the second lap but, for once, the Gods were with me and his engine succumbed to the thrashing he was giving it. I had a feeling he was pushing too hard when he passed me, so I chased him as hard as I could to put the maximum pressure on him and his bike and was delighted when, for a change, he became the victim and had to abandon the race. When I saw him suddenly sit up and grab hold of his clutch, I knew that he was finished. My Honda covered the six laps without the slightest problem; I had at last achieved my much-needed first victory of the season.

My success in the TT did not stop Phil defeating me in Holland, in the next GP race at Assen. There, after problems with my gearbox, I had to let him go and finished in second place behind him. In return, during the following GPs at Spa in Belgium and on the Sachsenring circuit in East Germany, my Honda proved its reliability and immense potential and I carried off both victories. Each time, Phil took second place, which was not too good for me.

At Sachsenring, because the 250 race was much more exciting than the 500 race (which was just a formality for Mike Hailwood on the MV) it was decided to run the 250 after the 500 as the last and most important race of the day. It was a wet day, the first since resurfacing of the famous Sachsenring track, so we had no idea if the surface was good or bad. Remember, the old surface was cobblestones through the villages, of which there were several, so the FIM had insisted on a complete resurface in order to grant World Championship status to the circuit.

I was keen to find out how good the surface was in the rain but wanted to be the only one who had this information. Then I had an ingenious idea about how to out-fox Phil Read. I asked Mike Hailwood to stroll down past all of us, when he had finished on the podium, as we lined up for the start of the 250 race. I would call out to him and ask how the track was and he would shout back the exact opposite. So, as he walked back past us I called out "How is the track in the wet, Mike?" to which he replied "Be bloody careful, it's fucking slippery," which, of course, really meant the opposite. As I had hoped, Phil heard the exchange and when the race began he started out very cautiously, expecting to come across some very slippery sections, whilst I shot off like a rocket getting a tremendous lead on the first lap. This ploy definitely helped me win this race as I had around a 15 second lead on the first lap; the secret was getting such a good early lead that Phil would not try as hard as he would if we were close together. Nevertheless, despite

Two Wheels, or Four?

this win, my overall problem remained the same: Phil had a comfortable lead on me in the championship and it was going to be difficult to catch up and win back the title. On top of this I also had to defend my 350 title, which was under threat from Ago, although thanks to my last four results, I had at least a slight lead over him in the 350 class, but it was not all over yet - quite the contrary ...

At the Ulster GP the weather was usually deplorable. The circuit was situated in the main rain catchment area of Belfast so it was often pouring, resulting in flooded paddock and pits. The working areas were for the most part fields which became a sea of mud, with spectators squeezing into the pits and around the teams and bikes like sardines. There were no comfortable covered areas with decent pits in which to work and repair our machines properly. The toilets were a disaster and it was a struggle to find something to eat.

Around 80-100,000 people turned out to watch the GP, but only a few paid for grandstand seats - entrance was free as the race was held on public roads - which meant the organizers were always struggling to find funds. A major part of their revenue came from the cars which parked in the fields surrounding the circuit, or from those that paid for a seat in the grandstands or a ticket to get into the paddock. The crowds were very enthusiastic about their racing and very knowledgeable about everything to do with GP racing. They turned out in their thousands in the most appalling weather and were lovely people. The organizers, especially Billy McMasters, did their best to meet all the needs of the different teams and tried as hard as they could to keep this circuit a part of the GP calendar. They met all their commitments, which was not very easy considering the conditions and difficulties they encountered.

I detested the conditions we had to endure for this race and yet I loved the people. Despite the bad weather they kept a sense of humour: they said if you could see the mountains of Scotland it was going to rain and if you couldn't it was already raining! For someone who had become accustomed to the sunny skies of Rhodesia and South Africa, I found all this rain depressing.

The Ulster was bad for me that year as I had the same type of accident that I'd had in the German GP. This time though I was alone in the lead and on the last lap of the 350 race, and well ahead of the other riders. I came round a very fast bend to find that the rain had turned the circuit there into a sea of mud. People with mud on their boots had been crossing the track on the straight just before that corner all day, which did not matter while the circuit remained dry, but after a sharp shower it became a disaster area. The marshalls were good as they saw the danger and ran up the road towards the corner, waving their flags to warn oncoming riders, but I had a good lead and arrived there first before they could run far enough up the road to give a decent warning. I slid madly on this mud, could not keep the bike up

Jim Redman

on its wheels and fell fairly hard, but was on my feet as soon as I stopped sliding down the road as I knew I had time to get back on and still win the race, such was the lead I had. I picked the bike up and saw that the front mudguard was jamming the wheel. As I tried to bend it back off the wheel, I noticed that the wheel rim was badly bent - I had no chance of riding this last lap and winning.

Once I gave up I started to feel the pain in my shoulder and realised I had broken my collarbone, which made me very cross as I knew the injury would stop me taking part in the 250 race later that day. Even more importantly, I would probably not be able to ride in the next GPs in Finland and Italy. To my shame I turned my anger on the doctor that arrived to check me out, saying "Come on, let's get the figure of eight bandage on my shoulders so that I can get back to the pits and get things sorted out." He was very calm and nice and told me I should go to hospital for an x-ray, but I wouldn't hear of it and told him it was just a waste of time: we could all see the collarbone was broken so he should shove the bandage on my shoulders and I'd be on my way. I was beside myself with rage and blamed my own stupidity for letting the conditions catch me out as they had. I punished myself with the pain of staggering around with a broken collarbone.

Phil Read was declared World Champion in the 250cc category, even though there were still three GPs left on the calendar in which to compete. I was in complete despair and even though my collarbone was not completely healed, announced my intention to participate in the Italian GP at Monza after missing the Finnish GP. Aika San persuaded me not to ride at Monza and made it easier for me by announcing that none of the Honda team would race in this GP. Despite this, at the last minute the 350 was transported to Milan but, since I wasn't there, it never left the packing case ...

After all these disappointments and accidents, I felt I needed some space in which to get back on my feet again. I wanted some peace and quiet most of all, and who better to provide this than Elvio, my good Italian friend, who I knew could raise my spirits and help me get my body back into shape. So, as we had done every year, Mike Hailwood and I went to Elvio's hotel for a well-deserved rest.

In a motoring magazine that Mike was reading one day there was an article about a new Ferrari. Mike turned to me and said "The new 2+2 Ferrari looks just right for us, we should buy one each." Elvio, who claimed he knew everyone, said to Mike "If you want to buy this new model Ferrari, I will telephone my friend Enzo Ferrari and ask him to drive his one down and let you try it out." True to form, this was Elvio; slightly larger-than-life and very flamboyant, exaggerating just how well he knew people and saying on this occasion "Enzo is my big friend, he'll come down for lunch." Without believing this story for one minute, we replied, a mite sarcastically, "Of course, Elvio, you tell your friend Enzo Ferrari to come down here with his car for us to try; he's bound to want to drive a couple of hundred kilometers just to see

Two Wheels, or Four?

us." Elvio didn't falter, just went to the telephone and phoned Enzo Ferrari, owner of one of - if not *the* greatest - racing car stables in history. Elvio came back a few minutes later to say that Mr Ferrari had accepted his invitation and would come to lunch with us in a few days with his latest Ferrari ...

On the morning of the day in question, Elvio told us not to forget that we had agreed to have lunch and spend part of the day with Mr Ferarri. Of course, we still thought it was a joke and that at most a salesman would appear with the car but not the great Enzo himself. You can imagine our amazement, then, when the magnificent Ferrari that Mike had seen in the magazine pulled into the hotel driveway. To cap it all, Enzo Ferrari stepped out of the car, a big smile on his lips, his hand outstretched to shake Elvio's and give him a bear hug. He came across to shake our hands and told us how happy and proud he was to finally make our acquaintance as he had been reading about our exploits for years. What a fantastic shock; meeting this living legend left us speechless, but to discover that he knew all about us and was proud to meet us (whilst we considered the honour to be entirely ours) was astounding. He was a real gentleman, too: quiet and modest about his achievements, not at all like the public impression he gave of being the authoritative proprietor of the most famous car factory in the world.

Enzo was quite surprised that Mike and I should spend time together on holiday when we raced for two completely different teams, and he was very interested in everything which concerned our world of motorbikes, asking particularly pertinent questions about this subject that fascinated him so much. After lunch, he gave us the keys to his car and invited us to try it out. Because it was Enzo Ferrari's own car we pushed it to the limit, knowing full well that Mr Ferrari would have no trouble having even the slightest mechanical fault repaired at his factory. Back at the hotel we told him what a really excellent car we thought it was. He said that if we'd each like one he could let us have them for a very good price. Jokingly, we told him that as we were motocycle World Champions we should get them free of charge. Pouring him another glass of wine, we said "Come on, Enzo, you can spare two cars for us." Sipping his wine he said "OK! You buy one and the other I'll give to you ..." We couldn't believe our ears. Mike and I looked at each other, astonished, and immediately accepted the deal, paying half each, before he changed his mind. Delivery was fixed for early in the 1966 season, and so, that year we found ourselves the proud owners of a brand new Ferrari each!

But back to the 1965 races. I had only to finish in second place in the 350 category at the Japanese GP in Suzuka to win the World Championship in this class, and I didn't want to blow this and finish the year with no title at all. Even if Ago won the race, as long as I was second I would still take the title. I had to do everything in my power to beat him or get second place, and with Hailwood in the race on his last ride for MV I had my work cut out to finish second. There was going to be no help from Mike either; he'd made

Jim Redman

no secret of the fact that he was going for a win and we'd have to fight it out. Honda took this race meeting very seriously, and besides wanting me to clinch the 350 title, badly wanted to beat the new 250 four-cylinder Yamaha which would be crowned World Champion at this GP in Suzuka, and which almost everyone thought was a bike capable of beating off all competition.

Also, before the GP in Japan, I had explained to Honda that if I was to race in three categories - 250, 350 and 500cc - in 1966, it was imperative I be given some help in the shape of a new team mate that was up to the task. Honda agreed so once again I put forward Mike Hailwood's name, which this time was accepted. I had at last convinced Honda that with Mike on the team, we would have one of the best riders in the world. Mike was not happy with his position within the MV factory team. Giacomo Agostini was taking over more and more and Mike had the uncomfortable impression that the mechanics, all Italians, were solidly behind Agostini and providing him with a better machine than they did Mike. At the MV factory - and unlike Honda - all the bikes were not identical and some were much quicker than others. At Honda each of us had exactly the same machine, and somehow Honda made them all almost identical in speed and all-round performance.

During the time I was recovering from my Ulster crash I discussed Mike at great length with Honda. In September 1965, Mike received a 'surprise' telegram from Honda Team Manager, Mr Hisakazu Sekiguchi, inviting him to join the team and ride, amongst other machines, the famous Honda 6. Unfortunately, Mike discovered he had a contractual problem with MV, to whom he was tied right up until the last race of the World Championships. Of course, he was obliged to respect the contract and give Agostini all the help he could so that he could win the 350 title. Under these conditions, riding the 6 seemed difficult for Mike but, because traditionally the 350 race was on the first day of racing in Japan and the 250 race on the second, he could do it. It must have seemed strange for Mike during practice as he was in both camps, riding the 250 for us and the 350 for MV. After the 350 race Mike would be free from his contract and the next day we were both to race in the 250 class, riding modified, upgraded 6s which had been specially prepared for the Japanese GP.

Our fans were, of course, extremely important to us and we valued them highly. However, they did annoy us slightly when we were really in a hurry trying to get a bike ready and the crowds would actually get in the way when we were trying to get the job done. This happened in Japan, although the culprits were mostly journalists who were so anxious to get a story about Mike and his impressions of the Hondas that they crowded around him as he came in from his first practice. They asked what he thought of the 6 and he told them "Loads of power," and the handling, they asked, to which Mike replied "Bloody awful." I told him "Hey, Mike, it's taken me two years to get you into the team so don't stuff it up in five minutes." Mike told the reporters "I now appreciate what a good rider Jim is for riding these things all these

Two Wheels, or Four?

years and not complaining about the way they handle."

With regard to the 350 race, my attitude had been this: I was up against Mike, the rider with the most natural talent the world has ever seen in the history of racing (including modern-day riders like Mick Doohan.) My job was to beat him, and to do that I had to take an unconventional approach. Honda's bikes were shorter, lower, lighter and had more power than the MV, which made them quite twitchy to ride. I had learnt to cope with this over the years, finding that with the extra acceleration and speed the bikes had, I could make up on the next straight anything I lost in the corners. If the race went right down to the wire I could make an extra-special effort towards the end of the race when I knew just where the bike would leap around over the bumps. Luckily, that did not happen too often as my extra speed usually got me away, especially on the 350.

In Japan in the 350 race I was alone against two giants: Hailwood and Agostini. I knew that my Honda would do the job and I'd always liked Suzuka circuit, so was pretty confident I could beat at least one of the MVs if not both. Honda prepared a 350 6 for me to use especially for this race, which was a forerunner of the bike we would use against the 350 MVs in 1966. But I felt it safer to use the tried and tested 4 to be sure of finishing at least second, if not winning. I rode a few laps on the 6 in practice to test it out but, despite superior acceleration and top speed, felt the handling needed more development. So I rode my old 4-cylinder in the race and left the 6-cylinder in the hands of the house test rider, Kasuya, who, by the way, finished third in the race. Mike won this race, his last for MV, whilst both Ago and I had problems. Early in the race the three of us were dicing together when, suddenly, I felt what seemed like a stone in the side of my helmet just below my goggles. I did nothing about it but then felt a sharp pain in the side of my face and realised it was a bee or wasp, not a stone, I bashed the side of my face with my fist and managed to kill it before it did any more damage but my face was very sore as I raced on. Luckily for me, shortly after this Ago was forced to drop back with a problem with his bike, allowing me to finish just behind Mike and carry off, with the greatest of pleasure for me and Honda, the 350 title for the fourth consecutive year.

I almost didn't finish the race as toward the end my eye had closed up completely from the bee sting, as you will see in the photo which was taken just after the end of the race. Fortunately for me, the swelling had been a gradual process and I was able to adjust to the steady loss of vision. By the end of the race, I couldn't see a thing out of this eye and was just happy to cruise around and take my safe second place to win the title. When I arrived at the Honda pits the team was very excited that we had won the title again, but as soon as I took off my helmet their faces dropped in horror at the sight of my face. The swelling was huge and it looked worse than it was because of the marks of my goggles still on it and the dirt from the race. The doctors cleaned me up and gave me an injection but, of course, it was obvious I could

Jim Redman

not ride in the 250 race. In any case, Phil Read had already been declared World Champion in this category. However, it did serve to illustrate just what a good decision it had been to have Mike join the team as he went out and won the race for Honda. All-in-all it was a nice result for Mike as he'd fulfilled his obligations to MV by winning the 350 race the day before, and pleased his new Honda team from Mr Honda down by winning the 250 race for us!

Previous to all of this, I had been very happy to see Ralph Bryans pick up the World Championship title in the 50cc category on his minuscule Honda. Honda had asked me to chose an unknown rider for this class who was small in size and not too well known, but capable of winning the 50cc World Championship title. My choice was Ralph, whom I'd noticed at the Ulster GP, where he had ridden superbly on his Norton 500 with the right amount of aggression mixed with the temperament necessary to make a World Champion. Seeing him take the title on the tiny Honda 50 gave me almost as much satisfaction as winning my own title. Honda made a special point of congratulating me on my 'excellent choice,' as they put it. I knew they'd be even more pleased with my choice of Mike for the big bikes.

Honda also invited me to chose an unknown young rider to race the 250 and 350 production machines, with a view to preparing him for the factory team later. This individual was to ride for me, but Honda would give me the bikes and the spare parts so that I could sponsor the rider as my protégé. I chose Bruce Beale, a fellow Rhodesian, who could perhaps carry on the Rhodesian tradition of Amm, Redman and Hocking and who was also from Bulawayo like Gary and myself. I knew Bruce was a good rider with the right approach to his racing and serious enough about it to go to the top in a few years' time. Bruce had very good results during the 1965 and 1966 seasons, all on the 125, 250 and 350 production twin racers but, unfortunately for him, Honda decided to reduce the size of the team, and it was for this reason that he was replaced by a more experienced rider. Thereafter, Bruce was not able to obtain a factory ride and retired from racing at the end of 1966.

The 1965 season had been full of surprises, right up until the end. However, it was nothing compared to what was going to happen the following season ...

Right from the start Mike had problems with the Honda's handling. In some respects the way the bikes handled was my fault, as years before I had elected to keep the Hondas shorter and lighter than the MVs. This gave them more acceleration and top speed and, as I knew I had Mike to beat, I figured this was the best way to do it. The bikes jumped and wriggled a bit but, over the years, I had got used to it and I loved the way they responded coming out of the corners. In the early part of a race they sometimes gave you a few good frights, but as the race progressed you got into the groove and handled it. And the extra speed and acceleration meant you won races.

Mike came along, used to the way the heavier MVs handled, and was straight in at the deep end. He did not like the jumping and wriggling one

Two Wheels, or Four?

bit, which was especially obvious with the 500. I thought then - and still do now - that the bike handles very well; I'm much happier on the 500 Honda than on the 500 MV and feel sure I can go faster on the Honda. I am amused that everyone who tests the 500 considers it an unrideable monster just because Mike said it was. It just goes to show the respect everyone has for him. I seem to be the only person in the world who thinks it's a good bike and handles well. Because it had received such bad press, when I got on it again at Suzuka in 1996 I was a bit apprehensive, as I thought maybe I could not trust my memory. Happily, once on board, I found it to be the same bike I remembered from 1966, which goes like mad for its age and handles very well. Of course, I could not do it justice now, but I did at Assen in 1966 and you just can't ride as I did that day on a circuit like Assen if your bike does not handle well.

It was really great to have Mike as a team mate as we'd always got on well right from when we met in South Africa in 1957. We understood each other so well and trusted each other implicitly. We were looking forward to 1966, especially me as it was great to have Mike to take some of the pressure off me. I'd been on my own for a long time on the 250 and 350 Hondas but now, not only did I have Mike to help me, I did not have to go out and try and beat him either! I looked forward to a good year, one where maybe I could take life a bit easier, with a leisurely win in the 500 World Championship, the way Mike had on the MV for a few years. As it happened, it turned out to be a really bad year for me as my season ended so early in the year at Francorchamps. And not just my season, either, but my entire career ...

Mike had said some nice things about me to the press in relation to my riding of the Hondas. After the first tests, his comments were, to say the least, somewhat cutting: "These bikes are absolutely terrifying to ride. How did Jim ever ride these things for a whole season, in fact, for years, without complaining? Redman is a superb rider, I am telling you, much better than any of you press guys have given him credit for ... To be able to ride these things one has to be a hero. He should get a Victoria Cross." Mike rambled on and on, and when Honda people were not there I loved it. The press had not been very magnanimous towards me throughout my career and here was the greatest motorcycle rider the world has ever known, bar none, singing my praises to the tree tops.

After riding the very heavy, very stable MVs, Mike was completely lost on the Hondas and asked for enormous modifications on the machines for the upcoming 1966 season. These modifications were only rarely done as it was felt that Mike would get used to the handling of the bikes the way I had. In any case, Mike was not very good at communicating exactly what it was he wanted, so a lot of the time the engineers were completely baffled, especially when they asked me if my bikes were alright and I said they were fine.

Apochryphal stories abound about how Mike and I worked out that he would go for the 250 and 350 titles in 1966, and I would go for the 500, and

Jim Redman

most of them make me out the big bad wolf who pulled rank. The truth of the matter is that, whilst in Japan for Suzuka 1965, I said to Mike that since he had had it easy on the 500 for a few years now, and as one more 500 title was neither here nor there to him (and as he was younger than me), he should do the hardest job and win the 250 and 350 titles, whilst I took it relatively easy on the 500. No-one knew then that MV was going to come out with the triple, so the 500 title looked the easiest, just as it had been for MV for the last several years with Surtees, Hocking and Hailwood all having an easy time. Mike laughed and said okay, and that was that. I was looking forward to my turn for an easy year and to capturing my first 500cc World Championship.

Mike and I often made a deal about the last five laps when we were obviously the only two in the race who could win (usually in smaller races and not Grands Prix). This arrangement was good for the sport and the crowds, as they got a big kick watching us passing and re-passing each other in the corners. It was good for both of us, too, as it took a lot of the danger out of the race; it's quite amazing how easy it is to ride together, lapping just fractionally slower than your best, and concentrating on passing and re-passing each other. You feel as though you could go on all day without any risk of a crash, and yet you are still going fast enough to stay well clear of the rest of the field. Then, for the last five laps, we give it one hundred per cent. Mike and I would not do this with some of the other riders who wanted to as we did not trust them the way we did each other; in fact, Mike told me a few times that he really only liked doing this sort of 'deal' with me, as he trusted me completely.

13
The Final Crash

The 1966 season began very well for Honda. The first race was the Spanish GP, where Mike won the 250 and Luigi was second in the 125 with Ralph third. Then at the German GP at Hockenheim, all the categories were on the program. Mike and I considered riding in the three main ones - the 250, 350 and 500. Unfortunately, two incidents prevented this. First of all, under FIM rules the combined mileage of the races exceeded the maximum allowed in a day. As Mike's priorities were the 250 and 350 events he had to concentrate on those, whilst I rode the 250 and 500. We calculated that the 350 Championship was going to be the easiest for Mike to win so I chose to back him up in the 250 in case I could be of some help. Secondly, the gearbox broke on my 500 during practice which meant that Mike's bike was used for spares. On the extremely fast Hockenheim circuit, I caused the biggest stir by winning very easily from Agostini with the new Honda 500 in its first ever race, while Mike won the 250 and 350 races. However, to do this he had to put up an unrelenting fight against Phil Read in the 250 and Agostini in the 350 race.

The French GP at Clermont Ferrand was next on a track that was both superb and yet very difficult and very long, winding for eight kilometres through the Auvergne mountains. Right from the 250 practices, Mike made the best times and he, Phil and myself were each faster than the old 250 lap record.

I led for the first lap, then Mike caught up and passed, leaving me standing, to win the race by a total of forty five seconds. Phil finished third nearly one and a half minutes behind Mike and forty seconds behind me. Mike's supremacy during this race was phenomenal, he was so relaxed and made it look so easy and yet no one could catch him; I rode my heart out just trying to follow him, and congratulated him after the race on his brilliant ride. The following race was another formality for Mike: on his 350 he simply pulled away from Agostini and me, at the same time setting a new track

Jim Redman

record. This was a brilliant double for Mike.

For the next GP at Assen, Holland, things would be a lot more difficult for me in the 500 race as Agostini was on the new MV 500cc 3-cylinder for the first time. To my surprise the MV was as fast as the Honda, its speed down the straight now practically identical. From the start of the race I took an immediate lead, but then going full-speed down the first straight Agostini passed me with disconcerting ease. I was very surprised, as my bike at Hockenheim was much faster than his old 4-cylinder MV and I never dreamt that the 3-cylinder MV would be that much faster. I had to take my hat off to MV for coming up with such a vast improvement in only a month, although I guess they had been working on it all winter. By beating Ago so easily in Germany I had hastened the triple's appearance in a race.

All this went through my mind as I tucked in behind Agostini down that first long straight, and I realised the season was going to be a lot more difficult than I had anticipated. Mike had made a lazy start but got close enough to 'get on to terms with us' about halfway through the second or third lap (the races were shorter at Assen, allowing Mike to ride in all three classes). On a fast right-hander behind the pits, Mike tried to pass me on the outside to take his turn at having a go at Ago but, as we changed direction for the following left-hander, he dropped the bike and slid down the road right next to me. He was sliding along next to me at an angle that was closing the gap between us, pushing me more and more to the right when the corner coming up bore left. Luckily, I managed to avoid hitting either Mike or his bike but, by the time I had extricated myself, I had lost a lot of ground to Agostini.

I then made the mistake of trying to catch him too quickly and rode very badly, braking too late and going fractionally into the slip road at the next sharp right, losing more precious time. As I passed the pits I received the signal "minus 15 Ago" and the official lap board said 20 laps to go. I metaphorically shook myself by the scruff of the neck: "Settle down Redman, and do it right, you have to pull back a second a lap on Ago." I started braking a bit earlier, got on the gas a bit earlier and pulled myself together. Little-by-little I got back into the race, consistently pulling back a second a lap. I was going well and was back in the groove, pulling back a second a lap for six laps. However, as I got the signal 'minus 9', Ago made a supreme effort and the next lap was minus 9 and the next, but then the following was minus 7 and I knew I had him. I began to see him in front of me, a corner or two ahead: just the extra motivation I needed. Two laps from the end I took the lead by slipstreaming him and then nipping out of his slipstream and passing on the outside in the flat-out left-hander just after the start and finish line. A hundred metres later we ran into a cloud burst which seemed like a wall of water. I was mad as hell: I'd done all this hard work and was in the lead but it had to rain like never before! I was, above all, fearful of going too fast and making a mistake. You can imagine the state I was in but I tried to keep calm. After riding a few hundred meters in this downpour, I saw three riders ahead dicing with

The Final Crash

each other and thought if I could pass them all braking for the next corner and leave them in Ago's way I would have the race won. I braked as late as I dared and shot past all three of them on the brakes, with the bike getting a bit sideways in the corner as I was going slightly too fast in the rain for the tyres to grip. I thought to myself "That's done it" and as soon as I got the bike back under control, accelerating hard, I looked back, hoping to see Ago behind these three riders. You can imagine my disappointment when I looked over my shoulder right into the eyes of Ago, who had followed me through on the brakes!

A few kilometres further on we found ourselves back in bright sunshine and on a dry surface, so were flat-out again. As we passed the pits with a lap to go we were plunged back into the downpour again. These weather extremes were a great strain on the nerves as they made it difficult to judge how hard we could press on in the wet without doing something stupid, with me under the most pressure as I was in front and had to judge the pace - Ago could wait and see if I made a mistake and finish up on my arse. I was very relieved as we came out of the rain halfway round on the last lap as I knew then that I could get to the line first, which I did, winning by two seconds from Giacomo.

I knew I'd ridden well and felt a deep satisfaction. I felt that this was definitely one of my best and most incredible triumphs. Giacomo came to shake my hand and said "Well ridden, you are very strong." To which I replied "Not bad for an old fart." This was a reference to an earlier conversation between Mike and myself when Mike had said that he'd better get to the gym as Ago was fit and six years younger than he was. I'd asked Mike how he thought I felt as he was six years younger than me and Ago twelve! Mike said he always forgot that and thought of me as being the same age as himself as we'd been racing against each other for years. I was very pleased and flattered by Ago's compliment though, make no mistake.

There's a very interesting sequel to this race, too. In those days we always used to go to Mallory for the post-TT meetings on the Sunday. John Cooper - "Mooneyes", as he is known - was a Mallory Park specialist. When I rode a 350 there, John would ride his heart out trying to catch me - a hopeless endeavour as my four was much faster than his single. What no-one knew was that, at that time, Honda did not really want me to ride at international meetings in case I hurt myself and missed a GP because of injury. In order to keep Honda happy I used to ride extremely carefully at these meetings, doing just enough to win. Consequently, John used to see me just ahead and feel he could catch me as I was not riding very hard. He told a lot of people that he could ride the Honda much quicker than me. I didn't know him well enough then to put him in the picture by telling him he need not waste his time: if he became a threat I could always go a bit quicker!

In June at Assen John was one of the three riders - the other two were, I think, Stuart Graham and Franky Stastny - we passed on the second to last

Jim Redman

lap. They were competing for 3rd place when we lapped them. John said to me after the race "You bloody ride bloody different over here, don't you?" I told him that this was where it's all at; Grands Prix were where I had to really go to work to win my titles and 'Holiday Racing' at Mallory was different.

In October 1996 John Cooper and I were both at Daytona riding for Team Obsolete, and over dinner we laughed about those times. What's great about talking of those days now is that there's no pressure - like there was then - and we can just relax and tell it as it was.

I arrived at Spa Francorchamps in Belgium full of confidence after my win at Assen, sure that I could win again after such a good on-form ride the weekend before. I had no idea that this was to be my last GP ...

In the 250, Mike won from Phil Read, with me third. Then came the 500 race. The weather was uncertain, which made us all very nervous as we'd not raced at the super fast Francorchamps circuit in the rain and had no idea what to expect. As we went to the line we were all looking up at the sky, wondering if it would rain and trying to guess what to do about tyre pressures; we had to try and guess right as in those days the race just went on and if you made a mistake you either lived with it or stopped and lost time doing something about it. It's different today as the race is stopped if it rains and the riders are able to change tyres or wheels. I think this is wrong: it should be the same as in F1 where the individual driver or rider decides for himself which tyres are most suitable.

In our case, the only change we could make was in tyre pressure, but we knew that if we started with the correct pressure for the dry and it rained, the bikes would be sliding all over the place, as we had to have very high pressures at this circuit because of the high speeds at which we rode. On the other hand, if we let the tyres down for the rain and it stayed dry, it would be very dangerous as the tyres would then overheat far too much. We made the decision to run the tyres hard.

As we waited on the starting grid, the commentator announced over the speakers *"Il pleut a Stavelot."* which even I knew meant "It is raining in Stavelot." I called the Dunlop technicians immediately so that they could release a little bit of pressure from my tyres and all the other riders followed suit.

Then the start, delayed a minute or two by the tyre pressure adjustments, was given. As the circuit was soaked and we had no idea what to expect, I decided to play it cool and sit behind Mike and Ago and await events. My reasoning was that I had won both of the first two rounds and if I finished third here in Belgium it would not be a disaster for me as I would still be leading the title chase comfortably. It also occurred to me that, in these conditions, there was a good chance all three of us would not finish. I wanted to be there at the finish so decided that if Mike and Ago left me behind I would not try too hard to catch them. My guess was right, but it was me that crashed out ...

Sitting behind the two of them after a few laps I was completely blinded

The Final Crash

by spray so decided to pull out of their slipstream for a few seconds to see what the road looked like. It was nerve-wracking riding along in the spray and seeing nothing, not even their back wheels. If either had fallen I would have hit him before I'd seen him; I wasn't even sure they were both still there, conditions were so bad.

My caution was my downfall because, as luck would have it, at the very spot where I decided to pull over to the other side of the road there was a lake of water which I hit before I even saw it. The bike aqua-planed on top of the water and down I went doing over 250km an hour. I hardly knew what had happened but as I hit the road, with my left arm down to save myself, knew that the crack I heard and felt was my left wrist breaking. As I slid on my back, going backwards on the wet tar, it felt as though I was accelerating rather than slowing down. In a crash you have to keep thinking and working to try and save yourself. There are three things to think about: first, to survive coming off the bike; second, survive the rest of the crash, avoiding impact with anything solid, and thirdly - the hardest of the lot - survive the first aid. As I slid backwards I began trying, by pushing with one hand and pulling with the other, to turn myself round, the idea being to slide feet first as there would be more give in my feet and legs than my head if I hit something solid. Before I got anywhere with this however, I saw the bike sliding toward me. Just as it got close, going faster than me, the tyres dug in and it lifted off the ground and would have crashed down on top of me. I frantically lashed out with both feet and managed to give it a hard enough kick to send it sailing over my head, but caught it awkwardly with my right leg and felt intense pain shoot up my leg from my shin. Broken leg to go with the broken arm I thought, but there was no time to worry about that as I slid off the tar on to the grass verge and started to go end-over-end, losing all sense of direction.

I found out afterwards that, as the bike flew over my head, it demolished one of those low, solid concrete milestones, exploding it into a thousand pieces just split seconds before I slid head first over the spot where it had been. That would have meant, at the very best, a very serious headache!

I finally came to a standstill, half submerged in water and feeling very sore. I looked around and saw a big hole in a wooden fence. "Gee," I thought, "the bike made a big hole there." Looking again, however, I could see the bike further down by another hole in the fence and realised that the first one had been made by me as I crashed through the wooden fence. There was no time to worry about that though as, having survived the first two things in my list, I could see a group of spectators running frantically towards me and knew the hardest part was yet to come: survive the well-meaning but often panic-stricken first aid. As they got to me and reached to drag me out of the water, I held up my good right hand in a fending off gesture and, for some unknown reason, yelled *"Langsam"* which is German for "slowly." I have no idea why, in Belgium, I used German instead of French; maybe the big leather coat that the leading guy was wearing made me think he was German, but it

Jim Redman

did the trick and he stopped dead in his tracks and held out his arms wide to ward off the rest of the mob. One guy tried to grab me and yank me from the water, but my benefactor shoved him away and told him what I had said. In broken German, English and French, I explained that my left wrist and right leg were broken and got them to drag me out of the water by my right arm and left leg. My man then took off his big leather coat and wrapped me in it as best he could as shock was starting to set in and I was wet through and shivering violently. I know this saved my life but I never found out who he was, so if he reads this or someone who does tells him, I would love him to contact me so that I could buy him a beer or two and thank him.

It took forever for the ambulance to arrive. During this time and unbeknown to me, my good friend Frank Perris had shouted for the helicopter from the pits to be sent for me. The answer he got was "Do you know how much it costs to send this thing for him?" Frank replied "I don't give a shit how much it costs, what's it there for, a fucking ornament?" It was all to no avail, however, and I was finally picked up in the ambulance which for some reason took me to the pits instead of rushing me to hospital. Marlene and Frank were told at the ambulance that it was Derek Woodman inside and not me, but Marlene pushed past, recognized my boots and shoved her way into the ambulance. Frank's wife, Rita, looked after Jimmy and Marlene went with me in the ambulance to the hospital.

My wrist was set and my leg examined (it was horribly bruised but not broken, although I still have an indentation in my shinbone to this day). But worse was to follow. I slept and when I awoke I could feel that my wrist was not right; the plaster was too tight. I waited for Marlene to visit and she helped me to dress and get out of there. Ophie Howard, another Rhodesian rider, had crashed a couple of days before me and Marlene had gone in the ambulance with Ophie and his wife as she was panicking, so Marlene was getting to know this hospital well. My bill for one night was much more than Ophie's had been for three nights, and the reason for this was that Marlene had come to fetch me in our Ferrari, whereas Ophie was a privateer in a van. Ophie didn't have enough money to pay his bill and the hospital was adamant: no pay, no leave hospital. It was up to me to pay the ransom and bail him out so that he could leave at the same time as me.

Eventually, all was settled and we headed for the coast and the first ferry to Dover. My wrist was hurting atrociously so Marlene got hold of a doctor who was going back to England. He took one look at the state of my hand, wrist and arm - they'd doubled in size where they poked out of the plaster - and said he didn't dare touch me, but advised I head straight for hospital in London, even though it would be the middle of the night when we got there. He was concerned that gangrene would set in if I waited.

We went to the hospital - St.Thomas's, I think it was - where surgeons cut off the plaster and reset my wrist properly. When I woke up from that operation I knew it was right so we headed back to South Africa for some

The Final Crash

rest. I knew that an excellent doctor in Durban would get me back on my feet as soon as possible so that I could return to Europe and take up the challenge once again.

I'd calculated that if I could finish third in the Ulster GP (which I thought I could do, even with a half-mended wrist, as Mike and Ago were the only serious opposition), I had only to win the TT and the Italian GP in Monza to give me enough points to win the 500 World Championship. Confronted with my determination and insistence, the doctor in Durban took off my plaster and replaced it with a new, very much thinner one which would allow me to move my wrist. Five weeks later in Belfast, I did not let anyone see that I was wearing an even thinner plaster, which would fit under my leathers, as I knew full well that if the organizers found out I would not have been allowed to start.

I went out for the first practice session trying hard, whenever possible, to favour my left hand, but it was hopeless. The Belfast circuit was well known for being very bumpy and very fast and the 500 Honda was a handful even with two good hands, so my left arm was having to work hard just to hold it. I had to stop after a few laps because my wrist was incredibly sore; I could see I had buggered it up again as it had doubled in size. I went to the hospital immediately, where the doctors and nurses shouted at me for being crazy. The plaster was again cut off but a new one could not be put on until the swelling had subsided. Obviously, I could not ride as planned, but all the same went to the TT with the Honda team which was being held in September that year instead of the usual June because there had been a seamans' strike in June. I knew I couldn't ride in the TT but wanted to go there with the team and consider my future.

I had - more or less - made up my mind that if I won the 500 title I would retire, so knowing that I would not ride again that year meant it was time to make the big decision. I knew my arm would become a factor in the future as I had messed it up badly by trying to ride at the Ulster. I was 35 years of age; did I want to carry on? I had a long discussion with Honda, during which I formally advised them that I was putting an end to my career in the racing profession. Being a devout coward, I've always had a strong desire to retire whilst still alive!

A few days later, I was invited by Honda to go to Japan for a Sayonara Party as Mr Honda wanted to thank me personally for my contribution to Honda's success in motorcycle racing. Several functions were held in my honour, one of which Mr Honda attended and gave me a beautiful painting of Mount Fuji as a parting present and thanked me profusely for all I had done. It was a sad but pleasant time, saying farewell to all my friends at Honda, especially Aika San.

I received an unexpected invitation to a lunch at the home of Mr Fujisawa, Vice-President of Honda Motor Company. I was very surprised at this invitation for two reasons: although I had met Mr Fujisawa he had never

Jim Redman

had anything to do with the racing team, and it was a personal invitation to his home; the Japanese custom is to be invited to a restaurant, never to the home. When everyone was present at the lunch (guests had been carefully chosen), Mr Fujisawa started to speak, initially in a most disconcerting way - through an interpreter. "Personally, I don't like racing. I don't think it helps that much to sell motorbikes and I think that we can be the biggest motorcycle company in the world without racing, just advertising and publicity campaigns and the quality which characterizes our machines. But, then again, I am only the Vice-President of this company, and Mr Honda is the President, he thinks quite the opposite to me. He loves motorcycle racing and sincerely believes that winning races helps enormously to sell Honda motorcycles all over the world. (The reader should know of the relationship that existed between Mr Honda and Mr Fujisawa. Back in the early days Honda was fitting ex-war department stationary engines into bicycles, Mr Fujisawa went to Mr Honda and told him that although he was a brilliant engineer he was not as good at the sales side of the business. Mr Fujisawa proposed that he take care of sales whilst Mr Honda concentrated on development. Many years later this division of areas of expertise still applied.)

Mr Fujisawa went on: "So far, Honda has won 97 GPs and 12 World Championship titles. Jim San has won 46 of the 97 GPs and 6 of the 12 World Championship titles, more or less 50 per cent, with the twenty or so other Honda riders making up the rest. So, although it is true that I am against Honda competing in racing since Mr Honda would never allow me to change that, I wanted to say to you, Jim San, that as we had to go racing I am glad it was with you. I want you to know how happy and honoured I have been to have had you in our team, and to have had you represent Honda so brilliantly. All the while magnificently representing and defending the interests of the other riders in our team while you were their Captain." I was overcome with emotion, but he wasn't finished.

After this speech, Mr Fujisawa invited me to follow him into a special room in which was displayed all sorts of *objets d'art* he had carefully collected over many years. He spoke to me about his passion for this pastime and asked me to choose one of these treasures for myself. In a low voice I said to the interpreter "It is out of the question that I take one of these objects." The interpreter replied that it was not possible for me to refuse as to do so would be a terrible insult. All of these treasures, he said, meant much to Mr Fujisawa, which made it all the more important that I did as he asked; for him, it was proof of respect, friendship and affection. Mr Fujisawa was a rich man, who could have bought me anything I wanted. Taking a treasure from his private collection meant so much more to us both.

Following this explanation I decided to do as Mr Fujisawa asked, and chose a beautiful round bowl. Mr Fujisawa looked at me for a minute without speaking, then said "Not only are you a great rider, you also have good taste." He was probably only being kind as everything in the room had been

The Final Crash

personally selected by him and was probably just as valuable, in money and sentiment. The interpreter told me it had hurt Mr Fujisawa to lose such an object, but he was comforted to know that it had gone to me.

My farewell to Mr Honda and everyone in the company was an event of incredible warmth and great dignity. Sadness and pride were the emotions I felt as I entered the plane that would take me back to South Africa, where a new beginning awaited ...

14
Honda

It was whilst riding for Honda that I was FIM World Champion six times which is still - over 32 years later - the most World Championships any rider has ever won for Honda. To win those World Championships I achieved 46 GP victories, along with another record - the first rider in the 90-odd year history of the TT to win the same two races three years running, and on a circuit recognized as the most difficult and dangerous in the world. A feat recorded in *The Guinness Book of Records* for over 30 years.

Even if my old TT record is beaten in the future, it will still stand to a degree, as it was set when the TT race counted towards the World Championships, a fact which made the race much harder as the pressure to win was really on. Many years ago the TT lost its status as a GP with points counting towards the World Championship as modern riders believe it to be too dangerous and refuse to ride there. It speaks volumes for the TT race that not only has it been able to survive this, it's also gone from strength to strength.

Riding Hondas, I also set another world record as the first rider in the history of racing to win three GPs in one day, setting three new race records and three new lap records in the process. This was at the Dutch TT in Assen in 1964 and, to this day, only one other rider, the legendary Mike Hailwood, has matched this record. There's a good chance it'll be a long time before anyone else joins us as the modern trend is to ride in only one class. With races cut to about 40 minutes duration, instead of the compulsory hour-plus they used to be, GP riders have a lazy life these days: it's no wonder they need a retinue of people to motivate them and advise on diet and exercise - they have nothing else to do!

In my day, most riders rode at least two - and a few of us rode three - classes, so we were race fit and our motivation was good as, initially, it was to win enough to be able to eat. Later on, once we became works riders, the motivation was to keep our places in the team from the hordes of other riders waiting to take them. An interesting side note here: in 1996, Chris Carter interviewed me over the public address system at Donington. He remarked that having disappeared for years, I was now around every week and suggested I should take up GP racing again. Chris went on to ask which class I would choose if I did, and I told him I would probably do as I always did and ride 125, 250 and 500. He looked very thoughtful as he replied, "That's right, you always did do that." I could see he was wondering why no-one does it today.

Another thing which has changed is that our earnings were so small, compared to modern-day riders, that we continued to compete in international races other than GPs in order to earn extra money.

Honda was responsible for my route to financial success. Had I not been chosen by Honda I may have remained one of those privateers fighting to survive, while hoping for better days. But then, on the other hand, I would also have definitely quit the world of motorbike racing a lot earlier than I did. Honda gave me the opportunity to be captain of the most fabulous team one can imagine. We travelled thousands of miles a year, visited places we had only dreamed of seeing and had a lifestyle the envy of every dyed-in-the-wool motorcyclist the world over.

Wherever we went in the world, to whichever country, the name of Honda was always special. The crowds came to expect something unusual or exceptional as soon as our bikes appeared on the race tracks; looking back I can say they were almost never disappointed. As soon as our bikes entered the arena, people crowded around to admire them and try to touch them, and often we would hear someone call out "The Hondas are here!" In the beginning all this attention was a bit disconcerting, but we soon got used to it and were certainly very proud as we did try to do our best everywhere, for the crowds and for ourselves. I can't remember a single event where we didn't get a triumphant welcome. The fans were not wrong: the Hondas were by far the best racing motorbikes in the world and deserved all the admiration they got. If I had not been a professional rider I'm certain that I would also have been a part of the ecstatic crowd of fans.

15
Back to Normal Life

Marlene and the family took the news of my retirement casually and calmly, without expressions of either joy or sadness; they simply thought I'd had a long and marvellous career but now it was time to move on to something else.

Once back in South Africa I tried to resume a normal life while all the time people kept asking me what I was going to do next. To tell the truth, I had no idea! My life up to this point had been spent living at a hundred miles an hour, obsessed by the need to make money firstly to bring up Peter and Wendy, and then to ensure my family had everything it needed and everything that I didn't have when I was a child. I also wanted to make sure there was enough cash if I did get written off in racing.

Now I wanted to go slow for a while, to experience the simple pleasures of being with my family, no plane to catch or race meeting to get to. We had a great house in Durban, we all had good health, my family were well and happy and we had lots of friends. What else could I ask for? Perhaps I would just live the life of a retired motorcycle rider. I took up golf and played every morning, thinking that this was what people did when they retired. I hated it. Then I tried fishing with some friends who lived for their fishing, and that was worse. So I read a lot and enjoyed the luxury of being at home without any particular schedule.

Many people came to see me to tell me how they could make me rich with my money. I told them I did not really need the extra money so they should do it and make all the money for themselves, as none of their projects really interested me. Then my friend Charlie Young came back again with his new proposition.

Previously, when I was visiting Japan regularly, Charlie had asked me to persuade Mr Honda to give us the Honda concession, with exclusivity for South Africa. At that time Charles was selling English motorcycles - Norton,

Back to Normal Life

Matchless and AJS - and some Italian bikes, but realised the way ahead lay with the emerging Japanese motorcycle firms long before most people woke up to this. Of course, our friendship helped as I was feeding him all the news of my trips to Japan. He suggested that if I could secure the Honda franchise for the whole of South Africa, while I continued to race he would manage the business so that afterwards, when I retired from racing, I would join him full-time in the business, with each of us owning fifty percent of the business.

However, when I suggested this to Mr Honda he flatly refused. He wanted me to concentrate solely on my racing and not be distracted by other business interests. I respected his wishes and forgot this idea and another company took up the Honda concession for South Africa (and later became the biggest motorcycle importer in the country, selling 800 machines a month). In the meantime, another shipper had imported Yamaha bikes and was looking for a motorcycle firm to handle them. Charles was the ideal man. He was not sure of Yamaha at that time so took the bikes on a consignment basis. In no time at all he became the Yamaha importer for South Africa with a network of dealers right around the country. He was very successful and was selling about a hundred Yamahas a month, which made him the third largest motorcycle importer in the country after Honda and Suzuki.

In 1966 Charlie made me such a good proposition that I could not turn it down. He would sell me one third of his business at two thirds of the share value to have me join him: he wanted my energy and name in the business. However, I could not accept this very tempting offer immediately. For many years, as leader of the Honda Team, I was well aware that although Mr Honda was on good terms with Mr Suzuki, owner of the Suzuki factory, he had never had any time for Yamaha. I thanked Charles for the offer, but told him that before I could accept I felt honour-bound to go to Japan and discuss the whole situation with Mr Honda.

I took the first flight leaving for Japan. Over dinner, Mr Honda asked me why I had made such a long journey to see him and if I needed any help? I assured him that all was well with me and told him I had received a very good offer of business in South Africa. He immediately asked "Motorcycle business?" and when I said "Yes." he asked "Japanese motorcycles?" "Yes." "Then it's definitely not Honda, or you would not be here asking my advice." When I quietly mentioned the name Yamaha, his immediate reaction was to say no, it was out of the question that I join Yamaha. He was both shocked and surprised that I would consider Yamaha, and asked me why I wouldn't rather join the Honda dealership in South Africa. I replied that I had been contacted by Honda South Africa but that the proposal was in no way comparable to that made by Charlie Young; Honda had offered me a job, whereas Charlie had offered me a third of the business. Mr Honda suggested that I move to Los Angeles and he would arrange a suitable position for me in Honda America, which belonged to him. But at that stage of my life I did not want to move to Los Angeles, I wanted to stay in South Africa. After

Jim Redman

long, lively - but friendly - discussion, we separated on good terms and I joined Charlie Young with Mr Honda's approval and his sincere thanks for having the courtesy to go all the way to Japan to discuss it with him before committing myself.

During the five years that followed the business grew throughout the whole of South Africa. Charles and I made a good team; he was too conservative and I was too reckless, so the balance was right and sales went from 100 to 500 bikes a month in that time. Our business was based on certain solid ethics and, in particular, never to run down Honda and its bikes, whilst still being as honest as possible with the client. Soon after I joined Charles in the venture, without any warning, Yamaha Japan sent us a racing bike which arrived one day out of the blue. It was one of the RD 56, 250cc twin cylinder bikes I had raced so hard against in 1964. It was sent with a message,: "Just in case Mr Redman is tempted to take up racing again in South Africa." Naturally, I could not resist the temptation to make a few laps on this bike. The spirit of competition was still very much alive and kicking inside, but now I was able to indulge in the pure pleasure of riding a racing motorcycle - at least, that's what I tried to tell myself, and Marlene. When I get on a bike in a race, though, something goes 'click' and I have a need to win; that's always been my problem.

So, my first race on the Yamaha was in Cape Town, where my main opponent turned out to be a certain Mike Hailwood, riding the famous Honda 6. It felt very strange to be riding a Yamaha against a Honda. I didn't dare suggest "Last five to count" to Mike as I was so rusty and having so many problems getting the bike right I just assumed that Mike would beat me. Tommy Johns, previously SA Champion riding Yamaha for Charles, was in charge of the technical division of Charlie Young Yamaha. Tommy was the finest tuner in South Africa and he came down with me to help with the bike. He worked very hard to get it right for the race, but we had no information about it and this was our first race, so had no experience to call on.

It was a tight race, Mike and I taking turn to lead several times. Since I had no experience on Yamahas, I had no idea - and even Tommy could not be sure - which plugs we should use on this tight circuit so we had to make a calculated guess. Nevertheless, I stayed with Mike and we kept overtaking each other during the race. It was the good old days all over again but no last five to count this time as Mike did not think I would keep up. Then, with me still just leading at about half distance, the motor suddenly cut right out opposite the pits and I cruised in to retire; we had used too hard a plug.

During this race I came to appreciate just how easy it had been for Phil Read on his Yamaha Twin to race against me on my Honda 4 back in 1964. The Yamaha's acceleration was superb which, on this tight little circuit, made it possible for me to stay with Mike on a 6, never mind the 4 that I was riding in 1964. For years Phil had said how much more difficult it was to ride a two stroke and I was a little worried before the race because I had no previous

Back to Normal Life

experience of them, but I found there was little or no difference, they're all just motorcycles.

Earlier in 1966, just after I joined Charlie Young and Yamaha, I went to Bulawayo for the Rhodesian GP to fulfill a commitment made to ride the Honda there. The stress was enormous because practice was going so badly, and I knew that if I was beaten riding the Honda against Yamahas people would say I had lost deliberately because of my involvement with Yamaha. In the end, everything turned out fine; I got the Honda right and won the race easily. Lots of people said to me "You don't give a damn about business, you race only to win." and they were right: winning gave me the greatest satisfaction.

Early in 1969 after racing the Yamaha in about twelve races all over South Africa, I was racing in Pietermaritzburg, our local circuit close to Durban. During the race I kept looking back at the riders behind who were still quite close. I should have been winning this race easily as I used to, but it was getting harder and harder to beat the rest. I realised that if I carried on for another year the other riders would begin to beat me, and that was something I didn't want to happen. After the race I told Marlene I was quitting racing completely. Of course, she didn't believe me at first but when I told her I did not want to race on and get beaten, she saw the sense in that. I did not race again until 1995 - twenty six years later. Over the previous eighteen months I had ridden the Yamaha in about a dozen races and won them all, except for the first one against Mike. I should mention that, subsequently, Mike Hailwood went back to race in Europe, so I didn't have too much competition from the other riders.

During the five years I worked with Charlie a lot of my friends pestered me to sell them four-cylinder road bikes; everyone at that time wanted something to ride with four cylinders. Unfortunately, Yamaha built only twin-cylinder bikes, while Honda was having a lot of success with its fours, both 500 and 750 models. Even though I did not really want to, I sent them over to the Honda dealer, knowing full well that my friends would find what they were looking for. I told Yamaha that it was not possible to sell twins when everybody wanted fours. Yamaha understood my dilemma and tried to correct the situation as quickly as possible. Yamaha was much more competitive in the 50cc class, because the machines were very popular with the youngsters, who preferred them to Hondas because of their greater reliability. We always tried to put forward the good points of Yamaha rather than criticize the Hondas. I know that my ex-employer appreciated this attitude, and in this way I have managed to maintain excellent relationships with both companies.

In 1971 I started feeling weary. I'd channelled all of my energy into the business, which was successful, and I felt the need to rest and break away from the business world, at least for a while. Shortly before this one of our staff, Kelvin Thomas, came to see me looking for an increase in salary. I'd explained to him that the way he was working he was not worth any more money; to be worth more he had to take more responsibility and the way to do that was to make the decisions he was currently coming to me for. In other words, make himself indispensable to me and then come and demand more money which I would be forced to pay. He listened and did this, which meant I felt confident about his ability to take over from me.

I had a long conversation with Charles in which I admitted I was fed up with staying in the same place all the time and doing the same job for five years. I need one or two months' break to get away and have a good time and wanted to go and visit my old friend Mike Hailwood. Charlie, a really good, understanding person, said to me "Listen, Jim, for five years now you've been working non-stop, your trouble is that you only have one speed, flat-out, I don't think a couple of months is enough; why don't you take a whole year off and enjoy yourself. You have Kelvin at the stage where he can now do your work, so go, have a good time, enjoy yourself and come back completely refreshed and give Mike my fondest regards." What a partner to have! He knew our business was very successful, sales had multiplied by five since I joined him, but this wasn't down to just me: we were a good team.

Throughout my entire career I didn't stop travelling around the world, all year, every year. I travelled from the top to the bottom of Europe, to South America, then on to Japan, coming back to South Africa and finally Australia and New Zealand. I'd always wanted to be one step ahead of winter and roaming the world showed me new horizons, and whether life was better elsewhere in case I ever wanted to settle somewhere else when my international career was over. When I decided to end my GP career it meant that my travelling days were over, which was a total relief. At last I could take some time for myself and my family and not be constantly on the move and under pressure. At last I was going to be able to enjoy the present and watch time pass little-by-little, and experience simple everyday things like sleeping in my own bed.

For five good long years I was able to find myself and see my children grow up. But it seems I was not meant to remain in the same place for long and the need to move on became more and more pressing. I felt stifled and wanted to breathe the air of new challenges or new places, and some of the places I knew well and had not visited for five years.

My itchy feet had returned. Marlene and Charlie understood it well enough and set me free, and off I went to Europe for a couple of months to look up my long-time friend Mike Hailwood. I stayed with Mike and together we went to the races and had fun like a couple of kids. I looked up some of my old contemporaries, breathing in the unique atmosphere found only in the pits, paddocks and workshops of the racing world. After a good break and a nice holiday I returned home to Durban.

Waiting for me was a letter from an ex-racing motorcyclist whom I'd raced against in Australia. He told me of the imminent opening in South

Back to Normal Life

Africa of a company called 'Golden Products' which, for the last year, had enjoyed phenomenal success in Australia. I rang him and he told me that two Australians, Graham Caldwell and Bill Binns, were coming to South Africa shortly and he would telegram their schedule. Very curious to find out what it was all about, I flew to Johannesburg to meet with them.

At that stage the company employed a pyramid-type, direct-sales scheme with only five cleaning products in its range, but proposed to expand into health products, vitamins, toiletries and beauty products. The idea was quite revolutionary in 1971 without adverse publicity and the whole concept was new to me. Caldwell and Binns were convincing about their sales method and the success of the business, explaining that the financial rewards were exceptional. Plus, if I climbed the ladder of success with them, I would be required to do a lot of travelling, which suited me very well - especially at this particular moment.

Before I made any decision, I had to find out just how solid this Golden Products company was. I had my bank make a few enquiries about it and was told that the company seemed financially sound; it paid its bills on time and looked OK. I decided to join Golden Products as an independent distributor.

I was used to people wanting to use my name to endorse a product, and this makes sense for them, but, I asked, what was my special deal? Graham and Bill explained to me that if they gave anyone a special deal it went against their system of promoting people for their efforts and results. I would be running my own business within the Golden framework, but there were no free rides, not even for me, although if I was any good the sky was the limit.

I told Charlie what I intended to do and he couldn't believe it. I offered to give him one-third of my Golden Products business, which was only fair if I was going to put my energy into Golden whilst he was concentrating on our existing business. Charles had no confidence in this new style of company and thought they may be fly-by-night people. He said I had to choose between him and Golden Products.

I chose Golden Products. Charlie was completely at a loss to understand this and said I was foolish to join them and perhaps ruin my good reputation. This reminded me of when I had been called foolish for starting in motorbike racing. Charles bought back my shares of the company on the same basis he had sold them to me, which gave me a profit, and we separated on good terms. He and his wife Hazel have been and still are extraordinary friends for whom I have great affection.

A lot of people thought I had made the wrong decision because there were many companies, of the same kind as Golden Products, which were not reliable, who gave the direct-sales sector a very bad name.

I started as a distributor for Golden Products in October 1971. Sales bonuses were extremely high and, in a few months, I had under my control

Jim Redman

the cities of Durban, East London, Port Elizabeth and Cape Town - the four largest cities on the coast. I was promoted very quickly and became Sales Coordinator for Durban, then Regional Director of Natal, then National Sales Director and finally, in November 1972, Vice-President for South Africa.

In the early 1970s, selling direct to the consumer was not very fashionable in South Africa. Our method of recruiting a large number of independent distributors to sell our products either on a full- or part-time basis was regarded very sceptically by a lot of people. This was because a few companies had abused the system right at the time Golden started. The big difference between us and the other companies that employed this style of merchandising was that we distributed quality products, and our greatest priority was to sell at retail, Bill Binns was very strong on that. Not many people were as confident as I was and our distributors would ring me when other companies folded and bleat about what would happen if Golden collapsed, too. Distributors and consumers were always asking themselves who would be the next to go? I told everyone not to worry as we all knew it was a good business and if ever Golden did let us down, I would arrange to manufacture the products myself and keep the business going. Of course, that didn't happen and twenty-six years later Golden Products has become one of South Africa's most important direct selling companies and is still expanding, with sales currently about R25 million a month. As rules and legislation changed, of course, we had to modify our marketing plan, but it seemed that every time we did, things just got better.

I really appreciated all those years spent with Golden Products. As the company got bigger and bigger we would organize weekend seminars to which we invited several hundred people. The seminars were a way of bringing together the entire sales team in order to motivate and encourage. I gave my career and experience as a racing motorcyclist as an example of how motivation worked as I had obviously not won six World Championships simply by clicking my fingers.

All "How to be a Success" books talk about achieving your goals; I've never read any of these but achieved my goals simply by instinct. The world of racing was not, in essence, so very different to that of any business. Re-telling my experiences and successes managed to captivate a large audience, especially when I went into details about a particular race. It made me happy to see their rapt faces as they listened and, in motivating others, I was motivating myself.

Golden asked me if I would go to the UK and start a company called "Gold Power Automotive." Bill Binns was offered the post but refused, preferring to play safe by staying in South Africa. It was early 1973 and this new challenge excited me. Without hesitation I accepted and a few days later put my house up for sale, thinking we might never return to South Africa.

Soon after arriving in England, I realized that pyramid selling had a very bad reputation, especially with governmental bodies, and it soon

Back to Normal Life

became illegal. This was crazy as it re-appeared as multi-level marketing and, when that became unfashionable, as networking. People have tried to tell me there is a difference but that's not true, it's all the same, direct selling in some form or another. I tell people: if the product is good, the owners of the company are thinking long-term and have a good marketing plan, then it's fine. Many companies had gone bankrupt because of government pressure and, in this respect, England had become the strictest concerning this type of sales venture. We had a lot of problems just trying set up our company and to work normally, even though we had the best of intentions, as had been proved in many countries throughout the world.

In the end it wasn't my problem as after just six months in England I was asked to rescue the Italian company that had started the same time I went to England. I left Richard Place in England to run Gold Power Automotive and left for Rome in October 1973 to replace the managing director who had been fired because of very bad results.

When I arrived, I was quite depressed at the animosity displayed by the company's own distributors, not so much towards the company but the previous MD, Rick Spranzo, and their dislike for him transferred to me as I had taken over from him. The company was in a sorry state; there was no money in the bank, no products in stock, and half the staff had not been paid that month and it was already the 7th of October. Our reputation was at its lowest and I knew I had to move quickly to improve the image of Golden Products to stop it disappearing completely from the Italian scene.

I called a meeting of the 130 distributors working for us in Rome twenty-four hours after my arrival. Because of a very bad sales policy, these individuals found themselves in a disastrous financial situation which, I explained, was in no way the fault of or representative of Golden Products, especially in South Africa where the company had a remarkable image. Elsewhere in the world the company worked wonderfully, and I was going to work flat out myself to get it back on its feet.

At first, they bayed for my blood and wanted to get their money back from me as quickly as possible. I asked them to make one last concession: work hard with me for the next thirty days, at the end of which, if nothing had changed, I gave them my guarantee that I would personally buy back all of their stock, right down to the last penny. I told them the story of Engineer Carcano, the famous designer at Moto-Guzzi, who, when the press asked him what made his motorbikes go so fast, even with the lowest horsepower, said "Very strong Italian horses." The Italian distributors loved this sort of story - and, evidently, my sincerity - because they agreed to give it a try and placed their confidence in me. A month later the company was back on track, and later on became the most powerful company in the Golden Products Group.

That first night, when I met with the distributors, I was still working with them in the head office at about midnight when the phone rang. It was Bob Brassfield, Vice-President of the International Group, asking how things were. When I replied that they were fantastic, he said how could that be? I told him because there was no way this company could go down as it was already at the bottom, so could only go up. He asked if there was any money in the bank, any product in the warehouse and had all the staff been paid, to which I replied no on all counts. He offered to transfer US$250,000 to get me started but I wanted to show what we could do. I told him not to send money, just containers of products and we would trade ourselves out of trouble.

Without asking for one single Lire from the banks, we developed remarkably well. The only desperate case was that of a young man who didn't have any money and whose wife was having their first baby. I gave him some of my own money that first night, and told him it was not a loan but a gift from me. Later on, this young man repaid me by becoming one of our best distributors worldwide.

I remained at the head of Golden Products Italy for four months, by which time the company was back on track and going very well. In February 1974 I was able to hand over to Mickey Shapiro, who had worked as a regional director under me in South Africa, whilst I moved on in order to head up a new venture. So, I did not have to reimburse anyone, due to those Italian distributors who, once they had confidence, could sell, and they still are selling since Italy is, I think, still the largest company in the Group.

At the end of 1973, the company had decided to branch out into another revolutionary concept: the vacation business or, rather, a new type of holiday resort with some type of membership, but weren't exactly sure how or where to do it. Once again, I was chosen for this new project and was able to select the country in which we would start. Of course, I chose South Africa as I was tired of living in Europe - once Africa's in your blood it's hard to stay away.

I flew home to South Africa from Milan on the 28th February, collected a station wagon that Golden South Africa had purchased for me to use and drove straight down to the Edengrove Hotel, a country hotel and farm I had found during the Christmas holiday break and which I thought would make an ideal ranch, the theme Golden had chosen. Before I went back to Italy after Christmas we had bought it. We were officially taking over on the 1st March 1974.

I thought this new venture was a great idea with lots of potential, so was already imagining a chain of ranches around the world. But, boy! I had no idea what I was letting myself in for. There I was, with a 200 bed hotel and a 2000 acre farm with 200 head of cattle and 400 sheep and not one day of farming or hotel management experience. I've always considered myself quick on the uptake, but had really been thrown in at the deep end here, especially when, as a result of my new ideas, all of the staff except two resigned within a few weeks. I was left with the hotel receptionist, who was

Back to Normal Life

over seventy but a wonderful person and a very hard worker with a great attitude, and the farm manager plus, of course, Marlene. Naturally, we struggled, but it was character-building and we came out on top but I still had to put the new project together as well. Bear in mind that this was 1974 and the concept of time-share didn't exist in America until the late 1970s, so we were real pioneers.

After researching many ideas we finally decided to register a public company and sell shares in it, with the shareholders receiving cheap holidays instead of dividends - and it worked. We sold 25 per cent of the company for four times as much as we'd paid for the entire property, and by then had nearly 2000 shareholders who used the ranch for weekends and holidays all the time: we had some great times for the next 12 years. The shareholders accounted for about a third of our business and the public and conference facilities roughly a third each. I still think that for the shareholders Sierra Ranch was, and still is, the best time-share-type operation in the world. There are no levies, so when people get tired of coming, they can just stop for a few years and start again when they feel like it.

In the '70s and '80s Sierra Ranch was the 'in' place to be and with singles weekends and theme weekends there was never a dull moment. I had solved the problem of losing money on the farming operation by selling all the livestock and farm implements and leasing the land to the farmer next door. With the cash realised in the bank earning interest, and the rent for the land I was one of the few 'farmers' in that area making a profit at that time.

When we bought the Edengrove it had never made a profit for any of its owners. When I put the public company together and went to the registrar of companies to register my first prospectus to sell shares he was amazed. He said "You're going to try and sell shares in a company with a 100 per cent record of losses every year, and yet your shares at R1500 each are the highest priced in the history of South Africa. How do you expect to sell them?" I said "That's my problem, but I'm going to tell everyone that we are going to change this and put it right if they invest; your job is to make sure I've set this out in a legal fashion with full disclosure." The registrar approved the prospectus and wished me luck, but I could see he thought I was mad. You can imagine his surprise when I was back three months later with a new prospectus offering shares at R1700, as all the others were sold.

The Ranch was completely transformed. Jimmy and Brett could not wait to get home for holidays as there was so much fun at the ranch. Since they've grown up I've been delighted to learn that they will both always be grateful to me for their time at Sierra Ranch It certainly was a marvellous environment to grow up in, with tennis courts, swimming pool, bowling green, horse trail riding, motorcycle trail riding, squash court, airport, and farm animals. We had three miles of river frontage with hay rides down to the river every Sunday. The shareholders and guests loved holidays there as they never saw their kids and never had to worry about them.

Jim Redman

It was here that Jimmy and Brett, adolescents at the time, started riding motocross and they loved it. The legal age in South Africa for youngsters to start riding MX was twelve years, but today it is much younger. Brett badgered me for months before his twelfth birthday to have an MX bike and start racing. I had been very low-key about my racing career and this was the first time that either of them wanted to race bikes in any form, but I guess it had to come. From this point on, I went from World Champion to van driver and pit mechanic for my two sons. Lots of Sundays were spent at motocross races all over the Natal Province. I worked non-stop on the bikes in the pits, and it became my turn to feel deep down inside the agony and fear that my family must have felt when I was racing. I was much more nervous than when I had to go out and race myself.

One day I really impressed the pair of them. It was just a few minutes before the start of a race and Jimmy had jumped on his bike ready to go to the start when he saw his tyre was flat. He had been having a good day and was so disappointed at not being able to compete. I tore out the wheel, ripped off the tyre and put in a new inner tube so quickly that before he realized it he was with the rest on the starting line. He was amazed and so proud of me that he couldn't stop thanking me. I was proud to show my boys that I could still do it and they appreciated my work. There has always been a lot of respect and love between the three of us; we are a very united and professional team. However, it became apparent to all of us that Brett was more gifted than Jimmy, who gave up MX because of this and turned to road racing. Brett had the passion and the will worthy of the great champions.

It was at this time that I met Kwezi Kennedy, a little eight-year-old girl whose step-brother, Mike Wilson, rode motocross as well, so our two families came to know each other quite well at the races. Then when we decided to construct our own motocross circuit at Sierra Ranch and hold races, they were naturally at the ranch a lot. Later on Kwezi, when she reached the age of fifteen, had a crush on Jimmy who, more than twenty at the time, was not interested as she was too young for him.

Each year at Sierra Ranch we saw the same faces - especially at Christmas and Easter - so Brett and Jimmy knew all the shareholders' children and had, over the years, formed two distinct groups, each with its own following. We spent our time playing all sorts of sports, and were all in good shape. Life was beautiful. We participated in all the sports events organized at the Ranch, and later on instigated theme weekends, something which attracted a lot of interest. Sometimes it was a Cavalcade of Sport weekend or a 'Western' weekend, sometimes a 'Roman' weekend, when the customers had to come to dinner dressed in costume, which meant wrapping themselves in sheets to make Roman togas. Then we removed the tables and everyone ate on the floor - they loved it! Finally, we organized weekends for singles which became so popular we had to have separate ones for 20-year-

Back to Normal Life

olds and over 26-year-olds. The latter group became known as the 'Grab a Granny' weekends, but you should have seen some of those 'Grannies'!

These singles weekends quickly became the talk of South Africa: they were incredible and completely mad and alcohol flowed freely. We left the bar open until the early hours during these weekends and the Ranch beat all the records in takings; in one week we took more money than some of the big hotels, so were very proud of ourselves. We were situated 15 miles from Mooi River, a small town in the middle of nowhere, and local inhabitants didn't give a hoot about what we were doing so nobody bothered us. We were able to give our customers the time of their lives, and let them stay up partying all night if they wanted to ...

One of the first things I established when the Ranch was completed was a landing strip for small airplanes, for anyone wanting to arrive by air. We had room to park plenty of planes so it didn't matter how many arrived, and was a very practical way to travel. From Durban to the Ranch was a two-hour drive, whereas by airplane it took only thirty minutes. From Johannesburg was a four-hour drive but an hour by plane. Soon after I stopped motorbike racing I took up flying and, like magic, flying soon became a passion. The Ferrari that I had bought some years before came in very handy, too. After I had driven it during the 1966 season, I brought it back by boat to South Africa. Once back in my country, of course, I had the greatest pleasure driving this magnificent machine - up until the day I discovered airplanes, and the exhilaration of flying. I then sold my superb Ferrari, replaced it with a Ford Mustang and bought my own airplane, a Piper Cherokee 180, a single-engined plane. The Cherokee did not last long as I soon traded it in for a Mooney, a very beautiful and rapid little aircraft. From the time I bought a plane I used it as much as possible, especially during the years when I worked with Charlie Young and we visited Yamaha dealers all over the country.

As I became more experienced at flying I entered the 'State Presidents Air Race.' This was a very popular event in South Africa with a huge entry of aircraft of all sizes running on handicap. On one particular occasion we had to spend the night in a hotel in downtown Port Elizabeth. Not far from the hotel a reception given by the Mayor had been organized in honour of the race competitors. Upon leaving the reception, slightly tipsy, we came across a double-decker bus which was parked nearby whilst the drivers were changing shift. We hopped on the bus, with one of our crazy group behind the wheel, and decided to go for a little drive around town. Here and there, we stopped to pick up passengers waiting at bus stops: it didn't bother us that it wasn't the right bus for where they wanted to go, we would drive them wherever they wanted! Growing tired of the joke, we drove back to our hotel, double- parked the bus outside and went for a nightcap at the bar. What we didn't know was that the police had been searching the city trying to find the bus, hoping to arrest the revellers ... So, there we were at the bar

Jim Redman

in the hotel, having one last drink, when someone rushed in to breathlessly warn us that the hotel was full of police who were looking for us!

Two of us went to speak to the police and were told that they had descriptions of two of the ring-leaders - Pat Clarence and Ed Carbett. We quickly sent someone to warn the pair to hide but it was too late as they were both already in the elevator. When the doors of the elevator opened a policemen shouted "There they are!" Thank God, Pat and Ed were quick enough to press the elevator button and disappear again. The rest of us went to bed smiling innocently.

The next day at the airport the police arrived just as we were getting ready to take off. Vern McWilliams, another member of the 'band,' went to meet them and ask what they were looking for. When the police told him they were looking for Pat Clarence, Vern said that, of course, he knew Pat very well and would point him out. He pretended to look for Pat as the plane that he and I were flying taxied out to the runway. As the plane took off, Vern exclaimed "Oh, there he goes!" Of course, the police called off the search and never twigged that Vern had delayed them deliberately at the airport.

On another occasion we were at the Wings Club in Durban, partying again, when a sing-song developed around the old piano in the bar. All of a sudden the pianist hit a few dud notes. To everyone's surprise, Vern went to the piano and asked the pianist to play the note again, whereupon Vern very sharply wrenched out the offending key! We decided (being quite seriously under the influence) that we should take the piano out on to the landing strip to see if it could fly. After pulling the piano out of the bar we were faced with a major problem - how to get it down the staircase? After a few moments' thought it all seemed too much trouble so we abandoned the idea and went back to the lounge for another drink. Some time later there was a deafening crash, and we rushed out to see the piano lying face-down halfway down the stairs. We all thought Oh, Oh, finished our drinks and stampeded out, putting our feet through the back of the piano as we trampled over it. Confirmed cowards that we were, we escaped as quickly as possible and headed home.

The next day everyone was summoned to attend a meeting at the Club which had been called by the executive committee, in order to discover the perpetrator(s) of this 'hideous crime.' We knew the 'guilty' person was one of the full-time instructors who was working for the Durban Wings Club, and we also knew that if the committee discovered this he would be fired on the spot. One by one we were called upon to testify - except, of course - the guilty party whom no-one suspected. We all admitted knowing who the person was but said that of course we could never denounce him. However, we had between us collected enough money to buy another piano, even better than the old one, an offer which was accompanied by our most sincere regrets, of course. But the committee was not very co-operative and were furious and frustrated. We were told that they wanted a replacement piano that

Back to Normal Life

was exactly the same as the broken one, and if they didn't get it they would impose some serious penalties. The committee was convinced that Vern, Pat and I were the instigators and we were each given a suspended sentence of expulsion from the Club which would take effect if we were again caught doing something naughty. We ended up buying a piano exactly the same as the original, which was far cheaper than the one we had collected for. So, with the leftover money, we decided to have another party ...

A few months later - again, after a few drinks - we decided to see if the new piano could swim. Because Vern and I were still under (suspended) sentence, we convinced two or three guys that, if they pushed the piano fast enough through the pub and through the big picture window, it would probably land right in the Club swimming pool. They started trundling the piano through the pub but Pat saw it coming and immediately guessing what was happening, kicked it over on its back as it went past him. It took several of us to lift it and carry it out onto the verandah where we balanced it on the railings. Unbelievably, Pat managed to persuade one the members of the committee, very drunk at the time, to be the one to topple it over from this first floor verandah. Once again, we bought a new piano for the club! We emerged from this escapade unscathed as the poor committee member had to own up that it was he who gave the piano its final, fateful shove over the top!

Years later, one of the club members painted a huge mural on one of the pub walls which comprised all the different types of airplanes, from the oldest to the most recent, that had been at the club. In the middle of this mural is a flying piano with little angel wings, which is still there today. So, if ever you're in Durban ...!

My new passion for flying took over my life. One morning I awoke after a party and Marlene said to me "So, you're off to America today then are you?" Apparently, whilst under the influence of alcohol (which, for me, doesn't take very much at all), I had told Vern McWilliams that I would go with him to Witchita, Kansas, to collect a new aircraft - a Beachcraft Baron - and fly it from the United States back to South Africa.

This was quite an experience as we had terrible weather throughout the whole journey, plus quite a number of other problems. We had to fly for between ten and twelve hours a day for five days, taking off early in the morning at around 3am, and flying right through until early evening, and each day brought a new problem. In Boston, we noticed a little too late that we didn't have the necessary customs documents, so had to telephone the Beachcraft factory, which got in touch with the customs officials and promised to send the papers immediately. Luckily, the officials let us leave on the factory's promise to supply the paperwork. Then, on our next stop-over in Torbay in Newfoundland, the weather was so bad that we had to ask the control tower for a GCA - a ground controlled approach - with the cloud base at 100 feet. Thick, dark clouds blocked our view and, right up until the minute the wheels touched ground, we were guided by the control tower. Vern flew superbly. The next day, officials wouldn't let single-engined aircraft take off because the weather ship, which housed the halfway direction beacon, had switched off its beacon to go and look for survivors from a ship that had gone down close by. We were allowed to leave as we were flying a twin, but some time after we were authorized to take off for Santa Maria in the Azores we found that our long range radio had broken down, and we could not communicate for some hours. Upon arrival at Santa Maria we discovered that we'd been on red alert because of the lack of communication. We were told that we could not take off until our radio had been repaired, which meant staying there for several days until the spare parts arrived from the United States.

This was out of the question! We waited until the air controller went off duty, and when his replacement arrived assured him that our radio had been repaired. He believed us and, after collecting our landing fees, gave us permission to leave. Unfortunately, as we were taxiing out towards the runway, the radio control room asked us to make a radio check to ensure our radio was now working properly. We tried to bluff our way through but eventually they demanded that we return to base so that they could make the tests themselves. Vern and I looked at each other for a second. Knowing full well that this meant we would be stuck there for ten days, I indicated 'go' and Vern opened the throttles and away we went. Vern warned me to have the torch ready as it was possible the control room would switch off the runway lights, throwing us into darkness with only the aircraft lights to see by, but this didn't happen and away we went. Over the radio the control tower came screaming through at us, saying our aircraft was not authorized for take off and we should stop immediately. But it was already too late and our plane cut through the air heading for Las Palmas. We had flight planned for Las Palmas as it was close but, in reality, we did not need to stop there as we had enough gas to take us through to our next stop, which was Bissau on the bulge of Africa. However, we did stop there only to run up against more problems with the officials who decided they needed to keep the original of our insurance certificate and would not accept a photocopy.

Well, we finally arrived in Durban, in one piece. Vern was a very experienced instrument-rated pilot, but he let me fly leg-for-leg with him. Another of our problems was that the automatic pilot would not work and we had to fly manually all the way ourselves. I was lucky in that Vern was very confident and easy-going and had confidence in me, so the trip gave me invaluable flying experience which stood me in good stead later. I loved it.

The Ranch was proving very successful. Approximately two thousand people bought Sierra Ranch shares so we were making money, which enabled me to pay off the loan from Golden. So, the ranch was debt-free and when I retired in 1986 I had R500,000 cash in the bank as well. Most of the original shareholders still hold their shares and, even today, their children

Back to Normal Life

benefit from the discounts and advantages granted to them.

My family and I had a great life on the ranch for twelve years and we were able to indulge in whatever made us happy. I spent a lot of time flying, going from owning a Mooney to a Bonanza to a Baron, and each week was flying either to Durban or Johannesburg to promote the Ranch. I had two teams of professionals helping me promote Sierra Ranch; one in Durban, headed by Peter Dornan, and the other in Johannesburg, headed by Jimmy Graham who is also a fantastic pilot. Both had their own planes and because of this there was always a lot of air activity around the Ranch.

One year the organizers of the South African Flying Championships chose Sierra Ranch as the venue for the Championships, as everyone in flying had heard about Sierra Ranch by now. Luckily, the piece of land adjacent to our landing strip was a field of winter feed grass for our livestock. When the organizers rang to ask how many planes we could park at the ranch, they were surprised when I said 300 (we had mown the grass and stored the feed to make the whole field available.) During the event about one hundred and fifty planes were there at any one time, with planes taking off and landing continuously. We used one plane as a control tower and the event was very successful.

I was also travelling for Golden Products, promoting the company and its products. Meetings were scheduled regularly, usually every three months, and were generally held in very exotic locations, such as Hawaii, Las Palmas, Switzerland, Palma de Majorca or California - Golden Products even have a ranch in California. During my first two years with the company I travelled throughout the world and the ten years that I spent handling Sierra Ranch meant I could more or less stay home.

One year at the end of the 1970s, we were in Geneva for a Golden Products convention. I had been invited to the Isle of Man to ride the Honda 6 for the parade lap. I couldn't leave Geneva until the morning of the parade lap but at breakfast was told by one of the locals that there was an air traffic controllers strike in the UK. After checking in at Geneva airport I got friendly with one of the ground hostesses and told her of my rush. She admitted that my flight to London had no chance of leaving on time so I immediately changed my flight to one to Paris on a plane which was leaving in a few minutes. From Paris, I planned to rent a small aircraft which could fly me to the Isle of Man. As I was arranging this in Paris, a loudspeaker announcement told me that the regular flight to Manchester was ready for departure. As this flight was quicker, I decided to take it and from Manchester rent a small plane for the Isle of Man. I bought my ticket and boarded, but as we taxied out it was announced that due to the backlog of planes waiting to take off, there would be a two-hour delay. Breakfast was served as we rolled slowly towards the runway!

Eventually I arrived very late in Manchester and knew I couldn't get to the Isle of Man in time for the parade. Disappointed, I called the Isle of

Jim Redman

Man to ask the organizers to excuse me for not being able to honour their invitation, explaining why I wasn't able to make it. I took the train that the airline company had provided for travellers wishing to return to London. As it approached London it started to slow and then stopped completely. I knew we were quite close to where I was heading and, having reached my limit of frustration and annoyed by the events of the day, took my baggage and jumped off the train. The train moved on and I found myself alone in the middle of the country, not knowing where exactly I was. I walked down the railway line to the road where I was picked up by a passing car which took me to the closest village. From there I called the friend I was supposed to visit the next day on business, who was amazed at my tale and at how I'd come to be there, and asked him to come and get me.

One of my most enjoyable trips was one I made to the Isle of Man in 1978 for Mike Hailwood's return to racing. To be honest, at the time I thought Mike was crazy to return to racing after such a long absence. I told him exactly what I thought; that he had everything to lose, that it would ruin his image should he not win, and that he really had nothing to prove anymore, especially since he had not ridden on the Isle of Man for eleven years. Quite amused, he said: "Of course I'm crazy! So what?" He went on to say that what had started as a bit of fun had gotten completely out of hand and had very quickly become serious. When the newspapers reported the story, several people had jumped on the band wagon - particularly sponsors - and Mike found himself back in at the deep end.

However, I was quite wrong about him disgracing himself, but no-one could ever have guessed that he would win in such a way, especially after an absence of eleven years, and in the TT! His victory there was extraordinary. Later, as Mike and I walked into the bar at our hotel, George Turnbull, the *Daily Telegraph* reporter shouted "Here they come, living legends!" to which I replied, pointing to Mike "Not me - him!" Turnbull said "If you'd been riding in the race, you would have been right up there with him as always."

It was said that Mike's extraordinary 'come-back' could only have happened on the Isle of Man circuit, because Mike knew this very long and very dangerous circuit better than anyone else, and had won it so many times, implying that he could not have done it on another circuit. A few days later the organizers of the Mallory Park circuit asked Mike to race in the post-TT meeting. Mike accepted and once again won fantastically. Following this further success I said "Maybe Mike won this time because the circuit was so short? Where should he race the next time? Perhaps on a circuit not too long or not too short?"

My son Brett climbed higher and higher up the motocross ladder. He went from Yamaha to Honda to Kawasaki, winning many South African Championships along the way, becoming one of the best - if not the best - motocross rider in the country. I remember his first motocross World Championship race, which was on a 250 in the 1984 South African GP. It

Back to Normal Life

was held in Johannesburg and all the best foreign riders were there. I found a spot on the inside of the first corner from which to try and pick him out amongst the fifty or so competitors. I had no trouble spotting him as he led right from the first corner; it was so exciting seeing him in front of this world class field ahead of the biggest names in that category. Brett was overtaken by two other riders but he wasn't about to give up that easily. He rode like a demon but with control; it was a pleasure to watch him. Normally, motocross heats in South Africa are of twenty-five minutes' length, but go on for forty-five minutes in GPs. Brett held onto his third place position for thirty-five minutes but as he went past me he indicated that he was getting tired and couldn't hold on much longer. I signalled him to try and hang in there but another two riders caught up and passed him. He finished in fifth place which was an excellent result, especially considering that this was his first race with foreign riders who were a lot more experienced and used to longer races than he was. Because he had earned points in this first GP of the season, he was invited to take part in the following GPs, as were all the other riders who had points in this race. However, Brett was the only South African to score.

Later that year we left for Europe, together with Brett's faithful friend and mechanic, Andrew Bell, and headed for the GPs in Austria and Switzerland. Brett did not like the cold, wet climate of Europe and soft muddy tracks on which these races were run - he'd always been used to hard, dry, fast surfaces. Neither was Brett a good traveller; he hated the language problems and strange cultures, and different organizational methods encountered. But, even though his results were pretty mediocre, he returned to Europe for other GPs throughout the season, but was definitely not at his best and not the same rider on these surfaces.

Brett decided to move to Los Angeles to try his luck there and Andrew went with him. The racing was better as the American circuits were more like those in South Africa. However, it didn't take Brett long to realize it would be difficult for him to make an impression in the States for the simple reason that he was not American. In the US sponsors were not interested in sponsoring non-Americans, however talented they were. And there were plenty of American riders to sponsor; riders they had seen grow and develop, and with whom the fans could identify. Brett was bitterly disappointed. He had been six times Motocross Champion of South Africa in the 125, 250 and the 500 categories and was respected in South Africa by the fans and the biggest motorbike importers, so it was very hard to be unknown and completely ignored. He decided finally to return to South Africa and continue riding on home ground. However, fate decided otherwise for Brett had two very serious accidents, both of which almost cost him his life. In the first crash he ruptured his spleen, which had to be removed, and in the second his arm was badly broken. This put an end to his racing career.

Although I am his father, and therefore biased, I consider Brett to have

Jim Redman

been the best motocross champion of his era. After motocross Brett took up jet skiing and became South African Champion at that, too. He raced in America, representing South Africa at Lake Haversu.

Whilst at Sierra Ranch I got involved in horse racing. At the end of the 1970s, Roy Meaker, a very well-known and respected Durban businessman, sold me and my friend and hotel manager, Jim Lawless, a race filly called Diamond Treasure. This was my introduction to the crazy world with which I was to become so deeply involved. Through Jim Lawless I met Ivan Pickering who at that time was Diamond Treasure's trainer. Ivan spent a weekend at Sierra Ranch so that we could talk about his profession, about horses and the horse racing environment because it was all very new and very different to me. I also wanted to discuss the Ranch with Ivan.

A few weeks later he returned with one of his patrons, to whom I explained the ranch project and who immediately became a shareholder. On the Saturday morning he arrived for breakfast, dressed in suit and tie, ready to go to the races. He suggested that we make a little bet on the jackpot run over four of the races this Saturday, and spend about R50 each. We would have won 50,000 Rand that day if Brian had not forgotten to include one horse - and a very good horse, by the way - in our bet. As he drove from Sierra Ranch to the Pietermaritzburg racetrack, Brian suddenly realized that he had made a big mistake by forgetting that particular horse. To make up for this mistake, he placed another very small jackpot bet which lost as well. He was very frustrated and kept saying that although he could pick the winners he couldn't make any money. We started betting together and made some money. Brian persuaded me that the best way to make money in the horse racing world in South Africa would be to buy a good quality horse in England.

The problem with this plan was that all the best horses were very expensive, and we could not afford to spend a fortune: Brian had no money so I would have to finance this. We had to find a horse with lots of talent but not one of the very best. After a lot of meticulous research, we found Foveros. Brian persuaded me to invest in this horse, which had not had the chance to prove what he was capable of because he kept coming up against Kris, the all-time champion then. When Kris's racing career ended, he was put out to stud at a price of 8 million pounds, whereas we were able to buy Foveros for R225,000.

Foveros spent six months getting acclimatized to his adoptive country and then won everything, including five Group 1 races. As we were intending to put Foveros out to stud when he'd done with racing, it was imperative he had these Group 1 victories. He was by far the best racehorse in the whole country, although his successes on the track were nothing compared to those on the stud farm, as we found out in 1982 when we put him to stud. He finally got his revenge on his old rival Kris by becoming a far better studhorse. He was Champion Stallion of South Africa for nine of

Back to Normal Life

the last ten years. One of his descendants, a horse called Singing Boy, was raised under the kind and careful eye of Jim Lawless at Sierra Ranch and won a total of R850,000 in stakes.

To some of us, Foveros was priceless, with plenty of class and personality. Vern Perry, a very solid friend of mine, used to sit with me and we'd rave about Foveros. Vern was also a shareholder and loved him too. Before the age of 48, I'd not even opened a newspaper at the horse racing section and yet suddenly race horses were a major part of my life. I can remember every race Foveros won; I'd shout him on so much that by the end of the day I was voiceless. I particularly remember some wonderful evenings spent celebrating each new victory, like the one in Cape Town following Foveros' victory in The J&B Metropolitan Handicap GR 1. Before this particular victory, we'd told the waiters and owner of a famous restaurant in Sea Point, Cape Town, to bet on Foveros in the upcoming meetings, that is to say The Queen's Plate and The J&B Metropolitan. We'd also told them that, in the event Foveros won the 'Metropolitan,' we would probably come there to celebrate, and that we would like a table for twenty right in the middle of the restaurant. As we had hoped, Foveros won and we began celebrating right away at the racetrack. We then headed off to the restaurant, arriving very late, and outside found a long queue of people, patiently hoping to get a table (the restaurant did not take reservations.) However, since the restaurant owner and personnel had won a lot of money due to our tip, they had kept us a nice table right in the middle of the restaurant as requested.

Later that night we went to one of the most popular nightclubs in Cape Town. As it doesn't take much alcohol to make me tipsy, I soon found myself sitting on the floor with my back to the wall, declaring that Foveros' next step was to win the famous Arlington Million race in Washington,DC in the United States. Of course, everyone thought that I was rambling. Two weeks later I had entered Foveros in the American race and paid the $3000 entrance fee. Unfortunately, we came up against quarantine regulations concerning all foreign animals entering the United States and weren't able to compete. However, the organizers of the meeting in Arlington were so impressed by our efforts to get our horse into the race that they reimbursed the full entrance fee.

We had a lot of fun at the races and regularly chartered a plane for twelve passengers to fly from Durban to the Vaal Racetrack for race meetings, where we were often successful. On some occasions, when we had made even more money than usual, instead of heading back home with our winnings we'd fly off to Sun City to play Black Jack, Punto Banco or Craps in the casino.

Last year Foveros' offspring won just over R5 million, a new record by a long way. He was a wonderful, magnificent animal, distinguished and incredibly strong. Unfortunately, he died in 1994 and from that point on I lost all interest in horses, selling off my horses and getting out of racing and breeding.

    I tasted the excitement of seeing my horses win races, and got an incredible kick out of it. I could understand now why there was no shortage of sponsors for bike riders, for I'm sure they experienced the same feelings when they saw one of their riders do well in a race.

16
Salt in the Wound

During a period of nearly twenty-five years, I had the most fabulous life and was a very happy man. A loving and united family; work that fascinated me; variety; financial security; sincere and loyal friends and, above all, an insatiable appetite for life. How could I ever anticipate the terrible events that were just around the corner. The loss of a dear friend and terrible betrayal by my family, borne out of their greed. In the blink of an eye the gloves came off and all the hardship endured, all the battles fought throughout my early life, were nothing compared to this, as throughout these earlier trials we'd been a united family. In fact, those early memories made my feelings of desolation and helplessness even worse.

I learned of the death of Mike Hailwood one day in 1981 as I was sitting reading the paper. There I read that Mike and his daughter Michele had been the victims of an accident and had both died practically on the spot. They had gone out to buy fish and chips and their car had collided with a lorry. Even now, it's hard to describe the pain I felt then. I was in deep shock, deeply revolted by what I regarded as an unjust tragedy. As tears welled in my eyes, I saw again the hundreds of images of Mike; our races - nightmare races, some of them, where there could be only one winner - our partying, where we let ourselves go completely, our brief private moments talking passionately about nothing but bikes; our unique complicity that bothered other riders but which united us forever; the mutual respect and admiration at the end of each race. What hurt the most was the way in which he had met his death: it was absurd. If he had been killed in a race, although my pain would have been the same, it would have seemed more appropriate; if he had to die he deserved to die in battle, on the circuits, in the TT.

I picked up the phone to make arrangements to go to his funeral, but then slowly returned it to its cradle. I thought of all the very many people who would be there: riders, company representatives, sponsors, journalists and photographers, plus, of course, his family and friends. There would also be those who attended purely to be 'a part of the event,' to see and be seen and steal whatever free publicity they could. The thought of this hypocrisy and insincerity sickened me and I decided to stay home. I hate funerals and have always preferred to show my respect to people whilst they are alive rather than when they are dead. Later, I went to see Pauline, Mike's wife, to help her with all the paperwork and problems that such happenings always cause. I knew that she would be needing help with the lawyers and with the businessmen. and, since Mike had been one of my best friends, I had to help her as much as I could. She seemed like a fledgling just fallen from the nest, abandoned and completely lost and distraught by what was happening.

I have so many memories of Mike. I remember one year he fell off his bikes sixteen times with barely a scratch. His way with his bikes was unique; it was all or nothing. That was his charm and maybe why he was so hugely popular with the media, riders and, well, everyone. I still miss him, this charismatic creature made up of shadow and light, who more than made his mark in motorbike racing.

The next knock came from my brother. Since their childhood, I had been practically a father to my young twin siblings Peter and Wendy. When our parents died, I promised myself that I would love them and help them as best I could, despite our very frugal existence. Of course, my older sister Jackie and I knew that we would never be able to completely replace the love and tenderness of a real mother and father, but we gave without counting so that the twins could grow up as normally as possible, teaching them to be stronger and more independent each day. The hardships we faced in England united us and made us more attached to each other. When I brought Peter and Wendy to Rhodesia after they had finished school, I took them into my new home, even though I was newly married, and under my wing, happy to have them close to me once again. I helped them find jobs in order to get them settled. Their wages were low but we felt we were rich, and the twins were so proud of earning some money.

I always supported Peter in any way I could. I helped him buy his first motorbike and later his first car. For his part, he didn't complain about giving me a hand, helping me repair my motorbikes in the evenings after he had finished work, and whenever he could, coming with me to some of the races. Later on I helped and encouraged him when he started racing, but his girlfriend, Annette, ordered him to quit the racing, and since he was deeply in love with her he obeyed; in fact, she ruled him. I found out later that she had promised to marry him on the condition that he give up any idea of motorbike racing.

Some time later Peter and Annette got married. Jackie told me recently that Peter borrowed money from her every time he visited. Jackie would take out her chequebook as he walked in, knowing that was the reason he was there. She didn't need the money then so wasn't bothered about it. Then, it

Salt in the Wound

was my turn. Peter came to me to ask for money when he wanted to set up a business in Bulawayo. Naturally, I obliged. Finally, when I retired from racing and decided to go and live in Durban because of the war in Rhodesia, Peter decided to do the same so, again, I helped him financially with the move. In fact, I helped him buy an Italian sports car which he brought to Durban and resold for a handsome profit.

Once we had established ourselves in Durban, Peter found a good job and began to handle his affairs much better. However, he was ambitious and wanted more than anything else to start another business as his first had not been a success. He started out very modestly by selling machine tools, presses, lathes milling machines, and the like, for another company. He did very well, but was always frustrated as he knew that he could make more money if he could buy the machines first, and then re-sell them rather than just getting a commission on his sales. I lent him the money he needed to expand his business and he did so well that a short time later he had an offer to buy half of his business. He was in a quandary: he wanted the company to grow, but did not to want to lose control of it. He came to see me and ask my advice. I told him to refuse the offer and keep the business in the family as I would help him financially again. I then bought a 25 per cent share of his enterprise, at the same time injecting more capital into it so that it could expand.

By this time Peter's marriage to Annette had ended and he had a new fiancée called Linda, who was soon to become his second wife. They both worked very hard and the business became quite profitable. Peter was ambitious for growth and asked me to invest more money to finance expansion into a branch in Johannesburg with an associate named Rodney Cook. Rodney owned 25 per cent of the branch, Peter 50 per cent and me 25 per cent. Even though the business ran very well, I continued to invest the capital necessary for its development and we became the fourth largest machine tool company in South Africa. At this particular time, a local bank called Volkskas decided to invest in industry and we resold 51 per cent of the two branches to VIB., the bank's industrial arm, for R1,050,000: to us, a fortune. Peter's company still owed me a lot of money, but Peter promised he would repay it as soon as possible, plus an extra amount that belonged to Peter, Rodney and me. We agreed that I should keep the extra money for as long as was necessary to accrue the interest I might have made had I invested my money in a concern which had paid interest. Only then should I give Peter and Rodney their portions of the additional amount.

For the moment, however, everything was going well. With the help of our new partner, VIB, we were able to buy out the oldest machine tool company in the country called Drury Wickman, which we renamed Drury Redman. With this acquisition we became the biggest machine tool company in South Africa. Peter and Linda - by now married and with two sons - decided to move to Johannesburg.

As well as being involved with Sierra Ranch and the racehorses, I had

Jim Redman

started an enterprise which produced chemicals and printing plates for the printing industry. One day our factory workers went on strike so we decided to hire school leavers who could not find jobs in order to keep the factory producing. A mysterious fire broke out and destroyed 50 per cent of our factory, started - we were certain - by the strikers who were very angry because we had hired school leavers in their places. The damage was considerable and loss of revenue substantial. If we wanted to recover our previous position, we had to reconstruct the factory as quickly as possible and so went straight ahead with this difficult and very expensive project.

At the same time I had over-invested in my horses as I had decided to buy some English horses using off-shore credit because interest rates were much lower than in South Africa. Unluckily for me, the political and economical situation in South Africa suddenly worsened, causing the Rand value to drop heavily against sterling. I had not taken any forward cover for this loan and did not have the facilities to bring it on-shore, so found myself having to repay it in pounds sterling - meaning I lost a fortune entirely due to my own bad judgement.

So this disaster, coupled with the fire in the factory, meant my financial position was somewhat unstable, to say the least. Peter was very financially secure, owning a large house in Johannesburg and another in Durban, so for the first time in my life, I went to ask my brother to help me out. As soon as he heard of my predicament Peter said he would sell his house in Durban and lend me the money I needed. I told him I didn't need such a large sum and he said, in that case, he could help me out immediately; quite frankly, I didn't expect any less from him. Besides all the help I had given him in the past, just before our agreement with VIB., the South African economy was not in particularly good shape, and I had signed personal guarantees to help the machine tool company survive, putting my house and all I had at risk. At the time Peter was so stressed and worried that he couldn't sleep at night, afraid of losing everything and going out of business. Every day I went to cheer him up and give him support. He well knew that if things did not improve, I would lose everything. Mostly because of our refusal to give up and his hard work and my scheming the situation returned to normal, but it was a long haul and I'd risked a lot for him.

When I went back to Peter for the money he had promised to lend me he said he didn't have it any more as he had invested it. I was devastated and asked him why. He said that a good deal had come up and he had taken it. I slept on this but woke in the middle of the night and asked myself how I could be so stupid; I thought Peter was lying to me, though I could hardly believe it.

The next day I rang Peter's bank and asked for his account balances; everyone says we sound the same so I knew the bank would think I was Peter and give me the figures. Then I rang Peter and told him what I had done. I gave him his account balances (which were much, much higher than

Salt in the Wound

I wanted to borrow) and asked him why he did not want to lend me the money? He was clearly very embarrassed but said that, as he did not think I could possibly survive, he did not want to lose any of his money and so was not going to help me. I could not believe my ears: what an arsehole! After all I had done and risked for him and he would not help me at all. Then it dawned on me. His first, instinctive reaction to my request had been to offer to sell his house in Durban, but now he was balking at lending me a small amount of cash from his account, something or someone had changed his mind and I wondered if it was Linda. Was Linda the problem? I was speechless and at that stage not even cross, just simply amazed. Then I remembered how weak Peter had been with his first wife, Annette, when she had forced him to choose between racing and her.

I realized that Linda, in ordering Peter not to help me, was getting her revenge on me. A long time before, I'd had an affair with Linda: she was introduced to me by a single guy who was having an affair with her and her sister at the same time. When Peter broke up with his first wife Annette, I suggested an affair with Linda to cheer him up. But Peter fell in love with her. At the beginning of their relationship everyone thought that it wouldn't last, nobody imagined it would become serious enough for marriage. This is the only reason I can think of why Linda would want to cause trouble between Peter and me: not only were we brothers, but also the best of friends and I think it's this that she never completely accepted.

Peter's refusal to help affected me deeply; not because of the money - I knew that somehow or another I'd survive - but because I had lost someone I'd considered my best and most loyal friend as well as my brother. This was like the world coming to an end, after all that we had endured and enjoyed together. Peter turning his back on the first occasion he had where he could help me for a change filled me with disgust and I started to look at him in a completely different light. I reminded him of the fact that Redman Machine Tools would not be the company it was if I had not lent him the money for expansion. Even when he did not think we were going to make it through our problems I'd still had confidence. When I began to threaten him with awful things I realized I was becoming as pathetic as he was. I knew our mother would be turning in her grave if she saw us destroying each other in this way.

One day in Johannesburg, it all came to an end. So thoroughly disgusted was I with this pathetic piece of shit in front of me that I told him to get out of my life, I never wanted to see or hear from him or his wife again. Apparently, Linda admitted to Peter that she had slept with me, although she couldn't very well deny it as I'd told Peter. I can appreciate why Linda never felt at ease with Peter and me, as I was the only one who knew the truth about her. If this was her problem she was wrong to worry, because I would never have hurt her, or Peter, in this way.

Peter let it be known we had had a huge argument about money, and it was for this reason that we were not talking to each other. I want to put the

Jim Redman

record straight here and now and say that he was completely mistaken. Yes, money was the thing that caused him to do this to me, but the main reason I shoved him out of my life was the betrayal, the lies, the let-down of finding out after all these years that he had been using me. That is what so completely destroyed me, I had lost at the same time my brother and my best friend. This all happened in the mid-1980s and for over ten years I did not speak to Peter. During that time I recovered financially as I knew I would, and luckily Foveros was profitable at stud, so my financial position became much more secure. As far as I was concerned I had an ex-brother and an ex-sister-in-law.

One day in 1994, I saw a film on television which told the story of a family that had lost both parents, and the older of the boys had to work hard to support his younger brothers and sisters - more or less our story. At the end of the film, feeling very sentimental I picked up the phone and called Peter and told him how I felt after watching the movie. I thought to myself, let's put this whole miserable affair behind us and pick up where we left off. I could tell when he heard my voice that he was very excited. He and Linda rushed over to visit me the next day but, regrettably, try as I might, I realized that my love for him as a brother and any other feelings I might have had were dead forever. He had killed that and now I did not even like him.

What I didn't know then was that Peter had made even more money with our business, and his *nouveau riche* attitude and snobbishness reinforced how I now felt about him. On top of that, I've recently discovered that after our famous quarrel, VIB decided to sell out its investment portfolio in various companies and had sold the shares in all of the companies in which they were partners. By mistake, also sold had been not only VIB's shares in Drury Redman but ours as well. This regrettable incident put the bank in a very difficult situation, because if it become publicly known, it would have been very embarrassing. Peter, with the help of his new partner, bought back the shares for the ridiculous nominal sum of R1000. All of this, of course, I found out much later by accident, during the course of writing this book, when I was reading the letters from Linda to Jackie that Jackie had kept. In one letter, Linda had written that Peter had been very lucky to be able to buy back in his own name this 49 per cent share at such a cheap price but that Peter was keeping it all for himself and Rodney and I were out of the business and out of the deal. More and more cheating; I was discovering one deception after another, years after they had happened. The letter was written with such relish that I knew for sure it was Linda who had come between Peter and me, but I still blame him for being weak enough to allow her to do so.

Whilst writing this book I telephoned Peter and asked if there was anything he wanted to say in it, in particular, perhaps, his version of our break-up? His answer was that he would have to think very carefully about it, which made me think "I bet you will as it would be hard to put anything down on paper." To be fair to him I rang and asked him four times to give me his side of the story but I'm still waiting for it. I would have liked to read

Salt in the Wound

what he had to say, it would have been very interesting; perhaps one day ...

Wendy came to Africa and visited Peter and Linda and was dumbfounded to discover that Peter had never told his friends he had a twin sister. He was, quite simply, ashamed of her, because he considered her inferior. During one of his trips to England, Peter admitted to Jackie that he hated talking about his poor childhood. He told her that he does not have many friends, preferring to make relationships with rich people capable of helping him or being useful to him, rather than remaining friends with his old buddies. That's what happened to me: everything was fine whilst I was useful to him, but when he thought I was no further use, he dropped me like a brick. Without money I was without interest. Of course, he was always proud to have a World Champion for a brother, but perhaps even this irritated him; to be only the brother of a star and not the star himself. Who was Napoleon's brother?

Everyone knows that Wendy has a twin brother, but a lot of them think it's me. Since her visit to Peter's house, she has only ever spoken of one brother. She was mortified by Peter's absurd behaviour that day and the change in him, and could not believe that he was so ashamed of his past and his sisters, who were not as comfortable financially as he was.

I know that Peter did want us to become close again; it showed when I tried to put what he had done behind me, as he was all over me. Now that I am back in the spotlight he'd probably like it even more, but as far as I am concerned it's finished. I've never really fought with Peter - and never would - preferring to simply treat him with the contempt he deserves. Now it's as if he didn't exist.

Peter even went to see Marlene to try to discredit me. Marlene's reply was along the lines of "You're trying to tell me that Jim is a bastard. Well, maybe he is in some ways, but not in the way you're suggesting." This was at a time when Marlene and I were not getting on too well and she was already thinking of divorcing me, so I was delighted to hear what she'd said as it showed that even though Marlene was aware of my faults, she recognized that, fundamentally, I was very loyal to my family and friends. Moreover, at the time when I had risked my house and all I owned for Peter when he was in great financial difficulty, Marlene had warned me about doing it, saying that Peter would never do this for me if the positions were reversed. I was so sure of him that I told her she was completely wrong, that my brother was very loyal and would never let me down whatever happened: how wrong can you be! She was so right and it's a pity I did not listen to her at the time. It was only a few weeks ago I found out that Peter had cheated me of my 25 per cent share of the company as well as the money. Still, that's all water under the bridge now as it happened years ago and I will never, ever see my share of the proceeds. Let him have it; at least I can sleep at night ...

So, my original feelings of revulsion and disgust and then sadness have been replaced by indifference. I hope one day that Peter will realize what he has lost forever and the heartache he brought to his own family, especially his twin sister who he thinks is beneath him. She is worth two of him, she has a heart of pure gold. May he one day remember the incredible love that united us all, until his actions dirtied and killed this unity, all for the sake of some miserable money. We, the rest of the family - Wendy, Jackie and I - are not ashamed of our poor background. We are proud that it forged our characters, made us stronger and better with greater regard for others. I ran into one of our mutual friends a few years ago who asked after Peter. When I said "You mean my ex-brother," he laughed and said "So, finally he caught you too. He caught all of us and we always wondered how you escaped, scot-free, without getting caught by him."

Even though it felt like I was drowning in my problems, I could still count on my sons, Jimmy and Brett, who stood by me no matter what and always told me that I would get back on top of all the negative things that were happening. They gave me the strength to fight on and not give up. At the same time as my problems with Peter, I could feel that Marlene was not very happy. She said she felt neglected and complained that I never took her out or was ever with her. It's true that most of my time was spent working and trying to settle all the problems that kept cropping up, but her complaint that I was never with her was a bit harsh as I worked from home. In fact, my working from home was another sore point with Marlene, but the reason she did not see much of me as because she was always out.

Marlene persuaded me to pay for her to have a face-lift. I agreed to this even though I found her attractive as she was and prefer people as they naturally are - a few lines show character. After the face-lift, and to keep herself busy, she started spending more and more time at the golf club where she was a member. She took off for a weekend of golf with some of her friends and when she got back she was acting very strangely. That evening she told me that she had to go out and see one of her girlfriends and would be back in about an hour. She didn't come back all night, I almost went crazy with worry not knowing where she was, imagining all sorts of terrible things - horrors - walking around the house, not knowing what to do. I guess I was naive or stupid not to guess the truth; her distant behavior, the face-lift, the time away from home - all the signs were there but I had so much trust in her that the truth just did not enter my mind.

Even when she stayed out that entire night, it never crossed my mind that she had had a weekend away with her lover. How naive can you get! The next day at around lunchtime she phoned me as if nothing had happened. I asked her where she was and why she had left me all night with not even a phone call to set my mind at rest that she was safe. She replied that she had spent the night with a girlfriend, because, apparently, she needed time to think. Think about what? I asked. She wouldn't tell me.

It still did not occur to me that she was having an affair, and with a much younger man. When she returned home, her attitude was more than distant,

Salt in the Wound

she didn't want me near, and after a short discussion she said she had to pop to the shops, but would not be long and then we could have a long chat about everything. Instead, after showering, changing and grabbing some things, she went to her lover again. I was completely shattered and devastated by her indifference, her coldness; she seemed to be doing her best to hurt me as much as she possibly could.

For years I had been a naughty bastard, having affairs, but was always very discreet so as not to embarrass Marlene; in fact, most of my affairs happened whilst I was in another country. Marlene had been a very good wife and mother and had seemed happy to stay at home and raise and educate the children, when she could not come with me on my travels. A lot of the Golden Products conventions included wives, in which case she always joined me and loved the excitement of travelling to new places. Despite an instinctive need to seduce and charm, I loved Marlene passionately and, oddly enough, had been a very good husband for some time: it had been many years since I had cheated on her. My love for her was just as strong, as intense, as when we'd first met. Of course I was guilty on all counts, but what really upset me was the way Marlene chose to leave me, it seemed as though she wanted to inflict the maximum hurt. Maybe this was intended as retribution for all my infidelities over the years. Perhaps because I had become a more conventional, stay-at-home loving husband she lost interest in me? Or maybe it was just that our marriage had become boring and routine.

Anyway, I discovered that she was having an affair and the identity of the man. So I started to give him a few headaches in his business. I discovered that he, too, was in a financial mess and it seemed to me that he was after Marlene because he thought he could get money from her in order to solve his financial problems. They quickly moved in together, in spite of the fact that he had another girlfriend he was still seeing regularly, and was calling on his ex-wife twice a week. He certainly was a busy man. I told Marlene what I had discovered and the problems I thought she would face if she stayed with him, reminding her that she was ten years older than him, and that in this relationship she could only lose. She would not listen to anything bad about him, even though in her heart of hearts she knew what I was saying was true, but she was infatuated and he was playing his cards well, hoping to get some money from her to help him out of his tight situation.

We were divorced and were like two strangers, walking past and not seeing each other. Losing Marlene, right after Peter, finished me off completely and succeeded in wiping me out. It hurt me more than the death of my father and my mother together and that is really saying something. I lost all interest in life and all confidence in myself. I'd worked my whole life to support the two families that I loved more than anything. Now, my wife had left to go her own way, and my children were grown up and independent. Why, then, should I continue to work hard and put pressure on myself and my health for nothing?

Jim Redman

I decided to resign from Golden Products and retire. The company was pushing for me to do this, in any case, as I was a shadow of my former self and useless in my present state. I was 55 years old and felt like the loneliest person in the world.

Thank God I still had Jimmy and his wife and family, and Brett, to whom I owe my salvation. They were the ones that brought me out of my deep depression. I couldn't eat and was slowly dying, little-by-little every day. The only thought in my mind was that Marlene should come back to me. I told her I knew I'd been a naughty bastard over the years, but that she had got her own back. I suggested that we call it quits, turn the page and start a new life together. She was not interested.

Jimmy took care of the reconstruction of the chemical factory after the fire and, at the same time, took over the management of the company which he still does. The company originally specialized in chemical products for the printing industry, but later Jimmy diversified the product line by going into household chemicals as well. Jimmy met with resistance to this plan from another director, who tried his best to discourage him from taking such a big risk - but when he saw the results, he regretted not having made the move before.

Marlene tried to push our divorce through as quickly as possible, and wanted to agree a cash sum of money that would be hers, so that she could help her boyfriend by lending it to him, but the opposite happened and things dragged on and on. Marlene was under the influence of her boyfriend, who kept pushing her to ask me for more and more money. Stymied by my refusal, he became more and more agitated. One day I received a 'visit' from two men, intended to frighten me. My reaction couldn't have been more unexpected to them: I laughed in their faces and told them that, in my state of mind, I was a lot more dangerous than they were because I did not give a damn what happened to me. In fact, I told them, I would relish this type of confrontation as I had faced possible death each time I had raced. I said that if they wanted to they'd better put a gun against my chest right away and fire, otherwise, get the hell out of my house. In any case, I told them, I had friends that would take care of Marlene's boyfriend should anything happen to me ... The pair left and I never saw or heard from them again.

Later on Marlene and I were able to discuss and agree on certain things, but each time her 'friend' interfered it all fell to pieces. Her friend didn't like my ideas; he wanted only to get money and as quickly as possible.

Then came the day that Marlene sold our beautiful house in Durban. We owned one of the nicest and most prestigious homes in Durban and had long ago agreed that it would never be sold but should remain in the family for Jimmy and Brett. If, for any reason, I was ever forced to sell it, we agreed I would pay off the nominal loan and give her half of what was left. To make her feel happy and secure, I had put the house in Marlene's name but had bent the rules to do so. Without warning she sold it, after receiving

Salt in the Wound

a stupidly low offer. I had already swallowed quite a few deceptions, but this was the last straw and I was furious. For the first time in a long while I reacted immediately and I must say that it made me feel better. I wasn't able to stop the sale going through but I did manage to get the buyer to pay a much higher price and as crazy as it may seem, this fight went a long way towards helping me recover my spirits.

I had opened a small casino in a section of my house with its own entrance, so now started a new career in the gaming industry. In the long-term it was not very profitable, but at that moment the idea of starting such a business was exciting. It meant that I met new people from different walks of life but, above all, would allow me to meet young and beautiful, uncomplicated women - exactly what I needed to build my confidence and give me a taste for living again. South Africa was undergoing a transformation and I was one of the first to open this type of casino. Obviously it was quasi-legal as there was a loophole in our new legislation, but neither that nor the possibility of being fined deterred me, nor did it stop the proliferation of other casinos. In fact, at its peak there were hundreds of them in the country. Strangely enough, it was legal in the Homelands, so though in Durban it wasn't legal, just 150 kms away one could gamble with impunity.

This double-standard is typical of South Africa at the moment which is a bit like the wild west. We are all guilty of looking out for ourselves, without noticing or thinking about the horrors going on around us. We read the newspapers, of course, but shrug and hope that nothing ugly happens to us and our loved ones. Practically the whole of South Africa is guilty of this; closing its eyes and pretending to live normally, ignoring the clashes, fights and violent crime that go on, managing our own lives and businesses as if nothing is wrong. I'm just as guilty as anyone; a long time ago I took the easy way and chose not to think about all the horrors that we can do nothing about. The reality is that for most of us who are neither politician nor criminal, there is nothing we can do.

Besides this, I was so crushed by my own disasters that I was able to concentrate only on myself and my new venture. The authorities finally decided that we had to close our little casinos. However, while my casino was running I was leading a crazy life; without family responsibilities I was determined to live each moment to the full. It was a very strange period in my life: on the one hand I was having a good time, not giving a damn about anybody or anything, but on the other was unbelievably lonely as I was just not used to being on my own a lot of the time. A lot of very glamorous girls worked at my casino but, deep inside, I didn't want this sort of life long-term.

To everyone I seemed happy and lively when really I was depressed and lonely. It was then that I met Kwezi again ...

17
A New Beginning

After having lost touch with Kwezi for a long time, by a stroke of good fortune I met up with her again. In the past she had often come to the Ranch and I had seen her grow from the age of eight to fifteen, when she'd had a crush on Jimmy who, in his twenties, was too old for her.

As soon as we met up again we went out to dinner. She had become a very beautiful young lady, gracious, sensuous, fine-spirited and quick, with a vivacious, well-defined personality. From then on we spent a lot of time together. Kwezi told me about her trips to Australia and her great desire to visit Europe, she'd always dreamed of going. A few weeks went by and we came to know and appreciate each other and got closer, a lot closer.

I offered to make her dream of seeing Europe come true so, in September, we headed for Italy - Milan to be precise - where we were received like royals by Giacomo Agostini. He had sent a driver to the airport to pick us up and drive us directly to Monza where the Formula 1 GP was taking place. At the time, Giacomo was running his own GP motorcycle team, sponsored by Marlboro and, because of this, we were their guests for the F1 GP. We were received in style and everybody from the Marlboro team was so welcoming, nothing was too much trouble. We had very good seats from which to watch the race, just above the pits and facing all the television cameras. Before the race, we were invited to the Marlboro company lunch with the team and drivers; we had a marvellous time.

Kwezi and I spent a few days at Giacomo's home in Bergamo. He was an outstanding host and also arranged for a friend, Paul Bushnell, to join us for the race and benefit from Marlboro's hospitality. Paul was a great Agostini fan and was in seventh heaven at the chance to shake the hand of his idol and experience the everyday life of his favourite team. Later on, Kwezi and I left for Switzerland in order to spend a few days with my old friend and Honda teammate, Luigi Taveri and his wife, Tildy. Again we were warmly

A New Beginning

received in their home near Zurich. Then we drove across Germany and France and arrived in England, where we visited many famous monuments and landmarks that in all my years of travelling I'd never bothered to see. On we went to visit Jackie and her husband Roly, and also Wendy and her husband Richard. Of course, they were all very surprised to see how young Kwezi actually was although I had told them she was younger than I. Kwezi was only twenty years old, and lots of people told me that our age difference was too great. I replied "Kwezi is under twenty-one years of age, and I'm over twenty-one, so the difference is not that great ..."

In London, I dropped Kwezi off at Buckingham Palace to see the Changing of the Guards and went to park our rental car. Needing some small change for the parking meter, I went to the closest newspaper shop. On the cover of the magazine *Classic Racer* there was a full-page photo of me with the caption "Jim Redman the Unpopular Champion." Of course, I bought the magazine to see what this was all about, and why, according to the magazine, I was so unpopular. The actual article - the title was *The Complete Professional* - was quite full of praise for me and related how I tried to win the my races as slowly as possible, as well as my totally professional approach to my motorcycle racing career. I took this to be a great compliment, especially as I'd started my career as "an accident looking for a place to happen."

We had a marvellous holiday in England, then returned to France and went again to Switzerland - Geneva this time - and on down to the French Riviera where we visited Cannes, Nice and Monaco. With Kwezi, I felt as if I had come to life again: we enjoyed every minute together. Despite all the travelling I'd done, this was the first time I'd done it as a tourist. I'd crossed the world from north to south, east to west and vice versa, but always at full speed, rushing from one circuit to another, having to arrive with enough time to prepare for the next race. Even when I was with the Honda team I had criss-crossed the world. When Jimmy had to go to school in Durban I was racing in Europe, travelling to and living in South Africa and testing out the motorbikes in Japan, returning to Durban each time there was a free weekend in order to spend ten days at home with my family. My life consisted of airports, racetracks and hotels; the only time I could ever relax was during the European off-season when I could go back to South Africa, or Australia or New Zealand to race as here the meetings were spaced further apart, and there was time to rest, go water-skiing, fishing or just generally hang out between race meetings.

So, for the first time in my life, I was a simple tourist with Kwezi, who taught me how to take my time, how to stop and smell the roses ... We went to gamble in the casinos at Divonne-les-Bains in France and in Monaco. At the main casino in Monte Carlo, we were stopped from going in as Kwezi was not 21. The doorman, seeing her sad face, kindly let us just quickly take a peek inside. We crossed the square and enjoyed a drink at the Café de Paris, by which time we felt so tired that we decided to return to our hotel to sleep. Later, I woke and, leaving Kwezi sleeping, went back to the casino to play. What a bad idea; I lost all the money we had just won in the casino at Divonne-les-Bains. In an effort to get it back, I played much longer than I had intended, but kept going until I had won back the money I'd lost, together with a profit.

I rushed back to the hotel but Kwezi had already woken. Finding me gone she tried to get out of the room and was surprised to find the door locked from the outside. She had a hard time trying to make the hotel personnel understand that she was locked in but finally managed to liberate herself and walked around outside of the hotel. Then, she started to get hungry but didn't have any money on her, so had to wait for me to get back in order to buy her something to eat. I got back late in the evening, and was not too popular as she was exasperated and worried, not knowing where I was although she had guessed. When she saw the money I had made, however, I was immediately forgiven!

For a long time when we travelled Kwezi qualified for student and youth fares, while I benefited from senior citizen rates. Many times I've been asked if Kwezi is my daughter, to which I reply "No. She's my granddaughter."

Returning to South Africa, we were still enjoying each other's company immensely, and decided that Kwezi would come and live with me. In the beginning, she kept her own apartment in case things did not go well, but soon gave that up. Months, and then years went by and we were still so happy together that we started to consider the idea of getting married. At first I told her she was crazy to want to marry me and that she should just live with me whilst my health was good. Then, when she met the right person closer to her age and with whom she got on well, she was free to go. I also added that I would always look after her financially because she meant so much to me. Her reaction was very quick "But it's you I love!" For an old fart like me it is fantastic to feel loved by someone so much younger - and as dynamic - as Kwezi. All of her friends accepted me very quickly and, because of this, I see my old friends only very, very rarely, since they have become too old for me! Of course, I still have my circle of old buddies, all of whom welcomed Kwezi. When I first met Kwezi she used to take me to her friends' 21st birthday parties, whilst I took her to my friends' 50th or 60th birthdays, or Golden Wedding anniversaries. Then it was her friends' weddings and my friends' funerals: four weddings and a funeral became four funerals and a wedding!

At the same time that I was experiencing this great love with Kwezi I was still interested in horse racing and breeding. However, in 1993 I could feel the end coming. We had invested in some of Foveros' yearlings, which were very expensive. We hoped that one of them would turn out somewhere near as good as Foveros so could replace him once he was gone. Unhappily, this plan was not successful. We purchased some lovely-looking Foveros colts, some ourselves and some in partnerships or syndicates. One of them

A New Beginning

was an exact replica of his father in looks, but could not run to save his life. We suffered substantial losses as a result.

Now that Foveros was getting on in years, his insurance premiums had doubled and were too expensive. As he was looking so fit and well - as if he would live for years - we reduced the cover drastically. At the end of 1993, Foveros developed a serious foot infection. I was not unduly worried as I had never heard of a horse dying from a foot infection. There was an American vet in South Africa who specialized in the treatment of ailments of horse legs and hooves, and he was brought in to examine and treat our horse. Foveros appeared well on the road to recovery but when the vet went away for the Christmas holidays, the infection came back. We were unable to save him and at the beginning of 1994 Foveros had to be put down. I couldn't believe it; I'd simply not considered the possibility that a stupid infection would cause the death of this extraordinary horse.

So, on top of substantial financial losses I had now lost what felt like a third son. Foveros had his own personality and I respected him because he had the conquering spirit of a champion. He always tried to win his races, and then turned out to be the best stallion South Africa has ever seen. Losing him killed my interest in horses and horse racing and left an emptiness inside me.

That same year I married Kwezi. We had a simple wedding ceremony, no formality at all and people were invited to come casually dressed so that everyone would be comfortable. We have been married for nearly five years now, and are just as happy as we were the first day. After nine years, we are still so very happy together, we take life as it comes, and we enjoy ourselves.

After my race in Daytona, offers for me to race on other circuits came flowing in from all over, but Kwezi said firmly "No more races, only demonstrations from now on." I agreed with this; I was sixty-three years old and even though I still felt good on the bike, with the same strong desire to win, my body was not as flexible and as agile as it once was. My reflexes were slower, and it was obvious that if I should fall or have an accident, it would take longer for me to recover. Most of all, I don't want the pressure. I want to be able to fully appreciate the electrifying atmosphere at the circuits and be relaxed enough to have time to meet and get to know the fans, something I'd been unable to do before. I had all the time in the world with nothing to prove and at last could enjoy the advantages of being a retired rider.

Daytona had been an extraordinary challenge and experience, but now I had nothing more to prove, either to myself or anybody else. My triumphant return to racing very quickly elicited an invitation from the Hungarian television star and comedian, Joszef Borocsky. He invited me to make an exhibition ride at the Hungarian hillclimb in the outer suburbs of Budapest.

Once more I found myself in a real race. I was to share the Triumph 750 with local journalist and racer, Imre Paulovics, who was also the owner

Jim Redman

of the motorbike. The first run up the hill I went quite fast on the deserted sections and waved to the crowds on the popular corners. They told me I'd made third fastest time even though I spent most of my time waving to the crowds as I took the bends. For the second run, now that I knew I was being timed, I tried much harder and could have achieved a better time but for problems with the brakes which right from the start were quite loose. Imre had tried to fix them but long before the finishing line I found myself on a motorbike without a front brake! Despite this I was the only rider in the hillclimb, out of the top few, to better my time on the second run and, with the points notched up during the two runs, managed to make third place. After this, I said, I will never enter or compete in a race again ...

Since Daytona, my life has changed a lot, with this new career opening up for me. Kwezi and I are invited everywhere and it's nice that she is always included. In fact, when I went to one demonstration on my own, I was told to teach Kwezi to ride the 6 so that if only one of us went it would be her! The first meeting we were invited to was the post-TT at Mallory Park. Returning to England in early June 1995 to again ride on this familiar circuit was unforgettable. It brought back a lot of memories, and being able to make a couple of laps on all the Team Obsolete bikes was fantastic. I rode the MV Agusta 350 and 500 (four-cylinder and three-cylinder.) Then I rode the Benelli four-cylinder and, of course, at last, the Honda 6. The crowd's welcome was out of this world. In the United States my welcome had been extraordinary, especially since it was the first time I had ever set foot on an American circuit. However, the welcome here at Mallory Park was no comparison; the crowd was fantastic. The organizers were over the moon as there had not been so many spectators in a long while, and were amazed at the attraction that these fantastic classic bikes still held, even in these modern days. These were truly machines that had·defied time ...

It was here that I met the very charming and charismatic owner of the Mallory Park complex, Chris Meek and his wife, Olya, who invited us for drinks in their home on the island in the middle of the circuit. They asked us to sleep over but we had to refuse this offer as we had already made other arrangements.

David Overend and his mother (who run all the events at Mallory) always look after us so well too, and it's thanks to them that Mallory has become what it is: a magnificent spot with a unique atmosphere which holds very special memories for me.

After Mallory Park we went to Assen for the Dutch TT; Holland is the only country, as far as I know - apart from the Isle of Man - that has called its GP a TT. The circuit here has always occupied a special place in my heart and is by far my favourite venue. I'm not sure if this is because I was so successful there, or because I was so successful there that it became my favourite. I just know that I really enjoy riding on this exceptional circuit. The tar has an abrasive quality which allowed us lean the bikes right over even

A New Beginning

on our old-fashioned tyres which, besides being very narrow, were not made of the best compound compared to modern tyres. We actually thought the new cling rubber was fantastic, but only when compared to what we'd had before! I was very saddened to see that at the request of present day riders who wanted to make it safer, the Assen circuit had been reduced in size by half. When I was racing, the circuit had already been halved in size, so this further reduction meant it was now only a quarter of the size it was originally. Even so, it remains a very good circuit today and rider safety should always be a main concern.

The public turnout was again incredible. Assen is one circuit where the spectators are close enough to the circuit to fully appreciate the speed, yet still very safe. During practice sessions we'd had experience of their kindness and incredible enthusiasm for the classic bikes and us old riders. On the day of the GP their warmth and enthusiasm was overwhelming and a lot of fans came to visit us as our area of the pit was open and accessible. It was just like a tidal wave and we met countless numbers of the most incredible fans, each one more passionate than the last. Most of them knew my career by heart and the Hondas I had ridden over the years, including the Honda 6. It was great to be able to talk with these people from all age groups and I was amazed at just how many of them - and especially the younger ones - had a lot of respect for our era of motorcycle racing.

A lot of the fans were simply curious and had come to admire and touch the Honda 6, which they would not have seen in its hey-day as they were too young, but we could feel their inherent love for these old motorbikes. Some came to see me because they had recognized me walking around the paddock, even after 29 years of being away from Assen. I was happy to know that I had not been totally forgotten and said as much to one of the fans. His reply was absolutely magnificent "As long as one of us who saw you race is alive, you will never be forgotten."

When we brought out the 6 the crowd began to press around it, realizing that we were about to warm up the 'animal.' As soon as I started the engine and they heard it rev up, the other GP mechanics threw down their spanners and ran out to find out where this deafening noise was coming from. For us oldies this was just routine, just the 6, but for all these young people who had never seen the Honda before, and had never heard a motorbike sound like this before, it was a real shock. And coming from such a small motorbike compared with today's modern machines, which are enormous, especially the 500s. At the end of our demonstration, several fans came to congratulate us and say goodbye as they were leaving to go home. When I told them that the GP was about to start, a brief shrug of the shoulders indicated that this was not the reason they had come to Assen. I could barely believe it; some of these young people could quite conceivably have been my children, or even my grandchildren, and yet their interest lay not in modern racing but the old machines and glories of a bygone age.

Jim Redman

The next meeting was at Scarborough where just me and a couple of other riders from the past were overwhelmed by the sight of the 20,000 spectators who had come to see us and the 6, instead of the predicted 10,000. The police had telephoned the organizers to have them make me wait a while before starting the demonstration, as there was a nine-mile tailback of cars full of people wanting to hear and see us queuing at the entrance roads to the city. The police said if I would delay my demo, they would go along the line of cars with a loud-hailer and tell the crowds not to worry as the demo would be delayed until 2pm. Whilst waiting for all these people to arrive, the organizers asked me to go and sign autographs for an hour or so. Three hours later, I was still signing autograph upon autograph and the only reason the fans eventually let me go was because it was time to go back to the pits to ride the 6. What surprised and fascinated me the most about the fans (besides the large numbers and their enthusiasm) was that they represented all age groups. The younger ones said they'd been told by fathers and grandfathers that they would never see Jim Redman riding the famous Honda 6. Admittedly, It made me feel my age but at the same time elated and all I could do was thank them. When I'm riding the 6 and feel the 17,000 revolutions-per-minute roaring, I become a youngster again. I talked about this with Luigi Taveri and we agreed we did not feel anything like our nearly 70 years; back on the bikes we feel 25 again. It's a magical feeling and the crowd's enthusiasm makes it even more so: we are at one with the machines and the fans.

The following year, 1996, at Scarborough, Peter Hillaby, manager of the circuit and Yorkshire's 'Mr Motorcycle Racing' took an enormous risk. He began by inviting Agostini and myself for a whole weekend event. Once he had publicized this and monitored the ever-increasing hotel reservations, he took a new gamble. He asked Barry Sheene to come from Australia, and then invited some English stars like Phil Read and Carl Fogarty and Irishman Joey Dunlop to come as well. What a master stroke! This prestigious line-up attracted more than 64,000 spectators to Scarborough and the event was a huge success right from the Friday evening, when more than 5000 people lined the beach front to see us riding our racing bikes - complete with police escort - along the promenade. The crowd cheered as each rider passed by, and then we gave interviews from the roof of an open-top tour bus which was fitted out with a PA system. I guess the public loved it, because I know that some of them telephoned their friends to come for the rest of the weekend.

We had the first demonstrations on Saturday which were a great success. Kwezi and I were driving to the circuit Sunday morning when she said to me how nice it was to be held up in so much traffic, Peter must be very pleased to see so many people and so much traffic arriving. Once we arrived at the circuit, shaking Peter's hand I said to him "I am sure that you will reach your goal of 50,000 spectators this weekend." To which he replied with a smile that said much more than words "I think that we already have, Jim, and it's

A New Beginning

only 10.30 in the morning." He was right, as I have said, as more than 64,000 spectators joined him to see the old machines and riders. The press headlines ran "Golden Oldies still bring in the crowds."

Peter Hillaby and his wife have always welcomed us warmly and it really is a pleasure going there. Recently, Peter told me I would always be welcome at Scarborough, and said if ever I felt like going I had only to pick up the phone and he would fly Kwezi and me in. He said the fans loved having us there.

I can't write about Scarborough without mentioning Tony Coupland, who has always worked very hard to contribute to the success of the meetings and the circuit, as has the whole of Peter's terribly efficient and professional team. These individuals always seem to have time to treat everyone with kindness and patience at all times, even when under the most intense pressure.

David Tappin too must be mentioned. David runs the Yorkshire Air Museum just north of York and not far from Scarborough. Besides ace pilots he likes to have guest motorcycle racers every month to give talks to the local enthusiasts, and there aren't too many riders who have escaped David's attention. David has invited me to host a "Tribute to Mike Hailwood Evening" on September 4th 1998, which I am sure will be popular with the crowds. To make the evening even more interesting he is inviting F1 drivers as well as motorcycle riders. It should be a good night and it will give the fans a chance to get near their idols and hear them speak. Scarborough is the same weekend so it means that the fans can take in this event, too.

During my week at Daytona in February 1996, Chris Carter asked me a question on his very popular live radio show which takes place during "Bike week." He asked "Jim, according to you, who is the best rider of all times, excluding yourself, of course?" My reply was unequivocal: "There can be only one rider that qualifies, Mike 'the Bike' Hailwood, and that does include me too." A year later the subject came up again on the same show, but this time I suggested that we write down some different criteria to determine who was the 'Best Rider The World Has Ever Known' and suggested some examples of what these may be. Two months later, whilst in Laguna Seca in California, a group of seven enthusiastic fans told me they had had their own debate after the radio show and had each written down their own criteria. According to them to qualify for consideration as 'Best Rider The World Has Ever Known' the rider had to have accomplished the following:

1. To have been World Champion in two different categories for at least two years, but not necessarily consecutively. This would prove that the best rider in the world was versatile and not just a winner in a particular class.

2. To have won GPs in a third category for the same reasons.

3. To have been at least five times World Champion in order to demonstrate the ability to race and win.

4. To have won a minimum of 100 other major international races apart

Jim Redman

from GPs.

They told me that when they took this criteria and applied it to riders past and present, only three names satisfied all the requirements: Mike Hailwood, Phil Read and Jim Redman. They then voted by ballot which gave the following final result: three votes for Mike and two each for Phil and me. So they, too, considered Mike Hailwood to be the best rider ever, with Phil and me joint second. Amused, I reminded them that they had not taken into account one thing - winning three GPs in the same day, an accomplishment that only Mike and I had ever achieved in the entire history of motorcycle racing. They agreed with this and said "OK! Mike first, Redman second and Read third." I told them that I was very happy to be joint second with Phil Read, especially as Phil is the only rider to have won races in the 1950s, '60s, '70s, '80s and '90s which in itself is a fantastic achievement. I also said I was very surprised that they did not mention any American riders, particularly as we were in the United States and they as Americans would be very patriotic. They replied that only Freddie Spencer had achieved the double in the same year, but that he did not fit the other criteria.

The Centennial GP at Assen in 1998 was a huge success even if it did put years on Ferry Brouwer. Kwezi and I arrived in Assen and were waiting for our documents at the welcome office when we were introduced to Luke Lawlor, whose bikes I was to ride at Assen. Luke introduced us to his brother, John, and we all got on like a house on fire right from the start. Luke was pleased to let me ride his bikes and I was very happy to do so once I had seen how well organized they were and how well the bikes were turned out.

Assen was a fantastic event with so many riders it was impossible to spend as much time with them as you wanted. Many I would have loved to have had a meal with to chat about old times, but it was impossible to do in just one weekend. I think there were over 300 riders present, and as many fantastic classic machines worth millions of pounds.

Honda was there celebrating Honda Motor Company's 50th anniversary, with Mr K. Kawashima, one of Mr Honda's first twelve employees, Aika San and Kunimitsu Takahashi, Naomi Tanaguchi, Teisuke Tanaka and Moto Kitano as riders. Remember, Mr Kawashima was the man who as Team Manager signed me for my first ride on the 125 Honda at this same circuit in 1960. He also signed Tom Phillis and myself for our first - and, incidentally, Honda's first - works rider contract in 1961. They all looked very young for their ages and I began to feel as if I was in my twenties again when I was riding the bikes, so it felt like the '60s rather than that we were all in our sixties! However, I felt the difference in the evenings as I was stiff from riding but still wasn't getting to bed until the early hours!

It was good to spend some time - even if it was all too short - with old friends we have not seen for so long. There was Frank and Rita Perris and Ralph and Jean Bryans, with Peter Pawson, Johnnny Anderson and Noel McCutcheon from New Zealand; Carlo Ubbiali and Umberto Masseti, and

A New Beginning

many, many more too numerous to mention individually and all of whom I have not seen for years. Then, of course, there were those we see all the time now, Giacomo and Maria Agostini, John Surtees, Phil Read and Wendy, Sammy and Rosemary Miller, to mention but a few.

Ferry Brouwer is to be congratulated as the Centennial Classic GP at Assen was his brainchild and he did a fantastic job of getting this major project off the ground and, ably assisted by his hardworking team, making it all work so well. The weather was cold initially but warmed up every day of our stay as if the Gods were smiling on these old riders who were really enjoying themselves. Ferry had his birthday party at our hotel on the Saturday evening with about 1500 guests, every function room, plus the foyer, housed a buffet table and bar and a great party was enjoyed by all. I was very touched when Ferry got very emotional as I presented him with my 1963 250cc Dutch TT-winning trophy as a birthday present. I was very glad I gave him this when I saw how much it meant.

A few personal moments that I enjoyed immensely were the five or six laps that Ago, Phil Read, John Surtees, Bonera and myself rode on Friday on ex-factory MVs. We passed and re-passed on nearly every corner and it was great to see each rider's fans leap in the air as their favourite took the lead. Then, in the pre-1960 500 race, I rode a Norton loaned to me by a Dutch rider. I had to start around 50 metres back in about the 8th row of the grid. We push-started the bikes ourselves that first day with no pushers, and I got my usual flying start and led into the first corner. Derek Minter on the very fast Summerfield Norton passed me on the back straight, as did Surtees on the MV, and it gave me a lot of pleasure to pass Derek a couple of times in the corners before the sheer speed of his Norton took him away from me. I must congratulate the Summerfield guys on how fast they have got their Nortons to go and the beautiful way they turn the bikes out.

Of course, the highlight for me was my two laps on the Honda 6, which it took all of Saturday evening to arrange. Everyone was calling me Henry Kissinger as I went from one group to another, ensuring it would not upset anyone if I went out on the 6. In the end, everyone agreed that the fans came first and I rode it on Sunday. Unfortunately, a big end siezed after only two laps, locking the back wheel in the fast left-hander just before the start and nearly throwing me off and leaving a huge black skid mark on the road. I should have got the clutch in sooner but my reflexes are not as quick as they were in the 1960s!

Kwezi and I had some lovely long dinners with Luke and John Lawlor, with others like Ralph Bryans and Stuart Graham joining us for a glass or two of port after they had finished their meals. Of course, the memories came thick and fast and, as always, I found it amazing how everyone remembers something different from the same event. I thought that Luke and John would get bored with it all, but they seemed to love every minute.

We came home to Durban for eight days after Assen and then I left

Jim Redman

for Montlhéry for the Coupes Moto Legende meeting organized on the old banked circuit near Paris by Serge Cordey. This is a meeting with a difference as hundreds and hundreds of riders take part so the pits are busier than a main street as the fans are allowed into the pits, too. It sounds chaotic - and it is! But it works very well the way Serge runs it and we all had a great time.

A very amusing incident occurred at Montlhéry. I had arranged to do a couple of laps on Luke's 250 Honda 4 and then hand it over to Phil Read, who had John's permission to ride it. I was then to have a few laps on a Swiss-owned 500 triple Honda of mid 1980s vintage. As arranged, I handed the Honda 250 4 to Phil and jumped on the 500 Honda standing next to us and was pushed off by a man I thought was the mechanic for the Swiss bike. I'd been told that first gear was down, so I pushed the gearlever down but the bike would not start. The mechanic insisted I pushed the lever up and I was surprised to find that this was correct; the bike started and away I went and had a fantastic ride on what was the most powerful bike I have ever ridden. Only after I came in did I find out that in error I had jumped - uninvited - onto Martin Jones' ex-Freddie Spencer 500 Honda which he had brought to Montlhéry for Phil to ride. Martin was real cool about the whole thing and must have thought to himself "If Jim Redman wants to try my bike, it's OK by me," and just pushed me off. We had a good laugh about it afterwards and have since become friends, travelling together from London to the Isle of Man. Of course, in the next session I did manage to get on the right bike and, with Phil on Martin's bike, we had a nice dice. I taught Phil a few new lines, cutting straight through the chicanes to catch him up.

Of course, my main objective in Montlhéry was to ride the Luke Lawlor bikes, but Luke was busy in Ireland making the money to pay for all this fun, so John drove down with a mad Irish friend, Austin Kinsella, who taught me to speak some Irish. Kwezi had decided to stay home in Durban for a little longer so, after a fantastic weekend at Montlhéry, John talked me into going back to Dublin with them. He offered to fly me there but I preferred to go with them in the van. We seemed to be laughing all the time and the miles just flew by; we caught ferries with just minutes to spare and in no time it seemed we were in Dublin where we were met by Luke Lawlor and Bill Sparling, a former Irish champion.

After dinner with Luke and John, Luke proceeded to show me Dublin while John went home to re-introduce himself to his wife and family before leaving again for Germany to take care of some business. During the time spent with John at Montlhéry and travelling to Dublin, and the time spent with Luke in Dublin, I came to know and like them both very much, they're such straight shooting guys and so keen on the classic bike scene. I was overwhelmed by their hospitality; they took care of everything and wouldn't even let me convert my money into punts. I'll get my own back, though, when they visit us in South Africa! We also had a great lunch with all the Dublin racing enthusiasts, former riders and journalists.

A New Beginning

Whilst I was in Dublin, Luke Lawlor persuaded me to go to the Skerries meeting and do a demonstration with Phil Read, Ralph Bryans and Sammy Miller, as well as Luke himself and Irish riders such as Ray McCullough and Austin Kinsella. When I saw the circuit, I joked to Luke that any promise made after midnight and a couple of pints of Guinness should not be taken down and used in evidence against me. I really did enjoy riding there, even though the circuit is so bumpy and narrow that it's known as "Scaries." I'd love for all the modern GP riders who complain about bumps on today's circuits to see it!

There are roughly three legs to the circuit, one is of normal width but the next two get steadily narrower and bumpier to the extent that there is a whole section where two cars cannot pass without both putting two wheels in the dirt. I had one of the travelling marshals take me down there to watch the riders come over the bumps, on the back wheel in the wet, down the steep drop of Gillie's Leap. It was a sight to behold, and that there has never been a fatal accident on this narrow lane is a tribute to the riders' ability to stay on their bikes. It is no wonder Irish riders dominate the Isle of Man races when they've grown up riding at Skerries.

Between races, members of the public are able to stroll down the circuit to change viewing position, but as soon as the commentator announces that the bikes are coming out for the next race the circuit is cleared in moments. It works well, and stops people walking through the fields and trampling the barley crop - very important as the barley makes the Guinness! This is just one example of how if people are treated as adults, they will respond and behave accordingly.

I cannot begin to describe the unique Irish atmosphere that exists at this circuit, so will leave this to the brilliant article that appeared in a major national daily, written in inimitable style by Andy Kershaw. I would like to mention a couple of funny incidents, however. Phil Read stopped at a restaurant for lunch around midday during his visit and was knocked out to see a sign on the door which read "Closed for Lunch." On another occasion, a couple walked into a bar at 10.20 in the morning but were told that the pub didn't open until half-past ten. However, they were quite welcome to wait the ten minutes until opening time and, by the way, would they like a drink whilst they waited?

Read on, as Andy's article says it much better than I ever could.

— Skerries motorcycle races - July 1997 —

"When we were little," said a Dublin-born acquaintance of mine, "we were told if that we didn't behave we'd be sent to Skerries." Well, if my weekend in the little seaside town just north of Dublin was punishment, I'm taking up S&M!

Festivities kicked off on the Thursday tea-time with the Classic Parade through the centre of the village. Signing-on was at a picnic table by the

Jim Redman

Ladies' toilets on the seafront. Stringy local youths - all in tracksuit bottoms and smoking Embassy Regals - milled around in the middle of the road. The first bark of an exhaust brought elderly residents tottering down to their front gates. Mums with pushchairs spilled off the pavements.

The classics weaved their way through. A double-decker bus blocked half the street and, throughout, the roads stayed open. Regular traffic, local shoppers and commuters returning from Dublin, mixed it with screaming Yamaha TD2s and clucking Manx Nortons. Nobody but me seemed to think this was out of the ordinary. In fact a Country & Western line-dancing team - a vision of synchronicity in black Stetsons and electric blue shirts - kept right on twirling and clapping in front of the Carnegie Free Library as the bikes blasted by. It doesn't bear thinking about but, until the 1960s, the *races* passed through the town centre.

In the Bus Bar, I raised a glass with a group of Skerries fans from the Isle of Man. "This place," said one, "is like stepping back into the 1950s." "Nah," said another, "more like the 1930s." Now, coming from a Manxman, this carries some clout. It's no marketing blarney, either, when the commentary on the promotional video from the Skerries Tourist Board tells us, "on the north coast of Dublin lies a village where time has slowed down."

"I tried to phone for a taxi," continued the bewildered Manxman. "There were only two. One was busy and the other fella had gone ice-skating."

"You see this wee bar here?" said Kenny Anderson of the Moira Motorcycle Racing Club, pointing to a vast drinking facility on Skerries main street. "'Well, last year we were queueing outside one morning, waiting for them to open at half past ten. On the dot at ten-thirty, they unlocked the door. We went in ... and it was *packed*."

"Skerries not only welcomes its visitors," promises the tourism blurb, "it opens its doors and hearts to them." Still opening its doors at half-past midnight - if you knew the right door to knock on - was Kenny's favourite pub. There was plenty of the open-heart stuff going on inside, though liver transplants have yet to be introduced.

So many pints of Caffrey's from total strangers were piling up, I needed a caddie - or to escape through a toilet window. You see, the singing had started.

With his guitar, Fire Officer for the races, Denis Martin, was leading the whole pub through 'Wild Mountain Thyme' and something called 'Yellow JCB.' I was, at first, dreading them roping me in, though by the time I left town on Sunday I realised I'd sung most of the Merle Haggard catalogue in public. At 2.00am, tottering back to Mrs Wilde's excellent B&B, we were very much in a Skerries state of mind. I knew this when we passed the pub I thought we'd been in.

Before Friday practice, feeling not fully race-kitted, photographer Mac and I went for a sighting lap or two in his van. Mac had been to Skerries once before, but remembered hardly anything about it, except that he knew he

A New Beginning

had to come back and something about the race commentator appealing for someone to "get that tractor off the circuit."

Even by Irish road-racing standards Skerries is bumpy, scary, fast and narrow - in places very, very narrow. Legend has it that when the Grand Prix tough-guy, Alex George, came here in the 1970s, he pulled up on the lane out of the paddock and asked a local for directions to the circuit. The local looked at Alex like he was daft. "This is the circuit."

I'd seen the photos. I'd read the awestruck reports. I'd heard the Irish fans rate it the most spectacular. Yet I was no more prepared than Alex George for the insane reality of the Skerries track. There isn't exactly a ribbon of grass growing down the centre of the road but the surface was caked in dried mud and not-so-dried cow pats. Baldungan Corner, recently resurfaced in the sprayed tar and roll-your-own style, was covered in some places by loose chippings and, in others, by no chippings at all. (During practice I was hit on the head by a stone chip which came off a bike's back tyre like a bullet.) Steep grass banks line the course. Spectators line the banks. For the riders, it's like plunging down a chute. As a spectator you don't get any closer than this. There are no run-off areas. Only bales and sacks of Irish peat (each one sponsored by local enthusiasts or businesses) come between a tumbling rider and oblivion. At the outrageous Gillie's Leap the bikes are airborne for fifty yards at 140mph on a twisting bumpy lane just ten feet wide. It is astonishing that in 52 years of racing at Skerries there has been only one fatality.

R J Hazleton doesn't look much like a motorcycle racer. In Skerries Central Café it was tricky to connect this soft-spoken, balding, fortyish intelligent man-with-beard with the lunatic I'd gawped at in practice. RJ, who pulled the highest, longest wheelies over Gillie's and drew yelps of approval from the fans, reminded me of one of my university lecturers.

"Actually, I work in a fabric warehouse," he said. "Were you standing it nearly vertical on purpose?" "Oh, yes," said RJ, grinning on his chicken nuggets. "You don't seem crackers," I said, "not in here." He laughed. "It's more stable over the bumps on one wheel."

Newcomers, and those who still insist on using two wheels, are taken around the track before practice in a coach. I snuck on board to listen to the lecture from the travelling marshal, Ray Taylor. "OK," Ray began, "I'm here to show you right from left." And with that we rumbled off from Race Control (a shed in a farmyard), turning down a lane barely wide enough to take the coach - ordinarily the Skerries shopping bus to Dublin. At the first corner, the riders apex the bend in front of Fagan's Crash Repairs, a location chosen by Mr Fagan with naked, if not insensitive, opportunism.

"We've marked some of the rougher bits with white paint," Ray explained. At the back of the bus I was bouncing off the seat. We were touching 25mph. The fastest riders, Gary Dynes and Phillip McCallen, get round here averaging 103mph.

Because of the bumps and the twists and the cambers, agility, as opposed

Jim Redman

to brute power, is all at Skerries. McCallen's outright lap record was set on a lightweight, 250cc Honda two-stroke.

"Many of the driveways on either side," I pointed out to first-time visitor and classics competitor Chris McGahan, "are wider than the track." "And smoother," noted Chris.

Another rider recalled his debut at a similar Irish road race. "I went out in practice, did a few laps, thought 'I can cope with that,' went out for a race and we went the other way round."

Back at the paddock, Bob Jackson from Cumbria was heaving his Kawasaki from the truck. "We don't call it Skerries, we call it Scaries," he laughed. Bob is one of the quick men around here. His opposition was rolling into the paddock - the teams of Norman Gordon Plastering & Flooring, Wire Wise Electrical Contractors and Bill Smyth Heating and Plumbing. (Ever wonder where your builders disappear to?) Early arrivals queued at the scrutineering tent, tyres covered in slimy green cow dung. "Everything seems a bit bloody well ... er ... Irish," muttered an English tuner.

Roads specialist Mick Chatterton from Barnsley was ready to ride a track he loves but most would dread. "People at home say I must be mad to race at the TT but, actually,"... he paused to look around, "the TT is the safest track I race on."

I hurried to get into position. No-one else did. Between races and practice sessions, spectators stroll airily along the lane to the next vantage point. "Get off der track, folks," urged race commentator Big D. (This was when he wasn't fixing up fans with accommodation over the PA system.) "Der boiks are now on der road, folks! Please, get off der track! Respect proivate property along der course and for God's sake, folks, don't tread on der barley!"

Even when half the 20,000 Skerries crowd is as full as a bucket, they obey the familiar bark of Big D. Eventually. At the fast Duke's Bends I watched a man and two little girls still scrambling up the steep bank on the apex as Denis McCullough bulleted by, just inches away. More than once there were spectators strolling the track when the riders were on their sighting lap. Now I know what a sighting lap is for.

Just beyond Duke's Bends I chanced upon a uniquely rural racing hazard. In fact, I brushed them onto the verge with my foot. Potatoes. A couple of pounds of raw spuds scattered across the racing line. Such are the dangers of Skerries and would explain why I saw one travelling marshal rushing along on a big Suzuki with a broom under his arm.

But spillages of farm-fresh vegetables, chicanes of rich manure and weaving pedestrians couldn't stop the racing. The rain did.

During the Grand Final it poured down on the Skerries meeting for the first time in 46 years. The race was cut short but not before the Moira Club's Gary Dynes, declared the winner, blew apart the lap record - on a 250, of course. Kenny was ecstatic and hit on the idea of going to the pub.

A New Beginning

The hospitality was overpowering. I'd known most of these people for a matter of hours, now I was wondering how I could possibly live without them. Across the bar Denis was away again through the 'Wild Mountain Thyme'.

There's another race at Skerries, on the Killalane roads circuit, on 14th September. Before then, they are hosting - and you won't be at all surprised to learn this - something called The National Optimist Championships. Not much point in going home, really.

"They open in ten minutes," chirped one of my new chums, handing me another pint.

"They open *what* in ten minutes?" I asked.

"The bar." he said.

I chatted to the great Ray McCullough, uncle of the 125cc human-bullet, Denis, and one of Ireland's finest motorcycle racers of the 1970s. (Earlier, despite Kenny's warning that "eating defeats the object," I'd stood behind Denis in the chip shop.) A chubby little chap rolled between us, jabbed Ray in the chest and turned to bellow at me "Now, dere's a man who raced at Skerries before dey woidened der track."

Andy Kershaw
9th September 1997

From Dublin I flew to London to meet up with Kwezi. Whilst I waited I met with David Dew of Honda UK who very kindly arranged a car for me to use in England, and, in conjuction with Joanne Smith in Rome, arranged my trip to the Isle of Man to participate in the Parade Laps to celebrate Honda's 50th anniversary.

Kwezi insisted she did not want to fly to the Isle of Man but wanted to go by road and ferry, as she knew this was the way we had made the journey in the 1960s. We arranged to go with Martin Jones, as he was booked on the special Honda charter ferry which went back and forth for the two weeks of practice and race weeks, to make sure that all Honda owners and others were able to get to the Isle of Man when the other ferries were so heavily booked. Then, because Martin - who was taking his 500 for Freddie Spencer to ride - had to pick up his meachanic, Kwezi and I drove his van for the first 100 to 150 miles until Martin caught up with us on the M6 motorway. So, we left London the same way I had in my first years in Europe, in a smelly van with two racing bikes in the back, heading for the TT. It was fun but we were glad to hand the van over to John, Martin's mechanic, halfway up the motorway and jump into the Mercedes with Martin.

We were lucky to have a very smooth ferry crossing as it was an old ferry with a maximum speed of 14 knots. We even had to circle a few times when we arrived outside Douglas as something was wrong with the steering. In spite of bad weather the Isle of Mann was great and it was so nice to show

Jim Redman

Kwezi the circuit, as well as the rest of island. She was delighted with it all.

We must congratulate Bob MacMillan and his team from Honda Britain, and Silvio Manicardi and his team from Honda Europe in Rome as, in spite of logostical problems and continuous bad weather, the Honda 50th Birthday bash was a roaring success. At every turn they had to change their plans as races were postponed, throwing the whole schedule out. But their reward was notching up Honda's 100th TT win on the Friday so, of course, out came the 100th win T shirts which had already been printed for the occasion: there's confidence for you! We'd even joked that, if necesary, we would win the parade lap (which Bob Heath did so well on a Honda Fireblade) and add that to the existing 93 wins to make up the 100.

The Honda Britain guys impressed me as they're all genuine motorcyclists who rode the bikes from London to the Isle of Man. Bob MacMillan rode the big 6-cylinder F6C on the parade laps and rode it really fast and well, receiving an ovation from the crowd as he went round. They loved the fact he was having a real go and going very fast, especially on such a large cumbersome bike.

Fred Clark, who was commentating at Ramsay, said "Well, there goes Bob Heath, Charlie Williams and two other riders, plus Jim Redman, on the parade lap and now that the hooligans have gone through we will have to wait for some time for the rest of the parade." I was quite proud to be considered a 'hooligan' and justified this by making a mess of the second Waterworks corner, hitting the wall on the way out. Luckily, I was able to bounce off the straw bales and wave to the crowd as if it was nothing and keep going without falling off.

I worked out a great system for the parade laps; if I made a reasonable job of the corner I gave just a little wave to the crowd, but if I did a bad job, going much too slowly, I sat up and waved madly as an excuse for not getting the corner right. After all, you can't corner well and wave too, can you?

Whilst there I had the chance to meet the new President of Honda, Mr Nobuhiko Kawamoto, who was kind enough to tell me that he had watched me race in the 1960s at the second corner of Suzuka Circuit, and thought that no-one was as quick as I was through there. It's nice to know that the President of a large corporation like Honda is hands-on to that extent and so in touch with small details. Mr Kawamoto was pleased to learn that I would be in Japan for the main Honda birthday celebrations which would run from October 1st to 6th 1998, and I also had a chat to him about the Isle of Man event 1999. I explained that a lot of people had told me they were very disapointed that we had ridden the 1960s works bikes only as far as Crosby and then changed to road machines. There was a good reason for this, I know, as a full 37-mile lap is a long way for bikes which are so old and fragile. However, I asked him to consider letting me use the 500 4 and the 297 6 at next year's event and doing a full lap on the 500. I explained that the 500 was in better than new condition and would easily do a full lap, especially

A New Beginning

if ridden carefully, and Mr Kawamoto promised to consider this, as well as Goodwood next year. Who knows, maybe Honda will let me have the bikes for a number of events as the real birthday year starts in October 1998 and runs through to October 1999. I will have to talk very nicely to Mr Kawamoto in Japan in October 1998; after all, 1999 is the 40th anniversary of Honda's first race on the Isle of Man ...

Every day of the 50th birthday event (on the Isle of Man) Honda people would leave and be replaced by others. Mr Kawashima brought Mrs Honda with him and we were all very surprised to learn that she is 82 years old. As Mr and Mrs Kawashima and Mrs Honda were leaving the island their charter flight was delayed by the weather and poor Silvio Manicardi, from Honda Europe in Rome, was left with the possibility that an additional 70 people would require rooms for the night. Fortunately, the weather lifted but the three hour delay meant the charter flight had to carry on from London to Paris and Frankfurt as connecting flights had been missed.

Everyone agreed that two people were sorely missed at the 50th birthday event: Soichiro Honda and Mike 'the Bike' Hailwood.

We hope to have this book in print and ready for sale at Scarborough early in September 1998, then there's the Honda party at Twin Ring Motegi near Tokyo in October, the Bike Show at the NEC in Birmingham and the TT Riders' Lunch. After that, it's the Christmas break with, I hope, a very full year next year, especially if I can borrow the 500 4 and the 297 6-cylinder.

Epilogue

But, enough of the past; what of the future? Right now I am at a wonderful time of my life as I am really enjoying my new career with motorcycles. It's fantastic getting all these invitations to ride demonstrations and speak at various functions, and to have time to spend with my fans who have made me feel good by turning out in their tens of thousands to welcome me back. I want to thank them all from the bottom of my heart, and let them know how good they've made me feel. I feel thirty again as I zoom around on the fantastic classic racing bikes that I am so privileged to be invited to ride.

On the subject of family Kwezi and I invited the whole family to dinner - Jimmy and his wife Mandy with their twelve year-old son Ryan and eight year-old twins Bradley and Jade-Lee. Brett and Leane came with their son Travis. As I looked at them sitting around the table, I thought to myself how very lucky I was to have such a fantastic family. Jimmy and Brett have always been the best of sons; they are my most loyal supporters and we get on so well together. I have a good relationship with Mandy and Leane as well. Ryan said, as we sat around the table, that we were all champions, but that he had done better than all of us because he was the youngest champion in the family. He meant, of course, that he had become South African Triathlon Champion in the under 11 year-old category.

Brett had represented South Africa in two sports: he received his Springbok colours after being crowned South African Jet-Ski Champion, and had previously also been South African Champion many times in motocross, winning his first title when he was only fourteen years-old. Jimmy recently received his Springbok colours for representing South Africa at the National Biking World Championships. Being over thirty-six, Jimmy competed in the veteran class which means that not only am I a grandfather four times over, I'm also the father of a veteran!

Business-wise, I have many new projects to keep me busy as inventor

Epilogue

friends have asked me to help them get their new inventions off the ground. These include a new anti-theft system for cars, ten times better than anything available today, which has been patented in South Africa and in many countries around the world and which I hope to help launch, starting in the UK and America. It is unique in that it really does stop the car from being stolen in an inexpensive way, as opposed to being an expensive tracker system which locates stolen property rather than prevents it being stolen.

Another chap I met recently has invented a tyre monitoring system for large transporters. This is computerized and continuously displays tyre temperatures and conditions on a screen in the cab, and sounds a warning immediately any tyre overheats, loses pressure or starts to vibrate. Both of these will be ready to be marketed at about the same time this book goes to print so anyone who is interested can contact me via the publisher.

My favourite new project is with new friends I have made, Joe Campanini and Dr Sathisha Baijnath. We have opened a life extension clinic in South Africa, bringing to the public new products from America which I personally have found to be fantastic. The claim is that they will extend your life by one to two decades and judging by the way they have made me feel I am sure they are going to do this. On a trip to America late last year I had to take the long route via Europe, while Kwezi flew direct non-stop from Cape Town to Miami. After some time in Daytona for Biketober Fest, Kwezi spent a while with long-standing friends, Danny Steyn and his family in Fort Lauderdale, and then came straight home on the Miami to Capetown flight again. I had to go to Phoenix and LA, then back to Durban via London and Cannes, with gruelling schedules at every stop. When we arrived home Kwezi was feeling bushed and jet-lagged, whilst I was fine, and I am sure it was the course of treatment that was making me feel so good. Then Kwezi came down with a lousy bout of 'flu as well. Normally, when this happens, I would have immediately started taking lots of Vitamin C, but I felt so strong and well that I just knew the 'flu could not get me. I was right: I came through feeling fit and well and without so much as a sniffle.

The results of my blood tests, after only six months on the programme, show my body to be that of a man in his forties, and that's about how I feel. I've been told that these products need another ten or twenty years of testing, having had only ten years so far. My attitude is that, in twenty years' time I will be 86 and it will be too late. I'm not really bothered if my life is not extended; what I'm looking for is *quality* of life and these products make me feel at least twenty years younger. I get a fright every time I pass a mirror now as I feel so good I am surprised I do not look forty!

Of course, mixing mostly with Kwezi's friends also helps me to feel young as they are all in their late twenties and are all planning for the future, with big hopes and dreams, just like me. I have no thoughts of a conventional retirement - been there, done that and didn't like it one bit. I want to carry on living as I rode: fast enough to win but as slowly as possible to make it

Jim Redman

last, and I sincerely look forward to meeting as many of you, my fans, as I possibly can. Come along and say "Hi!" anytime you get the chance.

What Others Say ...

"I think that Jim Redman was a very intelligent pilot ..." — Giacomo Agostini

"In the mid-1960s Jim was the man you had to beat ..." — Phil Read

Giacomo Agostini

I think that Jim Redman was a very intelligent pilot. He knew how to take charge of everything concerning the competitions, perhaps the reason for him becoming Team Manager. His qualities of being well organised and an excellent negotiator led naturally to this position. As Team Manager he showed his maturity and experience and always had a smile on his face.

He was one of my toughest opponents, and we fought some remarkable battles.

He was the first to ask the organisers for a lot more money for pilots [riders] competing in international events. Before this they were paid very little, yet the risks were very great. This initiative made it possible for them to fulfil their passion and make money doing it!

Phil Read

Jim Redman had the reputation of being a hard rider. I found this out for myself in 1963 when I got my first ride for the Yamaha factory; in fact I had the chance to beat him in my first race, but my bike broke down.

In the mid-1960s Jim was the man you had to beat; he was always there, in all three classes.

Today (23 May 1998), I rode the 250cc Honda 4 for the first time, and I now realise what a fantastic rider Jim was, as the Honda is a delicate machine to drive really hard. Mike Hailwood said the same thing when he rode the

Jim Redman

works Hondas in October 1965, and I can now see why.

Jim set the professional standard of getting the best deal possible from race organisers. He made racing a business and a pleasure, whilst most riders were happy just to race. Jim was the first rider to bring lateral thinking to Grand Prix bike racing, and the lessons I learned from him have stood me in good stead right up to this day.

Luigi Taveri

As a six-time World Champion, it needs no words to understand that he was a good and serious rider. He was also a good and clever businessman.

We are so different, but after over thirty years of past racing we are still good friends.

Ralph Bryans

I always found Jim to be a very fair man and owe him a lot. He was probably the first World Champion who campaigned for a better deal from the race organisers on behalf of all the GP competitors in the 1960s.

As a young Honda Team member I found Jim's organising and team leader skills invaluable, The rest of the Honda riders only had to turn up at the GPs and ride. Jim organised the entries, start money and all the negotiations with the oil companies, plug suppliers, chain suppliers, etc., in an efficient and fair manner.

Furthermore, Jim was a brilliant rider who said that his objective was to win races at the slowest possible speed! However, when he had to ride hard he did and could be the most tenacious competitor, as his illustrious record proves.

In my opinion all GP riders of the 1960s are in Jim's debt for the good work he did in raising standards and making the organisers realise that without riders there would be no racing and that it was in their interests to deal fairly with the competitors.

All the best, Jim, and don't forget to keep it on its wheels and between the hedges!

Frank Perris

He [Jim] and I were team captains for our own teams, but this never came between our outside friendship.

As a private owner he was on a par with about six or seven top riders of the day. He got the opportunity of a works ride with Honda. He took this opportunity with both hands and lifted himself into the very top riders' league, on a machine that was the best of its time. He then showed that he was able to win 125cc, 250cc, 350cc and 500cc on these machines, which in my opinion made him one of the three best ever in the world.

Jim was the first rider to teach the other riders to stand up for better conditions from the organisers.

What Others Say ...

Stuart Graham (Honda)

Jim as a man? Personally I have always had the greatest respect for Jim: he was instrumental in me joining the Honda team after his accident in 1966, and helped me during my time there. Jim was also responsible for raising the level of professionalism and financial rewards for the riders during the 1960s, and was always very astute in his business dealings.

I admire the way he worked very hard throughout his career when it wasn't always easy, and he richly deserved his World Championships.

Jim as a rider? Very good; he was always very intelligent and could judge just what was needed to win championships. He could ride very hard when required, but more importantly knew how to win races. His long experience and development skills were very important to Honda - they respected him, which was important too.

I feel sometimes Jim was underrated as a rider - as were many - due to comparison with Mike Hailwood, but you do not win as many championships as Jim did without being very good indeed.

Jim Redman helped my career greatly; I thank him.

Nobby Clark

I have known Jim for many years. He used to live close by when we both lived in Bulawayo, Rhodesia.

I worked for Jim in 1963 as his personal mechanic. Jim was riding Hondas and had bikes which he used in international races, which I looked after. He was instrumental in getting me to work in the Honda racing factory team.

I think Jim's philosophy of riding just fast enough to win was great. He could nurse a bike home and still win. This helped the engineers and the mechanics a great deal. Jim could explain problems in a language which the mechanics understood. Before the Honda ride Jim used to work on his own bikes and so had a good knowledge of how engines worked.

Jim was the first rider to win three Grands Prix in a day: the Dutch TT 1964, 125, 250 and 350cc classes. The only other rider to do this was the late great Mike Hailwood. Jim is also one of only three riders who have won a Grand Prix in all four solo classes - *ie* 125, 250, 350 and 500cc.

Jim helped Honda a great deal in the early 1960s to get its name on the map and also helped to change the face of racing in the 'golden era.' He was the first man to ride *the* glamour bike of the 1960s, the Honda 250cc 6-cylinder.

Nanou Lyonnard

He always had a large outlook on his career and on his life, and that is why he became as great as in his dreams.

Jim Redman

Maurice Büla

I have been part of the motorbike race teams since the creation of GP in 1949 (changing rôles from spectator to sidecar passenger, pilot and photographer), I can confirm, without hesitation, that Jim Redman is one of the greatest pilots of the motorbike sport of all time. With his incredible talent he made his mark in the World Championships by winning GPs on 125cc, 250cc, 350cc as well as 500cc, which only Mike Hailwood and Phil Read have managed.

One of my memories is from Spa-Francorchamps in 1964, during the practices when I was permanently standing along [moving around] the circuit. Jim came to see me later to ask how many kilometers I had done during the session. He told me that he saw me here ... and there ... and there ... during each round, at 200kph, he had spotted me, no matter where I was. I could hardly believe it.

Rob Iannucci (owner of Team Obsolete)

How I managed to drag him [Jim] out of his retirement ...

My idea was to see if we could reassemble the Honda 6 for Daytona in 1995 and that Jim should ride it. As soon as he touched the motorbike he became a different man, as if he had never left it. After six rounds the 6 literally made him look younger ... He did some exhibitions for Team Obsolete in 1995, at Daytona on the MV Agusta and on the Honda 6 in Assen, on the 250cc Honda in Scarborough, then in Mallory Park. In 1996 he carried on, still in Daytona, but only on the 6 this time, then in Nürburgring and Scarborough, still with the Honda 6, to finish off in 1997 driving his fabled motorbike on the circuit of Laguna Seca. This motorbike is reserved for Jim and only he is allowed to do exhibitions with it. The day Jim stops, a piece of history will be gone ... I shall never sell the 6 unless Jim asks me to do so.

Reg Bolton

In a very competitive era, Jim was World Champion no less than six times. He is still the only rider to have a 'hat trick of doubles' at the TT. He won the 250 and 350 races three years running - 1963, 1964 and 1965. The GP racers of the classic era were a tough breed. The races were far longer than they are now. Jim regularly rode 125, 250 and 350cc races on the same day. He even managed to become the first rider to win three GPs in a single day.

Jim's first trip to Brands was at the Easter International meeting in 1958. He had sold up in Rhodesia (Zimbabwe) and come to Europe to seek his racing fortune. For such an unknown rider, even getting a race entry accepted was quite difficult. Jim's case was helped considerably by the fact that in South Africa he had broken the outright lap record - set by none other than Geoff Duke on a Gilera - at a well-known track on a 500 Manx Norton. At Brands the young Redman was out to impress, if only to ensure future entries, and to gain the attention of the press and therefore acceptance on the Continent. In the big race he finished second to 'King' Derek Minter, a fantastic debut. Also

What Others Say ...

racing were Bob McIntyre, Alistair King and even a youthful Mike Hailwood.

Jim is never shy to express his very professional attitude to racing: "I learnt very early that it was important to win at the slowest speed possible." This common-sense approach earned Jim a slightly 'lack lustre' reputation. However, you don't get to win six World Titles by being a slow rider and, when necessary, Jim could, and did, turn the wick right up.

Perhaps Jim's safety-fast outlook stemmed from the early deaths of three close friends in the same year, all of them great racers. Australian Tom Phillis, also a Honda works rider, fellow Rhodesian Gary Hocking, who was an ex-500cc World Champion and the greatest rider never to win a World Championship, Bob McIntyre. With the loss of three such great riders in 1962 alone is it any wonder that Jim began to have doubts about the wisdom of going 'all out' every time he sat on a motorcycle?

Joe Campanini (Life Extension Clinic)

What does it take to be a winner? What makes the difference between being number one and one of the rest? Skill? Undoubtedly. But many have equal skills and still there is only one winner. Luck? Yes, luck does play a small part - being in the right place at the right time, for example, does help. But, as Gary Player says "The more I practice the luckier I get!" Attitude? Most definitely. But what determines your attitude? Environmental factors? Surely. But more than that, attitude is a state of mind, and your state of mind is largely determined by your self-esteem, your feeling of self-worth. But what determines your self-esteem. Consider the following.

As we approach the 21st century, knowledge - and, in particular, medical knowledge - is increasing at an incredible rate. It is known that everything which determines how an individual will be is encoded in that individual's genes: hair and eye colour; height, weight and mental abilities, are all determined by genetic material. Even how we age, how our hormone levels drop with age, is determined by genetic factors. It has been observed that individuals with low testosterone and human growth hormone have lower self-esteem and, predictably, those individuals with high levels have greater self-esteem.

We cannot say with any certainty what Jim's hormone levels were as a young man, but in his sixties his levels are above normal for his age. Could this higher level now be indicative of a much higher level when he was a younger man? Could this be one of the reasons for his remarkable achievements, the 'genetic edge' he had over his competitors? All we can say with certainty is that since the Life Extension Clinic has been administering a cocktail of hormones and supplements which stimulate increased hormone production, Jim's biological age has reverted to that of a man in his forties.

As he has done throughout his life, Jim was able to embrace the new ideas expounded by the Life Extension Clinic. His enthusiasm to become actively involved in the new wave of medicine, anti-ageing medicine, age

Jim Redman

reversal and longevity, has been a valued asset in the continuing good fortunes of the clinic. And, who knows, in five years' time, he may decide to go for World Champion again!

Postscript

— Racing today —

Lately, I've been asked what I think of Mick Doohan as a rider and as a man, because a lot of people are talking about him now which, of course, is natural as he is winning everything. I have only met him very briefly on a few occasions, so it is not possible to give an opinion of the man himself. However, on the professional side, I have watched him win many races and because of this I think he is a great champion. I have often read about him in the press and have noticed he is quick to criticize the racing circuits, particularly from the safety viewpoint. At the moment he is the best rider in the 500 class, but how does he rate as one of the best riders of all times? This is difficult to say as Mick races in only one category. The reason for this could be explained by the enormous pressure applied to the riders by their sponsors.

During my time the situation was similar. We had to give the best of ourselves because there were so many other hungry private riders waiting their turn and hoping that the factory riders would commit the fatal error which would send them back into anonymity. Also, there were no sponsors and very few factory rides then, whereas now all riders have big sponsors.

I personally think that Mick should try to win the 250 and the 500 title in the two oncoming years. This would prove he is a real champion, comparable to legends like Hailwood, Read and Agostini. Maybe he will reply that today's world of motorbike racing has nothing to do with yesterday's, to which I'd say that, in effect, it's easier to race in only one shorter race today, than it was to race in three, which were much longer, all those years ago.

Today, the races last no longer than 40 minutes, whereas we raced for an hour at least each time. Then, of course, there was practice and we raced in three different categories at almost every GP. Plus, we had the pressure of racing on the dangerous tracks, like the Isle of Man, Ulster, Sachsenring and Brno, with their bad roads and cobblestones, and with roads sometimes

Jim Redman

bordered by houses, walls and telegraph poles, especially on the Isle of Man. I remember that on the corner as we passed through Ginger Hall, we had to move our heads away from the corner in order to avoid the telegraph pole. Later on the pole was moved, but nobody ever complained because that was how it was. Either we accepted the conditions or we stayed home and played marbles.

The most intense pressure came with the Tourist Trophy: over 37 miles of unforgiving road. The slightest error was fatal which is why this race was loved and feared by many riders, but also why it remained the most prestigious of all championship races. I was still a private rider when I first announced that I did not like racing in the TT. Racing there meant taking too many risks to win, which puts the most enormous stress on riders. When I won my first 'double' in 1963, the organizers and the press congratulated me, saying "We guess you like the Tourist Trophy now?" "No, not at all!" I replied, adding ironically "But why was everyone going so slow?" The TT was the circuit I respected the most. After racing there for nine years, most of the time in three different classes and despite all the practice sessions that I had to make, I never crashed once there.

I still hold an Isle of Man record: I am the only rider to have won the same two races in the 250 and 350 classes for three years running. This record is still in the latest Guinness Book of Records and has been since 1965. Even if the 250 record falls and a rider equals or beats it, he cannot do this in the 350 race as it doesn't exist any more, and my record was achieved when the TT still counted as part of the World Championships. This is something of which I am very proud especially as I did not like the circuit. Out of my last twelve races on Hondas there, six times I finished first, twice second, once third, once fourth, once fifth and once in sixth place. I can remember, after my triple double in the TT, journalist Vic Willoughby saying about me "Redman shows the talent of a true champion because he is always at his best when his back is against the wall."

In 1995 at Assen, a press conference was held to which Mick Doohan, Daryl Beattie, Kevin Schwantz and I were invited. The other three were introduced first and then I joined them. I was introduced to the audience as the first rider in the history of motorcycle racing to win three GPs on the same day. Kevin Schwantz said to me "Three GPs on the same day when I battle to win three in one year!" Kevin is very modest and really likable. He came with his father to admire the Honda 6 and the MV Agustas, and seemed fascinated by these machines from another era. I was amazed that Mick Doohan criticized the circuit at Assen by saying that the track was too bumpy, and that certain bends were a bit over-camber, and that the GP should not be held there any more.

Andy Kershaw, well-known BBC DJ and motorcycle journalist who also does TV travel programmes to off-beat places, asked what I thought of Doohan's remarks. I said "If it's bumpy and over-camber for Mick, then it

Postscript

must be the same for all the other riders and, in any case, I thought this was road racing not banked circuit racing - roads are often over-cambered and full of bumps ..." Later, Andy wrote an article about this subject in which he wondered aloud how Mick Doohan would have felt about racing a bad-tempered Honda 500 in the pouring rain on the old cobblestoned Sachsenring track on the hard rubber tyres of the 1960s? The priorities of riders on days like that was not to fall; try and at least remain in the saddle and maybe finish, and only then hope to win the race.

Modern motorcycles are so quiet and all tend to look the same. They do not have the magic, rareness and individuality of machines from past years, and I think the lack of any real noise is one of the reasons why the crowds have deserted the GPs. Conversely, we're told the opposite; that it was because of the noise the public became disinterested in motorcycle racing. But then how do we explain the great success of Formula 1 racing, where the noise is loud and beautiful? To me, the noise is one of the *raisons d'être* of the sport.

Perhaps declining public interest is also due to the fact that today's riders have become more and more inaccessible to the fans. They stay shut up in their motorhomes most of the time and it's very difficult to get an autograph. Anyone would think that this is a real chore, when it's their duty to meet their fans and spend some time with them; after all, it's these very fans who in part pay their enormous salaries. Today's riders seem to hide from the public, behaving like real *prima donnas*, and even sometimes during the press conferences like temperamental Hollywood stars. When I saw how Kevin Schwantz conducts himself I can easily understand why he is so popular with the public. It's simple: he always has a kind word to say to his fans and is always ready to please them.

The other riders should come out of their motorhomes and make themselves more available to their public. After all, they only compete in one race per GP so have more than enough time during the day to do so. At the Formula 1 race at Silverstone I noticed there's a special place cut into the outer paddock fence where the fans wait for autographs. Some of them seemed to stand there most of the day and there are always some waiting, which gives the drivers a chance to pop over and sign anytime they have a few moments to spare. Perhaps this should be done at all the bike GPs and Superbikes?

Yet another reason, perhaps, why the crowds are getting smaller is that they are placed too far away from the racetrack because of the wide security barriers that are now installed. The fans can *see* everything but are so far away there is no excitement and it's hard for them to feel part of the event, part of the show. At Assen, luckily enough, this is not the case, and the crowd are close enough to still feel part of the event; whereas, at the Nürburgring in Germany, one can only see tiny machines going silently by. After a few laps, I can tell you it is total boredom.

Lastly, the entrance fee is definitely too high for most pockets, especially

Jim Redman

for young people who have a passion for the sport. It's not hard to understand why they're staying at home and watching the GPs on the television: it's free, the racing is very close and very exciting. They don't mind paying for the trip to get there, for the nights spent in an hotel or camping, plus food, but, after all this, they then have to pay a huge entrance fee which at best gives them a place way back in the stands, where they need to have binoculars to follow the race - why bother?

Of course, riders earn good salaries, sponsors are more and more involved and have more and more control, but what happened to the atmosphere in all this? What part does the public play in the eyes of the professionals - besides a financial one? Despite everything, I am still convinced that motorcycle racing is a phenomenal sport with a great future. I am a motorcycle racer to the bone, and always will be. I think that the racing in 1999 is going to be very exciting. The 125 race is always very thrilling with about twenty potential winners on the starting line. The 500 class looks very exciting; Mick Doohan will be tested next year and we will find out just how good he really is.

I sometimes wonder how Mike Hailwood or Giacomo Agostini would have been today. I am sure they would have done well as they had the talent and also that will to win that comes from within. And would Mick Doohan or Kenny Roberts have done as well in our time as they have in theirs? The conditions were not the same, that's for sure, but individuals remain more or less the same; so I am sure they would have done well, too. The races are now a lot less dangerous than they were in the past, which is certainly a positive step. Hailwood and Read were very great champions and all of us would loved to have had the huge salaries and sponsorship available today - perhaps, then, we'd have only wanted to ride in one class, too!

I don't recall having heard of the death of a rider in any of the GP classes for years, and can't emphasize enough how happy I am about the enormous progress made in this area. I would have been even happier if, in our day, the Armco barriers had been replaced by sand traps as every year six riders lost their lives racing. This is definitely one of the greatest improvements carried out by the sporting community and it's crazy that it took so many years for it to happen.

Jim Redman's World Championship Results

— 1959 —

German GP, Hockenheim	6th	350cc	Norton
Swedish GP, Kristianstad	6th	350cc	Norton
Ulster GP, Belfast	7th	350cc	Norton
Dutch GP, Assen	5th	500cc	Norton
Belgian GP, Spa-Francorchamps	9th	500cc	Norton

— 1960 —

Dutch GP, Assen	4th	125cc	Honda
Belgian GP, Spa-Francorchamps	9th	125cc	Honda
Italian GP, Monza	4th	125cc	Honda
Dutch GP, Assen	8th	250cc	Honda
Ulster GP, Belfast	3rd	250cc	Honda
Italian GP, Monza	2nd	250cc	Honda
Dutch GP, Assen	7th	350cc	Norton
Belgian GP, Spa-Francorchamps	5th	500cc	Norton
Ulster GP, Belfast	5th	500cc	Norton
Italian GP, Monza	6th	500cc	Norton

— 1961 —

Spanish GP, Barcelona	3rd	125cc	Honda
German GP, Hockenheim	7th	125cc	Honda
French GP, Clermont-Ferrand	3rd	125cc	Honda
Tourist Trophy, Isle of Man	4th	125cc	Honda
Dutch GP, Assen	2nd	125cc	Honda
Belgian GP, Spa-Francorchamps	3rd	125cc	Honda
East German GP, Sachsenring	4th	125cc	Honda
Ulster GP, Belfast	4th	125cc	Honda

Jim Redman

Italian GP, Monza	4th	125cc	Honda
Swedish GP, Kristianstad	3rd	125cc	Honda
Argentinian GP, Buenos Aires	2nd	125cc	Honda
Spanish GP, Barcelona	4th	250cc	Honda
German GP, Hockenheim	2nd	250cc	Honda
French GP, Clermont-Ferrand	6th	250cc	Honda
Tourist Trophy, Isle of Man	3rd	250cc	Honda
Dutch GP, Assen	3rd	250cc	Honda
Belgian GP, Spa-Francorchamps	1st	250cc	Honda
East German GP, Sachsenring	2nd	250cc	Honda
Ulster GP, Belfast	3rd	250cc	Honda
Italian GP, Monza	1st	250cc	Honda
Swedish GP, Kristianstad	4th	250cc	Honda
Argentinian GP, Buenos Aires	3rd	250cc	Honda

— 1962 —

Spanish GP, Barcelona	2nd	125cc	Honda
French GP, Clermont-Ferrand	2nd	125cc	Honda
Tourist Trophy, Isle of Man	5th	125cc	Honda
Dutch GP, Assen	2nd	125cc	Honda
Belgian GP, Spa-Francorchamps	2nd	125cc	Honda
German GP, Solitude	10th	125cc	Honda
Ulster GP, Belfast	3rd	125cc	Honda
East German GP, Sachsenring	2nd	125cc	Honda
Italian GP, Monza	4th	125cc	Honda
Finnish GP, Tampere	1st	125cc	Honda
Spanish GP, Barcelona	1st	250cc	Honda
French GP, Clermont-Ferrand	1st	250cc	Honda
Tourist Trophy, Isle of Man	2nd	250cc	Honda
Dutch GP, Assen	1st	250cc	Honda
Belgian GP, Spa-Francorchamps	2nd	250cc	Honda
East German GP, Sachsenring	1st	250cc	Honda
Ulster GP, Belfast	2nd	250cc	Honda
German GP, Solitude	1st	250cc	Honda
Italian GP, Monza	1st	250cc	Honda
Dutch GP, Assen	1st	350cc	Honda
Ulster GP, Belfast	1st	350cc	Honda
East German GP, Sachsenring	1st	350cc	Honda
Italian GP, Monza	1st	350cc	Honda
Finnish GP, Tampere	2nd	350cc	Honda

— 1963 —

Spanish GP, Barcelona	2nd	125cc	Honda
French GP, Clermont-Ferrand	2nd	125cc	Honda

Jim Redman's World Championship Results

Tourist Trophy, Isle of Man	6th	125cc	Honda
Finnish GP, Tampere	5th	125cc	Honda
Italian GP, Monza	2nd	125cc	Honda
Argentinian GP, Buenos Aires	1st	125cc	Honda
Japanese GP, Suzuka	2nd	125cc	Honda
Spanish GP, Barcelona	2nd	250cc	Honda
German GP, Hockenheim	3rd	250cc	Honda
Tourist Trophy, Isle of Man	1st	250cc	Honda
Dutch GP, Assen	1st	250cc	Honda
Ulster GP, Belfast	1st	250cc	Honda
East German GP, Sachsenring	3rd	250cc	Honda
Italian GP, Monza	2nd	250cc	Honda
Argentinian GP, Buenos Aires	2nd	250cc	Honda
Japanese GP, Suzuka	1st	250cc	Honda
German GP, Hockenheim	1st	350cc	Honda
Tourist Trophy, Isle of Man	1st	350cc	Honda
Dutch GP, Assen	1st	350cc	Honda
Ulster GP, Belfast	1st	350cc	Honda
East German GP, Sachsenring	3rd	350cc	Honda
Finnish GP, Tampere	2nd	350cc	Honda
Italian GP, Monza	1st	350cc	Honda

— 1964 —

Spanish GP, Barcelona	2nd	125cc	Honda
Tourist Trophy, Isle of Man	2nd	125cc	Honda
Dutch GP, Assen	1st	125cc	Honda
German GP, Solitude	1st	125cc	Honda
East German GP, Sachsenring	3rd	125cc	Honda
Finnish GP, Imatra	3rd	125cc	Honda
Italian GP, Monza	6th	125cc	Honda
Spanish GP, Barcelona	2nd	250cc	Honda
Tourist Trophy, Isle of Man	1st	250cc	Honda
Dutch GP, Assen	1st	250cc	Honda
Belgian GP, Spa-Francorchamps	2nd	250cc	Honda
German GP, Solitude	2nd	250cc	Honda
East German GP, Sachsenring	2nd	250cc	Honda
Ulster GP, Belfast	2nd	250cc	Honda
Italian GP, Monza	3rd	250cc	Honda
Japanese GP, Suzuka	1st	250cc	Honda
Tourist Trophy, Isle of Man	1st	350cc	Honda
Dutch GP, Assen	1st	350cc	Honda
German GP, Solitude	1st	350cc	Honda
East German GP, Sachenring	1st	350cc	Honda
Ulster GP, Belfast	1st	350cc	Honda

285

Jim Redman

Finnish GP, Imatra	1st	350cc	Honda
Italian GP, Monza	1st	350cc	Honda
Japanese GP, Suzuka	1st	350cc	Honda

— 1965 —

Tourist Trophy, Isle of Man	1st	250cc	Honda
Dutch GP, Assen	2nd	250cc	Honda
Belgian GP, Spa-Francorchamps	1st	250cc	Honda
East German GP, Sachsenring	1st	250cc	Honda
Czechoslovakian GP, Brno	3rd	250cc	Honda
Tourist Trophy, Isle of Man	1st	350cc	Honda
Dutch GP, Assen	1st	350cc	Honda
East German GP, Sachsenring	1st	350cc	Honda
Czechoslovakian GP, Brno	1st	350cc	Honda
Japanese GP, Suzuka	2nd	350cc	Honda

— 1966 —

German GP, Hockenheim	2nd	250cc	Honda
French GP, Clermont-Ferrand	2nd	250cc	Honda
Dutch GP, Assen	3rd	250cc	Honda
Belgian GP, Spa-Francorchamps	3rd	250cc	Honda
French GP, Clermont-Ferrand	3rd	350cc	Honda
German GP, Hockenheim	1st	500cc	Honda
Dutch GP, Assen	1st	500cc	Honda

Sixty Years

Because of the demand for the German edition of my book, which, at the time of writing, is completely sold out, we decided to publish this new English edition too, to bring the story of my life completely up to date.

So many things have happened – my life has been very hectic – but I will do my best to keep these pages in chronological order. Forgive me, though, if the order of events is a bit mixed up.

During the late sixties I spent quite a lot of time in the UK, teaming up with Jim Blanchard at various shows and events. This worked very well for both of us. It was during this period, at the Motor Cycle Show at the NEC, that I asked Barry Hearn, one of Jim's customers, if he had any connections who could get me a hotel room. Honda had booked me for too short a stay. Barry immediately offered up his house, and thus it was that Barry, and then his friend Percy, joined me at events, and we travelled all over the UK and the continent together for some years.

In the early noughties, Jim and I had a stand at the TT riders' lunch. It was here that a man walked up to me and asked if I was Jim Redman. When I replied yes, he shook my hand and introduced himself as Charles March.

"Lord March ..." I said, "... what do I call you?" "My friends call me Charles," he said, and gave me permission to do so. He then asked me why I had never been to Goodwood, and I replied that I have never been asked. He said that he'd attend to that, and I promised to come next time. Of course, he then asked if I could get Honda to come. I replied that, once I'd mentioned the many important people attending, I was sure Honda would; I was right.

Later, at the actual Goodwood event, Charles thanked me for my help, saying that Honda would never have come without it.

Kwezi and I were invited to a dinner on the Thursday before the event. It was a small affair, for a few friends only, and we both met Lady March, 'Janet,' as she told us to call her, and we have been friends ever since.

Jim Redman

At the dinner Kwezi sat opposite me, at a very large round table, between Charles' father, The Duke of Richmond, and an Italian whom I didn't recognize. Once the plates had been cleared, the centre flowers removed, and we were at the coffee stage, Kwezi introduced me to Lucio, sales manager for Ferrari in Europe. She asked me to tell him the story of how Mike Hailwood and I met, and of how we persuaded Enzo Ferrari to sell us two cars at half price. That particular story is already in this book, so I will not tell it again.

Lucio could quite believe it, and had a similarly remarkable story, about a time that Enzo went for lunch at his favourite restaurant ... While the owner was fussing around him, Enzo mentioned to him that some guys who were sitting at a big table had nearly no money, and the owner was peeved that they were taking up space. Enzo asked if they owned the van and trailer of racing bikes outside, and, when the owner answered yes, said to tell them there was a competition running, which meant anyone who happened to sit at that table had all food and drinks on the house. Enzo instructed the owner to bring him the bill and that he would pay, but they must not know it was him.

So, somewhere in the UK, there are a group of riders that had a free lunch on Enzo Ferrari, and they still won't know; unless, of course, they read this.

Back at the table, a man to my left introduced himself as Klaus Bischoff, director of the Porsche Museum. I started to tell him my name, but he said, "You don't have to tell me, I am going to be the envy of everyone at Porsche that I sat next to Jim Redman."

Klaus then invited me to come and see the museum. I gave him the date I would be at the Glemsek Hotel, situated just round the first corner of the famous Solitude Circuit. He said the Glemsek was too small, and that he would fill it with people wanting to hear me talk. When I arrived I found he was as good as his word. Andreas, the owner of T&T (who, with his brother Frank, had translated my book into German) said: "I hope you're feeling strong, we're doing a talk tonight as well as the scheduled one tomorrow; Klaus had filled the room."

I was proud to see on the placards: "Jim Redman absolute record holder of the Solitude," and we had a great day with Klaus showing us everything.

During my talk I told the story of how Jack Ahearn's bike was stolen, and how Jack had then said he hated every German. The room went very quiet. Then, when I told them how the crowd collected buckets of Deutsche Mark coins and arrived at Jack's van with them – enough money to buy five Nortons – Jack immediately said he'd always thought that the German people were the best in the world.

Everyone had a good laugh; only Jack could get away with saying something like that. Rita Perris, who is German, was so angry – and when he changed his tune she was even madder – I thought World War III was about to start!

Barry Hearn and I went to Oschesleben for an event, where the Honda seized, throwing me off high-side, and I broke a collarbone. I discharged myself from hospital the same day, and we 'phoned Schotton to say that I could not come. The organisers wanted me there, even with the injury, and took me round on a sports car so that the crowd could see that I was there, but too injured to ride. The next event was the Goodwood Revival, and once again Lord March, or 'Charles,' as he told me to call him, asked me to come, and said they would take me around in a car to show the crowd I was really there. On the day, Charles asked if I could manage one lap on a bike he had borrowed for me, and I agreed to try, as long as I could find a suitable leather jacket. With my injury, I couldn't wriggle into one-piece leathers.

So, with jeans, boots, helmet, and Charles' jacket on, I climbed onto the bike. I couldn't reach the left handlebar, as my arm refused to stretch. I got off in order to hold the bar, before easing back on so that my arm stretched. Kwezi said I was crazy to even try and ride.

Now, Goodwood pit is out past the finishing line, so I had to do one lap to get to the start. I lined up with all the others on the front row, and managed to be first away. During the first lap I was expecting to be passed, but at the end of the lap I was still leading, so, of course, I kept going. On the next lap I was passed by Barry Sheene, Phil Read, and a couple of the other fit guys, so I went back in. Kwezi was so mad at me! She said, "Can't you fucking count to one?"

Of course I said she was right; I was stupid, but I was excited to be leading, the red mist came down, and so I did the extra lap. Charles came over with a big smile on his face, and thanked me profusely.

At one time, Rolf Korrmann came to South Africa for a holiday, and we invited him and his wife Gisela to bring their friends and come for lunch. Rolf and Gisela are crazy, like me. They met when Rolf, who had emigrated from Germany to South Africa, returned to Germany. Gisela, whose English was better than Rolf's, used to write Rolf's love letters to his then fiancée in South Africa. Rolf just wanted to say in his letters that he was going to Solitude one weekend, Hockenheim the next, etc. Gisela, however, told him that he should also say that he loved her, and was missing her, etc. Rolf was sure he couldn't do all that, and asked Gisela to do it for him.

A letter arrived from Rolf's fiancée to say that she had found someone new. Rolf thought that was typical of girls: they want a house, a fence and a baby or two. Gisela replied that she didn't want any of that, but to travel. Rolf then asked her to go with him to Canada, and off they went. On the way they went to Las Vegas, and while they were there they thought it would be a good idea to get married, which they did.

They have lived in Canada, and the USA, and are now back in Germany; retired from working, but not from travelling. As I write this they are both in the Channel Islands, simply because they have never been there before. When they get back to Monsheim, they are off to California to visit friends.

I've known Rolf since 1958 when I first went to Europe, and he has been involved in racing since about 1953, around the time I started racing in

Sixty Years

kept spinning loose, so that I kept losing it. It was so awkward that I gave up and used the engine as a brake, except for 'really stop' corners. The fans were loving it: I was changing down more and using the engine to slow down. So many people came up to me later and said that it was the best lap I had ever ridden on the Six ... I have never changed so many gears in one lap in my life!

When Kwezi divorced me I was shattered. She said that although she loved me, she was worried that if I were to die in 15 years or so, she would be alone, just like her mum was (Kwezi's mother was 27 years younger than her father, Judge Kennedy). Kwezi is 37 years younger than me, and, in addition, had found a new guy whom she liked a lot.

We had a fantastic 16 years together, and, when we were first divorced I just could not pull myself together.

The following year at Goodwood, I was shown the difference between a man and a woman. I bumped into Lady March as I arrived, and she put down the papers she was carrying and gave me a big hug. She told me she was going to look after me that weekend, so I would not be too lonely. Then, when I met Lord March, he said, "Sorry about Kwezi, old chap: get another one ... there are plenty here!"

I often had Sonja, Markus Halter's daughter (and grease monkey), helping to sell my merchandise at events, and to look after the table. I always called her my best girl friend. In 2005, as I hugged her and said that I'd see her next year, I realised that she had grown up. I asked her how old she was. When she said 14, I asked if she would marry me when she reached 18 ... I had just got divorced.

Sonja said, "Yes, yes I will, yes," and I was taken aback, especially as she came back and told me she had spoken to her dad! He had told her, that with his permission, she could marry me when she was 16. When I asked her if he had actually given his permission, she told me he'd said to ask her mum. Later in the day, I happened to run into Sonja's mum, Uschi. Uschi is another one who helps everyone in the paddock ... thinking about it as I write, she is the female version of Rolf Korrmann.

She said, "So, you want to marry my daughter?" I told her Sonja would get over it before she reached 16, but Uschi wasn't so sure. I started calling her and Sonja's dad my mother-in-law and father-in-law, and the news was soon all over the paddock.

This was the start of a fantastic friendship, and I am now close friends with all three of them. Often you are friends with a rider, and his family remains in the background. Well, I am proud to have them all as my friends; separately and together. I call their house my 'German home,' and if I am ever anywhere near them, I head over to visit.

In October 2010 I took my grandson Ryan there, and he was welcomed with open arms. He now calls them his German mother, father and sister!

Sonja is 19 now, and she did come to her senses before she got to 16!

The Sachsenring 80-year celebration in 2007 was fantastic, even though the Moto GP event was one week later, which must have used up the fan's

Jim Redman

spending money. Over 200,000 attended that event. Still, over 50,000 came to Sachsenring to welcome us. Sachsenring fans are really special: you have the grandfather, who tells the son, and the grandson about it, so the love of racing is sort of bred into them.

That year, at the re-opening of the Hohenstein Ernsthal museum I met and fell in love with a beautiful girl named Lisa. I signed a picture for her father, and asked her and her dad there and then if she would marry me. Her dad told us to go for it, but that I would have a problem convincing Lisa's mum. Lisa was stuck; she loves her home life and where she lives, and is not keen to travel.

Regardless, Lisa and I spent a lot of time with each other. I took her to the track, and to the various dinners and street parties that were going on.

We did a lot of riding over that weekend, and I rode some fantastic bikes – I really had a ball!

At one particular street party, people started asking for authographs as I came off of the stage. One girl asked me to sign her belly – you know how the modern girls like their bellies to show – and, well, that started something! I had to pull up the front of their tops to sign, and gradually I started lifting higher and higher ... Most of them did not wear a bra, so the guys watching egged me on, until in the end most of the girls were having their boobs flashed! The boys loved it, and so did the girls actually; as word got around more and more wanted to be signed. Everyone had a few drinks in them, so it was good clean fun ... but it did liven up the evening nicely!

Lisa told me that I had signed about 1000 autographs in one day, which is possible, as the fans could get to us in the pits – and they were there in force. I was proud that so many young people as well as old wanted an autograph or a picture with me, and a lot with Lisa and I together. I still see her every year when I go to Sachsenring.

John Hempleman was also at Sachsenring that year. He had not been back to Europe since he retired in 1959, but Frank Bischoff started a fund, and the fans all clubbed together to bring him over. Hempo, as I call him, showed the Germans how to drink beer, and he was fantastic!

Once, he overheard me asking Lisa to come and work for me. I asked her how much she earned at the hospital she was then working at, and she said not much. I offered to pay her double, at which Hempo roared with laughter and said that double not much is still not much! That was what he would take home with him: Redman offering to double not much.

I was then inducted into the Moto GP LEGENDS of Motorcycle Racing, at a big event attended by most of the 150 journalists and TV people that were at Sachsenring that year.

I told Lisa to sit with Rolf, since if there were pictures of her with me, her mum would be angry.

After the event, the journalists and photographers slowly drifted out. When she thought they were all gone, Lisa rushed over and flung her arms around my neck and kissed me. Click, click! went two cameras, and outside the rest of the journalists all heard, and rushed back to get pictures and the story. Rolf told Lisa that she would be in 150 newspapers and magazines, all over the world. It was lousy for her; the local paper put a picture of each of us on the front page and put underneath "17 and 74." Her mum was livid. I did calm her down, as it was Lisa's grandfather's birthday on the Saturday. I managed to pop over and have tea and coffee with him during a lull in the afternoon. He was gobsmacked to have Jim Redman in his home. I had brought him an autographed picture as a present, and he loved it ... I really get a kick out of the way they are so grateful.

In 2005, I rode at the Hamburg event on the Saturday, and afterwards we flew to Wien where Rolf and I were picked up by car. We arrived at 21.30 ... for a talk I was supposed to give at 20.00! I apologized for the plane running late, got on with the talk, and we all had a good night in the end.

The next day when our friend Karel Dobrodsky arrived with the bikes, I walked up the plank to greet him, but as I walked back down, the plank dropped with me on it. My hip was badly damaged, but not quite broken. I went back to South Africa on crutches, and then was unlucky enough to have a fall, which finished the job and broke it completely.

I flew to Durban and went straight into hospital, where I was operated on that same evening. The next morning I was fine, and the surgeon said I could go.

My son Brett picked me up, and we went to his house. The following Wednesday, the organizers of a race in Schwenningen, Germany, asked if I was OK to travel. They wanted me to attend the event, where I would be taken around in a car.

Off I went, and on the Saturday when they said they would bring the car, I asked them to bring the bike instead ... I was sure I could do it. Two big guys lifted me on, and away I went! I found it was too much to hold the left handlebar, so I held the petrol cap with my left hand, and rode with my right, changing up and down through the gears with no clutch. Of course I was last, but the crowd went wild as I passed. The commentator had told them what I was doing, and the spectators at the start and finish straight had seen me lifted on to the bike. I was the hero of the day: it had all been worth the trouble.

After this, during a visit to the Czech Republic, I met Jiri, who is a top surgeon there. He took one look at my x-rays, and told me how bad my hip was. The screws that had been put in had stopped the blood flow, and my hip was breaking up. That was the bad news. The good news was, he said, that he could shove a new hip in, my legs would be even, and I would have no pain. "I do 350 hips a year, but only one Jim Redman," he said. I immediately said, "You are my man," and he was as good as his word – the best surgeon I know.

I've been getting a little bit involved with some of the Moto GP riders. In 2004 I went to Valencia and was introduced to Nicky Hayden at the Honda hospitality. He told me I was his hero, and I replied by telling him he was the one guy who could take the Championship away from Valentino, perhaps

Jim Redman

not the next year, but in 2006, if he changed a few things. I said, "You can just say 'he is an old fart,' and walk away," but he suggested we get coffee and chat! I made a few suggestions; telling him to improve and really go for a win at Assen, where he always rides well, and again in Laguna Seca. He did it, and went on to win in 2006. When he won he said to me, "You were the first to tell me I could do it back in 2004." I always chat to him when I go to the odd Moto GP.

In 2009, in the Czech Republic, I was asked by the lovely Lorna Gibb, second in command of Castrol Europe, if I would go with Tony Elias and Andre de Angeles to the Castrol tent, where they were entertaining about 500 people. She told me they had some of my posters with them, and when we arrived I was quietly pleased to see that the line of people waiting for my signature was the longest. As we were signing I asked Tony – whom I had only just met – what his plans were for the next day. He had none, so I offered him a place on the Honda team, and he agreed. I advised him that Valentino, Lorenco, and Danny Petrosa would be tough to beat, and that he should aim for fourth position. Knowing that Lorenco could fall off, aiming for fourth meant Tony was still in with a chance of being on the podium.

As I was leaving Nicky Hayden on the grid the next day, Tony called me and asked for a photograph of us together.

I held out my fist and asked, "Podium?" He punched it and repeated: "Podium." Guess what ... Lorenco did fall, and Tony got the podium!

On my way to the trackside Grissini pit, I was waylaid by six beautiful girls. The girlfriend of our friend Karel Dobrodsky's son, Peter, was one. In total, there were four groups of six girls, employed by the organizers to walk around in their lovely, skimpy outfits, so fans could stand with them and have their picture taken.

Peter's girlfriend asked me to pose with her. Her friend, who took the picture, asked her why. When she replied I was six times World Champion, they all wanted a picture with me! The surrounding fans couldn't understand why such lovely girls wanted their picture with this old fart. It's moments like that which give our ego such a boost – and I love it!

In the meantime, everyone at the San Carlos Grissini pit was looking for me, and when we finally met up, Carlo said, "Jim, our hospitality unit is your home at Moto GP." He has been true to his word, and I can always be found there when I am at Moto GP.

At Sachsenring 2010, Honda had a great display of bikes, and I was invited to set up my table of merchandise. I sell this wherever I am, as well as on my web site, www.redmanracing.com.

On the Saturday, it was announced that Danny Petrosa would be there in the afternoon to talk to the dealers. I was asked to join him on the stand, and to say a few words to Danny. I spoke my mind, as usual.

Continued on page 299

Sixty Years

Parading at Böblingen, near Stuttgart, in front of Willi Marewski, who is a well-known collector of bikes. (Rolf Korrmann collection)

Another shot of the City Grand Prix at Böblingen going through the start and finish corner; note the lack of run-off area! (Rolf Korrmann collection)

With Gerhard Mitter (left), who is the organiser of the City GP, a great rider, and son of the late, great Gerhard Mitter, a German Legend. (Rolf Korrmann collection)

295

Jim Redman

Rolf, my Manager and good friend, and I admire a beautiful Honda replica; built by Norbert Prokschi and loaned to me by Willi Marewski. (Rolf Korrmann collection)

Giacomo Agostini asked me if I needed any help; just an excuse to talk to the beautiful Lisa at Sachsenring. (Rolf Korrmann collection)

Nice shot of the late Umberto Massetti with Willi and Rolf. (Rolf Korrmann collection)

296

Sixty Years

A happy shot, maybe as the beer was flowing in the Classic paddock. The picture is of the start of my last Grand Prix, the 500cc at Spa-Francorchamps 1966. (Rolf Korrmann collection)

With my broken hip still giving trouble, Rolf helps me get on board – just lift me on and point which way I have to go! (Rolf Korrmann collection)

Giacomo with me, Kwezi, and Rolf at the Solitude Revival. (Rolf Korrmann collection)

297

Jim Redman

Neli, wife of Andreas Ilg, the publisher of the German edition of this book, and owner of *MO* and *Klassik Motorrad* German motorcycle magazines, with Julia, who does a great job for *MO* at the events. (Rolf Korrmann collection)

Giving a little bit of friendly advice – probably "keep it on the wheels and keep it between the trees" – as Rolf looks on. (Rolf Korrmann collection)

Phil looks surprised that we even let him be in this photo! (Rolf Korrmann collection)

298

Sixty Years

I told him that he was in the same position I was; I had Mike Hailwood – the best rider of the past days – to beat, and then along came Ago as well. Danny had Valentino, his rival for years, and then along came Lorenso.

In the meantime, the Honda guy was panicking: he sent for help to rescue Danny from me; he thought Danny would be upset by what I was saying. Danny told them all to wait – he wanted me to finish what I was telling him. I said "You've beaten them before, so you can beat them again; I think you're going to win tomorrow."

The next day, after seeing Nicky Hayden and Casey Stoner, I went to Danny and shook his hand, telling him again that he would win. He rode a brilliant race and won well. The top man in Repsol said, "Jim, your second home is the Repsol hospitality."

In the last few years I have been riding a lot with Erich and Jurgen on three very well made 250cc Honda RC 163 replicas that they made in Stuttgart with their partner Heinz.

Heinz does not like to ride, but he very kindly let me ride his bike. All went well for the first few rides, but then when he saw me ride at Glemseck, Solitude, he said, "No more, Jim goes too fast!" Erich reassured him, and said, "He knows what he's doing, he's riding well within his limits," so Heinz relaxed after that.

Their bikes are beautifully prepared and maintained, and a joy to ride. Once again I give my sincere thanks for them letting me ride in what is now called "Team Jim Redman."

At the 100 years of the TT in 2007, on the Friday Lap of Honour, Neil Tuxworth, Honda Racing Team Manager, asked me if I'd like to ride the John McGuiness winning bike from the Wednesday race. I said that I would, although my hip was still bad at that time. I took three pain killers, and had to be lifted on, but then I was away down Bray Hill.

What a lap! The bike felt so good, and the power was awesome compared to our classic bikes, so I had a great ride. At one stage the zip of my leathers came open and I had to stop by a Marshal. He helped me zip it up, and then I was off again. I'm sure that if I had been fit, I could have cruised around on a fast parade lap and still lapped faster than I did in the '60s on our slower bikes.

When I came in, Neil and my son Brett helped me off of the bike. "Fantastic ride, this is a really fast bike," I said. Brett said, "We know ... they announced you went through the Highlander at about 350kph!" It is the fastest I have been on a bike in my life.

A few years ago Castrol invited me to Windsor for Castrol's 500 GP wins celebration. I was due to ride in an event in Kyjov, Czech Republic that Sunday. I told Castrol that if a flight was arranged for me from Vienna – the nearest big airport – to Heathrow, and then back to Stuttgart on the Wednesday, I could attend.

All went according to plan, and at the event Nick Harris, as Master of Ceremonies, welcomed everybody, and thanked a few specific people for

Jim Redman

coming, including James Toseland and John McGuiness, among others. He then said, "Finally, our Guest of Honour, Jim Redman, who with 46 Grand Prix wins, has won nearly ten percent of the 500 wins Castrol are celebrating."

We had a great evening, as it gave me a chance to get to know John McGuiness, who is a great guy, and to spend time with James Toseland (Tosy, as I call him,) who I have known and liked for years.

In 2008, I was invited to Imatra, Finland. I had previously committed to ride at Flacht Weide in Holland on the Saturday, so I told the Imatra organisers that I would come for Sunday if a flight could be arranged that would get me there for the morning.

Another crazy weekend, as I went to bed about 23.00 only to be woken up at 01.30 to be driven by the owner of our B&B owner's daughter, Dirka.

I checked in for the flight to Tampere, arriving at about 08.00. I met the guy with the "Jim Redman" board, and asked him how far it was to the circuit. He replied four to five hours. I staggered back; I'd not looked at the map, and had forgotten how big Finland was! Tampere is near the west, and Imatra is right over by the Russian border. In fact, the next day I went to the border and took a picture of me leaning against the warning signs: "No further this Russia."

As we got close to the circuit, they told my good driver to go to a nearby corner, where the safety car would come and pick me up. We left him to do the long drive around, and I jumped in the safety car with my leathers bag. I had a hair-raising ride, learned half the circuit at race speed, and was dumped at the VIP area in the paddock at 13.00. They told me to grab some food, as I was on at 14.00 and 16.00. Dinner was at 18.00, with a yacht ride at 20.00, and sauna at 22.00.

I walked in, got some food, and sat next to the only other person there: a beautiful girl named Johanna. We chatted throughout the day, and she invited me to visit her father's museum.

Phew, what a hectic day! I had been up since 01.30, and with the driving, flying, parading the racing bikes, and the calming yacht ride I collapsed into my bed at 21.00, even though I knew I would be missing the best event – a Finnish sauna is completely nude. I missed mixing with all those lovely girls, naked!

The next day I risked my life again on a rope slide, to cross the rushing rapids of the river running through Imatra; the flood gates had been opened for the occasion. My feat was soon made insignificant, however, when a 16 year old girl followed me, tied upside down by her feet. Oh dear, second once again!

Johanna's father, Ope, then took us to see his great museum, and then to dinner, during which I asked Johanna to explain to Ope that the going rate for a wife in South Africa was 15 cows, and would he accept that for her. I got a clout from her, and then he got one too, as he replied that ten was enough! He then offered me another deal: Johanna and his ex-wife as a package, plus two cows.

During the weekend, Johanna had told me that the relationship she had with her partner was cooling. I advised her to get out of it, which she did. As we parted at the airport I said, "How am I going to live my life without you?" "You may not have to," she replied.

Johanna has now been to South Africa twice, once with her dad, and has found a new guy. She is so in love she is glowing – at least I got that one right! Johanna and I are now very good friends.

This year I met Henna, another very beautiful and bubbly girl, who also happens to be from Finland. She has promised to come to South Africa this winter and visit, which is of course our summer.

I am writing this in October 2010; my season is almost over and I am spending time with my sister, Jacky, who turned 80 in May, and is in Worthing Hospital. She has been diagnosed with terminal cancer. My younger brother and sister, Peter and Wendy, both died of cancer. Only this morning, my brother-in-law Richard (Wendy's husband) 'phoned to say he has been told he also has terminal cancer, with no chance to operate.

In the meantime, life has to go on, so I still have the Stafford Show, then the Belfast show with a talk on the Monday, followed by Valencia Moto GP in early November. I am booked to return to South Africa on November tenth, but of course I may have to delay that. I left South Africa on May sixth, so will have been away six months with an event most weekends – sometimes two! Good job I am still young enough to do it!

I know my record of six World Championships, six Isle of Man TT wins, 46 Grand Prix wins and 97 podiums, and I am very proud, especially of being the first rider to win three Grand Prix in one day.

Because of the advent of computers, people now come to me with other facts. One, that I beat Mike Hailwood in Grand Prix Racing more times that he beat me, and another: if Giacomo Agostini and I both finished a race, I always beat him. I never knew these facts, although I always thought the first one was true.

Because of these stats, people have been kind enough to say that I am the best at what I do. When I disagree, and say that Mike was the best, they reply that the winner is the first past the post, never mind opinions. It makes me feel good when people say such things to me, but ...

As I am 80 next year, Rolf and I have compiled a list of about 30 events for me to ride in, plus a few talks. Wolfgang Strobek and his son Mario have promised me a good party at Salzburgring, and other organizers are offering to do the same. It looks as though 2011 is going to be one long party! I can manage it while I am still young, so I'd better enjoy myself before I get old.

***

It is now January 2013. My first race was in Rhodesia in 1953, so I've been racing motorcycles for 60 years so far.

I've had so much fun, and have made so many good friends all over the world, that I have no intention of retiring, and I will keep on attending classic events for a few more years.

I hope to see you there.

Also from Veloce Publishing Ltd ...

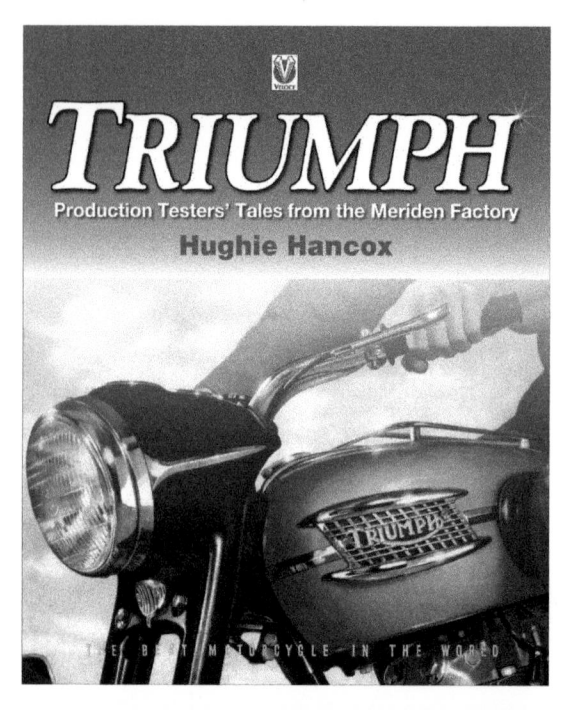

The story of one worker's time on the Triumph Production Testing team from 1960 to 1962, packed with amusing anecdotes about the obstacles and adventures associated with a tester's daily life. With guides to fixing problems still found on the 1960s models, this is an intimate and useful account of one of Britain's most famous factories.

ISBN: 978-1-845844-41-7
Paperback • 25x20.7cm • £25.00* UK/$39.95* USA • 160 pages • 183 colour and b&w pictures

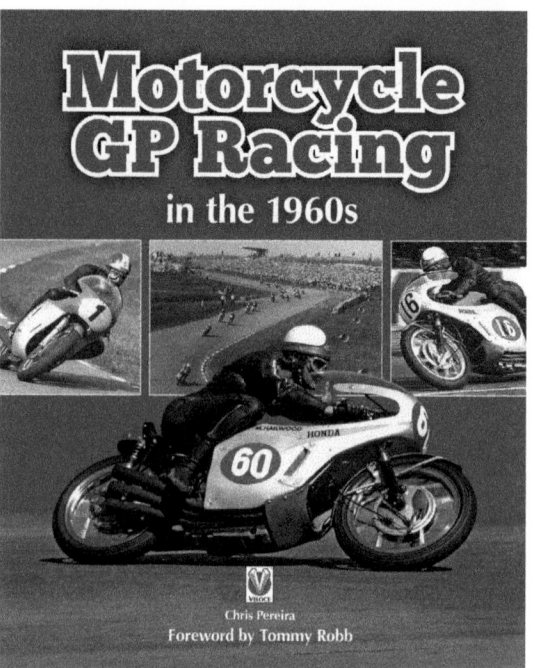

This book examines the classic period of Grand Prix racing from 1960 to 1969, and the men and machines involved. A fascinating exploration of the last decade of 'traditional' Grand Prix racing, before significant events changed the nature of the sport forever.

ISBN: 978-1-845844-16-5
Hardback • 25x20.7cm • £30.00* UK/$49.95* USA • 176 pages • 177 colour and b&w pictures

For more info on Veloce titles, visit our website at www.veloce.co.uk
• email: info@veloce.co.uk • Tel: +44(0)1305 260068
* prices subject to change, p&p extra

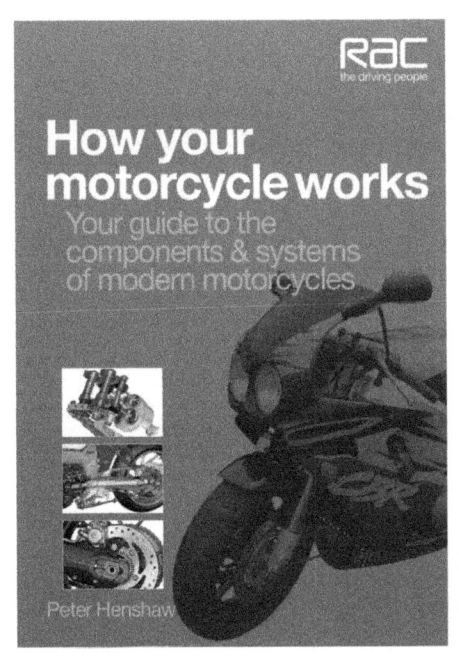

A fascinating and intricate piece of machinery, the modern motorcycle is easily as complex as the modern car. Clear, jargon-free text, and detailed cutaway illustrations show exactly how the modern bike works. From the basics of the internal combustion engine, to the wide variety of modern transmissions and ancillary systems.

ISBN: 978-1-845844-94-3
Paperback • 21x14.8cm •
£12.99* UK/$25.00* USA •
80 pages • 86 colour pictures

Taking the first-time buyer step-by-step through the entire experience of buying their first motorcycle, this friendly, clear, and jargon-free book explains everything they need to know to get the most out of their bike.
Covering practicalities such as the pros and cons of biking, and what type of bike may be most suitable, to training, insurance, and maintenance – even choosing the right kit, where to buy, and where to ride are covered by this invaluable guide – this book tells the whole story.

ISBN: 978-1-845844-95-0
Paperback • 21x14.8cm
• £9.99* UK/$19.95* USA
• 80 pages• 95 colour pictures

For more info on Veloce titles, visit our website at www.veloce.co.uk
• email: info@veloce.co.uk • Tel: +44(0)1305 260068
* prices subject to change, p&p extra

Also from Veloce Publishing Ltd ...

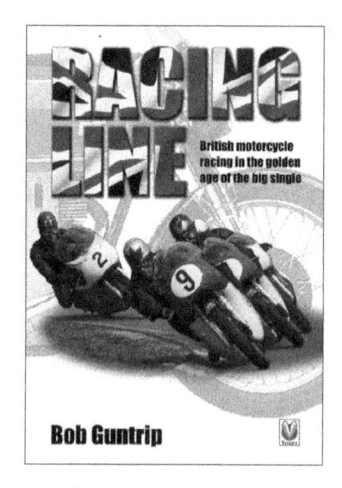

ISBN: 978-1-845847-93-7
Hardback • 22.5x15.2cm • £19.99* UK/$35.00* USA • 232 pages • 76 colour and b&w pictures

Racing Line is the story of big-bike racing in Britain during the 1960s – when the British racing single reached its peak; when exciting racing unfolded at circuits across the land every summer; and when Britain took its last great generation of riding talent and engineering skill to the world.

ISBN: 978-1-845848-96-5
Hardback • 24.8x24.8cm • £30* UK/$49.95* USA • 128 pages • 250 colour pictures

This is the first book to solely concentrate on the British-powered café racer motorcycle. Renewed interest in custom British café conversions is illustrated with stunning images of select sporting, racing, and 'café'd' British motorcycles. From single-cylinder to four-cylinder variants – see the 'café'd' side of British bikes!

For more info on Veloce titles, visit our website at www.veloce.co.uk
• email: info@veloce.co.uk • Tel: +44(0)1305 260068
* prices subject to change, p&p extra

Jim Redman

Rhodesia and South Africa. For the last ten years he has organised a lot of my events in Europe, and has become known as 'The Manager,' since he helps not just me, but everyone in the paddock! If a rider ever had a problem, Rolf would rush in to help them.

Rolf has a picture of me with him in the paddock in 1962 ... just two young boys.

He was born in East Germany, but wriggled his way out somehow in the early days, before the wall really came down, helped by a life-long friend. Even as a kid, when taken to the circus he always went around the back, or at motorcycle events into the pits. He knows everyone, and he has a fantastic memory.

A few months after that lunch with Rolf and Gisela, Rolf called to ask if I would ride in the Will Merewski team in some upcoming German events. I agreed, and a new relationship was born.

I had a great time with Willi's team. We had Dieter Braun, Ernst Hiller, Lother John, Norbert, not to mention Markus Halter and Heiner Butz, among others. These guys were sort of in the team, but rode their own bikes. I was sorry when Willi decided to cut back on numbers ... even more so when the team eventually stopped altogether.

We often had a big table in the paddock, and all of the riders and some of their wives would bring food and drink. We just sat around as the night fell, telling all the old stories and drinking beer; "The older I get the faster I was," that sort of thing.

Willi had some fantastic bikes, and as I had the chance to ride a lot of them, I was very happy – we had some good times.

Willi ran the team in his own way. He didn't really do much preparation on the bikes, unless we were at the circuits. This of course caused problems, especially as we were not given just one bike to ride. At first he gave me a four-cylinder Hocking era 500cc MV, which I rode every time. The bike was quite new, and as I am well known for being very light on bikes, it was fine. When Willi started letting others ride it, however, the bike soon went downhill in preparation and reliability.

Honda brought over the same 250cc six that I had won the TT on in 1965, so I could do a lap to celebrate my 50 years of racing. I mentioned to Alpine Star that this was going to happen, and asked if some new gloves could be arranged – mine had no plastic on the knuckles. When I arrived at the Hilton where I was to stay, there was a big parcel on my bed ... Alpine Star had sent me new leathers, boots and gloves, with a note saying that for my 50th year, I should be all new. I wet the gloves and got them a nice fit, then went up and sat on the bike and adjusted everything to fit me.

During the lap, I got to Quarter Bridge and reached for the front brake – but I could not get to the brake lever! The knuckles on my new gloves were too thick, so I quickly moved my hand to the end of the handlebar in order to reach the brake. Luckily, I had shut off early. On top of that, the front brake adjuster